W9-BRV-532

The Gilded Age
A History in Documents

The Gilded Age
A History in Documents

Janette Thomas Greenwood

Oxford University Press

In memory of my mother, Ferne E. Thomas

OXFORD
UNIVERSITY PRESS

Oxford New York

Athens Auckland Bangkok Bogotá Buenos Aries Calcutta Cape Town
Chennai Dar es Salaam Delhi Florence Hong Kong Istanbul Karachi
Kuala Lumpur Madrid Melbourne Mexico City Mumbai Nairobi
Paris São Paulo Singapore Taipei Tokyo Toronto Warsaw

and associated companies in
Berlin Ibadan

Design: Sandy Kaufman
Layout: Loraine Machlin

Published by Oxford University Press, Inc.,
198 Madison Avenue, New York, New York 10016
www.oup.com

Library of Congress Cataloging-in-Publication Data
The Gilded Age: a history in documents
Janette Thomas Greenwood.
p. cm. - (Pages from history)
Includes bibliographical references (p.) and index.
Summary: Uses a wide variety of documents to show how Americans dealt
with an age of extremes from 1887 to 1900, including rapid industrialization, unemployment, unprecedented wealth, and immigration.
ISBN 0-19-510523-0 (acid-free paper)
1. United States-History-1865–1898-Sources-Juvenile literature.
2. United States-Social conditions-1865 1918-Sources-Juvenile literature.
[1. United States History-1865–1898-Sources.] I. Greenwood, Janette
Thomas. II. Series.
E661.G45   2000
973.8-dc21
99-098194

1 3 5 7 9 8 6 4 2

Printed in the United States of America
on acid-free paper

Cover: On July 16, 1892, the Homestead
Riot made the cover of *Harper's Weekly.*
The use of force against striking workers
at the Homestead Steelworks epitomized
the labor violence that marred the
Gilded Age.

Frontispiece: In Pennsylvania's coalfields,
"breaker boys" sorted through processed
coal, picking out slate and other refuse,
for less than a dollar a day. Many miners
began their careers as breaker boys, often
before they were 10 years old.

Title page: In marked contrast to the many
Gilded Age Americans who suffered
extreme poverty, a few enjoyed fabulous
wealth. Cornelia Ward and her children,
depicted in this 1880 painting, led a
lifestyle very different from that of
working mothers and child laborers.

Contents

What Is a Document?

To the historian, a document is, quite simply, any sort of historical evidence. It is a primary source, the raw material of history. A document may be more than the expected government paperwork, such as a treaty or passport. It is also a letter, diary, will, grocery list, newspaper article, recipe, memoir, oral history, school yearbook, map, chart, architectural plan, poster, musical score, play script, novel, political cartoon, painting, photograph—even an object.

Using primary sources allows us not just to read *about* history, but to read history itself. It allows us to immerse ourselves in the look and feel of an era gone by, to understand its people and their language, whether verbal or visual. And it allows us to take an active, hands-on role in (re)constructing history.

Using primary sources requires us to use our powers of detection to ferret out the relevant facts and to draw conclusions from them; just as Agatha Christie uses the scores in a bridge game to determine the identity of a murderer, the historian uses facts from a variety of sources—some, perhaps, seemingly inconsequential—to build a historical case.

The poet W. H. Auden wrote that history was the study of questions. Primary sources force us to ask questions—and then, by answering them, to construct a narrative or an argument that makes sense to us. Moreover, as we draw on the many sources from "the dust-bin of history," we can endow that narrative with character, personality, and texture—all the elements that make history so endlessly intriguing.

Cartoon
This political cartoon addresses the issue of church and state. It illustrates the Supreme Court's role in balancing the demands of the First Amendment of the Constitution and the desires of the religious population.

Illustration
Illustrations from children's books, such as this alphabet from the New England Primer, tell us how children were educated, and also what the religious and moral values of the time were.

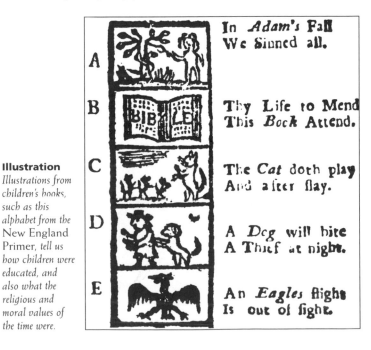

A   In *Adam's* Fall We Sinned all.

B   Thy Life to Mend This *Book* Attend.

C   The *Cat* doth play And after slay.

D   A *Dog* will bite A Thief at night.

E   An *Eagles* flight Is out of sight.

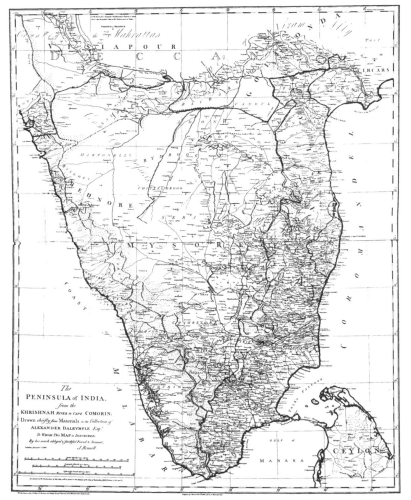

Treaty

A government document such as this 1805 treaty can reveal not only the details of government policy, but information about the people who signed it. Here, the Indians' names were written in English transliteration by U.S. officials; the Indians added pictographs to the right of their names.

Map

A 1788 British map of India shows the region prior to British colonization, an indication of the kingdoms and provinces whose ethnic divisions would resurface later in India's history.

Literature

The first written version of the Old English epic Beowulf, from the late 10th century, is physical evidence of the transition from oral to written history. Charred by fire, it is also a physical record of the wear and tear of history.

How to Read a Document

When reading any historical document, it is crucial to place the document in context. Every document represents a point of view, whether it be an essay, a newspaper account, a diary entry, cartoon, or photograph. We need to ask: Who was the author of the document? What was his or her message? Who was the intended audience?

The political cartoon of John D. Rockefeller and the photograph of the family in Kansas on the facing page are examples of two important types of Gilded Age documents. At the time, political cartoons were an especially effective means of shaping public opinion, as cheap mass-produced and mass-circulated magazines and newspapers became available to nearly all Americans for the first time. Photography also grew in importance as newspapers and magazines developed techniques to reproduce photographs on their pages. Technological advances in film, cameras, and the flash process made photographs clearer and more lifelike.

Other types of documents also fill this book. Pages from mail-order catalogs and house plans show how people dressed and lived. Songs and articles from popular magazines provide slices of popular culture, some of which may seem surprisingly familiar. Many of these documents reflect public discussions that raged in the United States during the Gilded Age. The nation's dramatic economic and social transformations sparked passionate public debate. Americans struggled with the meaning of justice and democracy in a new social setting as their nation became more urbanized, industrialized, and ethnically and culturally diverse, in short, modern. Similar issues—albeit in a different context—still consume the nation more than a hundred years later: What is a just society? What role should government and big business play? What strategies should the powerless employ to make change? How can Americans create a sense of community in an increasingly impersonal world? Who is an American?

Caricature

In order to make a strong and clear statement, political cartoonists use caricature, or exaggerated features. The author of this cartoon depicts oil tycoon John D. Rockefeller as a giant, towering over Washington, to represent his colossal power and influence. In contrast, President William McKinley cowers under the building, suggesting that Rockefeller dominates even the highest office in the land.

Symbols

Cartoonists communicate by using symbols that the reader can readily identify. Here the Capitol has been turned into an oil refinery, symbolizing Rockefeller's "ownership" of both the House and Senate. The moneybags surrounding McKinley imply that Rockefeller and Standard Oil can easily buy the President. The federal government, the cartoonist tells his audience, no longer represents the people, but instead is the private domain of the nation's most powerful company.

Subject

Even though a photograph might seem objective, as it captures "reality" within the camera's lens, the photographer's choice of subject conveys a particular message. The Shores family of Custer County, Nebraska, migrated to Kansas to flee the South's racial oppression. Their prosperous homestead testifies to African-American success in the West.

Pose

The family poses proudly, conveying strength and determination. Each member looks directly at the camera, asserting his or her equality with the viewer.

Arrangement

Portraying all three generations of the Shores family before their sod house, the photograph suggests the importance of family bonds and unity to their success. In an age of virulent racism, the photograph communicates the message that black Americans valued family and home just as many white Americans did and that given a fair chance, black people, too, could prosper in American society.

Introduction

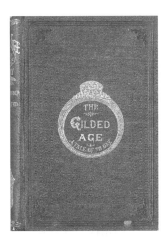

Co-authored by Charles Dudley Warner and Mark Twain, the novel The Gilded Age–A Tale of Today furnished the name for an era in American history marked by excess, corruption, and materialism.

An illustration from Warner and Twain's The Gilded Age, showing huckster Colonel Sellers enticing Washington Hawkins with visions of fabulous riches: "The colonel's tongue was a magician's wand that turned dried apples into figs and water into wine as easily as it could change a hovel into a palace. . . ."

Since 1873, when Mark Twain and Charles Dudley Warner published their satirical novel *The Gilded Age*, Americans have used the term to designate a distinctive period, the last quarter of the 19th century. The Gilded Age proved to be a resilient designation because it seemed to fit so well. Twain and Warner's novel scathingly satirized post–Civil War America as a land of craven materialism as well as hopelessly corrupt political practices. The United States indeed seemed to be gilded—covered with gold— in limitless moneymaking enterprises and business possibilities. But the gold casing often proved to be a thin veneer, covering up an uglier society—one of crass greed and excess.

For many years historians accepted Twain and Warner's characterization of the post–Civil War United States, an era dominated by robber barons—industrial leaders who fleeced a vulnerable public through questionable business practices—and fat cat political bosses who dispensed favors while lining their pockets with payoffs.

But robber barons and political bosses are only part of the story of the Gilded Age. As Twain and Warner suggested, it was indeed an era of extremes—a time of rapid industrialization coupled with cycles of crushing unemployment, of both unprecedented wealth and dire poverty. It was also an era of opportunity for millions of European immigrants who poured into the nation just as certain native-born groups, particularly African Americans and Native Americans, bore the brunt of racially motivated violence. It was also an era in which the downtrodden fought back, demanding that the United States live up to its ideals of equality before the law and justice for all, which had been lost in a flurry of industrialization and unprecedented concentrations of wealth and power in the hands of a few. It was a time when their loss kindled a blaze of social activism.

Chapter One

Big Business, Industry, and the American Dream

I n 1848, at the age of 13, Andrew Carnegie emigrated from Scotland to the United States with his parents and younger brother. The family settled near Pittsburgh, and young Carnegie quickly found a job as a bobbin boy in a cotton factory, working for $1.20 a week to help support his family. Educating himself by reading history and literature at a local library on weekends, Carnegie soon secured a job as a telegraph messenger boy and then as a telegraph operator for the Pittsburgh division of the Pennsylvania Railroad. He quickly rose to the position of office boy and then clerk; within several years he headed the Pittsburgh division. In 1865, when he was 30, Carnegie left the railroad to establish his own firm, Keystone Bridge Co., which manufactured and built iron bridges. Keystone Bridge soon expanded into iron and steel mills. By 1872 Carnegie, with the aid of investment partners, established his first steel mill near Pittsburgh. Twenty years later, Carnegie Steel had emerged as the largest steel company in the world, and Andrew Carnegie as one of its richest men.

Carnegie's success stemmed from his ability to cut production costs, allowing him to sell steel at a lower price than his rivals. Yet Carnegie's workers often paid the price for his obsession with economy, working long and dangerous 12-hour shifts for minimal wages.

In 1901 the former factory worker and immigrant sold Carnegie Steel for $480 million to banker J. Pierpont Morgan, creating the first

The steel industry emerged as one of the Gilded Age's hallmark "big businesses." Steel companies, such as Carnegie Steel, engaged in cutthroat competition in order to eliminate rivals, incorporating new technology, inventing new managerial methods, and keeping wages low—all to produce the best steel at the cheapest price.

An Age of Invention

Inventions, which proliferated during the Gilded Age, sometimes generated their own corporations. Thomas Edison, who invented the incandescent light bulb in 1879, founded the Edison Electric Illuminating Company in 1882—the first electric utility company—which supplied electricity to customers throughout New York City. By 1892 Edison Electric had merged with several competitors to form General Electric. Alexander Graham Bell patented the telephone in 1876 and, with several investors, formed the National Bell Telephone Company, which, by 1885, had become the American Telephone and Telegraph Company (AT&T), a massive company that dominated both local and long-distance telephone service. Together electricity and the telephone revolutionized American life. Other Gilded Age inventions included the phonograph and moving pictures, both developed by Thomas Edison.

Thomas Edison patented 1,093 inventions in his lifetime, far more than any other inventor in American history, including 195 for the phonograph alone. Edison ascribed his achievement to hard work, explaining, "Genius is 1 percent inspiration and 99 percent perspiration."

billion-dollar corporation in U.S. history, United States Steel. Believing that no man should die wealthy, Carnegie spent the remainder of his life giving away most of his fortune. He established public libraries, museums, and pension funds for steelworkers, railroad workers, and college professors as well as a foundation dedicated to international peace.

Carnegie's life story reflects many of the currents and crosscurrents of the Gilded Age. To some, he represented the self-made man and the limitless possibilities of the age, when even an immigrant boy, through hard work and determination, could become a powerful, world-famous millionaire, benefactor, and captain of industry. To others, he epitomized the evils of the age, of power and wealth concentrated in the hands of a few, of cutthroat business practices and the exploitation of workers. He was considered a robber baron who actually limited opportunity for average Americans.

Whether judged a hero or villain, Andrew Carnegie can tell us a great deal about the transformations in the U.S. economy that defined the Gilded Age. Railroads, such as the Pennsylvania, which employed Carnegie as a young man, provided the foundation for the second U.S. Industrial Revolution. By the mid-1860s ribbons of steel rails tied the nation together. The first big business in an era of massive industrial growth, railroads led the way for the growth of other big businesses. Keystone Bridge actually manufactured and built iron railroad bridges that spanned the Mississippi, allowing trains to cross the continent by 1869 and opening up vast markets for U.S. industry. The telegraph, which Carnegie mastered as a young man, provided a communications network that coordinated rail travel as well as the distribution of goods. A reliable transportation and communication system provided the foundation for modern, large-scale corporations, many of which produced a variety of products, such as Carnegie Steel, as well as clothing, shoes, and bicycles. All of these goods could be shipped by railroad to the most remote regions of the country.

To establish large industries and factories required tremendous amounts of money—more than one investor could provide. To establish the Carnegie Steel Company, Carnegie formed a partnership with several other investors. Other capitalists founded large, modern corporations that sold shares publicly to finance

their massive enterprises; shareholders, in turn, earned profits on their investment if the corporation prospered. Railroads, such as the Pennsylvania, were among the first to embrace corporate organization, but this form of enterprise spread to other industries following the Civil War, quickly dominating the American business world. Ownership of industries by shareholders, rather than an individual, became the modern enterprise structure.

Modern corporations were defined not only by their scale but also by their organization. A big business, such as Carnegie Steel, required an army of managers to oversee every aspect of the making and distribution of steel. Carnegie employed managers with specialized skills, who oversaw an array of divisions and departments. They monitored productivity, worked to increase efficiency, and cut costs in order to maximize profits and eliminate rival firms. Carnegie's emergence as the nation's leading steel maker was attributable mainly to the fact that he and his managers mastered the process of producing steel more cheaply than his competitors.

Cheap production depended largely on a corporation's ability to control all of its aspects. Known as vertical integration, this was the hallmark of the modern corporation. Carnegie Steel, for example, owned—in addition to steel mills—the mines that produced raw materials, such as coal, coke, and iron ore, needed for the production of steel as well as railroads to distribute it. Carnegie and his managers attempted to control every stage of steel manufacturing, from raw materials, to production and distribution, to the cost of labor itself.

Control of the manufacturing process alone did not account for business success in the Gilded Age; a competitive spirit often also prevailed. Carnegie's fierce competition with rival steel makers led him to enter into secret agreements with competitors, known as pools, in which steel manufacturers fixed the price of their products, allowing all to share in the market. But Carnegie, always seeking ways to dominate the steel industry, soon got a reputation for breaking pooling agreements and destroying his rivals by selling his products at a lower price.

Firms like Carnegie Steel contributed to the emergence of the United States as the world's greatest industrial power by 1900. By 1892 Carnegie Steel—a single American company—manufactured more than half of all the steel made by all the steel companies in Great Britain. Rapid industrialization and the emergence of large enterprises shaped nearly every aspect of American life in the Gilded Age—where Americans worked, the conditions of their work, what they ate and wore, and where they lived.

Even after becoming the world's richest man, Andrew Carnegie liked to think of himself as a workingman and as a champion of working people, although his own workers frequently challenged that view. Through most of the Gilded Age, Carnegie managed to maintain a positive public image. He frequently contributed articles to popular magazines and journals commenting on pressing political and social issues.

Wages and Efficiency

Andrew Carnegie's quest to produce cheaper steel affected the wages he paid his workers. At the turn of the century, most unskilled steelworkers, especially recent immigrants, earned from $1.50 to $2.00 per day. And while a family in the Pittsburgh area needed $15 a week to live, most workers made less than $12.50.

In addition to minimizing wages to undersell competitors, industrialists like Carnegie and their managers constantly sought to maximize the efficiency of their workers. They subscribed to the methods of "scientific management," as formulated by Frederick Winslow Taylor, who developed his ideas in relation to the steel industry. "In the past," he explained, "the man has been first; in the future the system must be first." To get the most from workers, Taylor insisted that managers investigate and observe, with stopwatch in hand, every aspect of a worker's performance.

No job was too lowly to be subject to scientific management. At Bethlehem Steel, for example, Taylor and his staff made a detailed study of coal shoveling that epitomized the principles of Taylorism, as it was popularly called.

First. Find, say 10 to 15 different men . . . who are especially skillful in doing the particular work to be analyzed.

Second. Study the exact series of elementary operations or motions which each of these men uses in doing the work which is being investigated, as well as the implement each man uses.

Third. Study with a stopwatch the time required to make each of these elementary movements and then select the quickest way of doing each element of work.

Fourth. Eliminate all false movements, slow movements, and useless movements.

Fifth. After doing away with all unnecessary movements, collect into one series the quickest and best movements as well as the best implements. This new method, involving the series of motions which can be made quickest and best, is then substituted in place of the 10 or 15 inferior series which were formerly in use.

While many industrialists in the Gilded Age enthusiastically embraced the "science" of management, workers deeply resented Taylorism and the stopwatch-wielding managers who hovered over their every move.

Big business and rapid industrialization seemed to symbolize progress and the emergence of the United States as a world power, but the rise of big business also made many Americans uneasy. They had never seen so much wealth and power concentrated in the hands of so few people. Some Americans asked probing questions about the consequences of big business and the rise of big businessmen. Did the rich and powerful, like Carnegie, rather than the people, now rule the United States? Did the rise of big business mean the end of small enterprise? Did success in business mean resorting to cutthroat competition and illegal practices? And did big business and industry mean more or less opportunity for the average American?

Captains of Industry

In his autobiography, published after his death in 1919, Carnegie discussed several of the innovations he pioneered in the iron and steel industry that allowed him to produce steel at a cheaper cost than his rivals. Attention to detail and an obsession with reducing production costs catapulted Carnegie to the pinnacle of world steel making. Gilded Age businessmen, like Carnegie, also revolutionized industry by carefully controlling every stage of manufacturing—from the raw materials needed to make their product to the production and distribution of their goods.

As I became acquainted with the manufacture of iron I was greatly surprised to find that the cost of each of the various processes was unknown. . . . It was a lump business, and until stock was taken and the books balanced at the end of the year, the manufacturers were in total ignorance of results. . . . I felt as if we were moles burrowing in the dark, and this to me was intolerable. I insisted upon such a system of weighing and accounting being introduced throughout our works as would enable us to know what our cost was for each process and especially what each man was doing, who saved material, who wasted it, and who produced the best results. . . .

The one vital lesson in iron and steel that I learned in Britain was the necessity for owning raw materials and finishing the completed article ready for its purpose. . . . [We were] the first, and for many years the only, firm in America that made ferro-manganese. We had been dependent upon foreigners for a supply of this indispensable article, paying as high as eighty dollars a ton for it. . . .

The experiment was worth trying and the result was a great success. We were able to supply the entire American demand, and prices fell from eighty to fifty dollars per ton as a consequence.

One of Carnegie's contemporaries, John D. Rockefeller, founded the Standard Oil Company in 1869, with several partners in Cleveland, Ohio. After careful observation of this boom and bust industry, Rockefeller concluded that control of railroads and pipelines to transport oil was the key to success in the oil industry. Rockefeller struck deals with railroads to offer lower rates to his company—known as rebates—for oil shipped in large amounts over long distances. Because Standard Oil was such a large company and provided the railroads with so much business, Rockefeller demanded drawbacks from the railroads; that is, he insisted that railroads hauling oil for other companies charge them more, kicking some of the money back to Standard Oil. Rebates and drawbacks, both secret practices, as well as outright intimidation, helped eliminate many of Rockefeller's competitors. Standard Oil soon monopolized the industry, controlling more than 90 percent of oil refining in the United States by the 1880s; by 1904, its profits reached a whopping $57 million. In *Random Reminiscences of Men and Events*, published in 1937, John D. Rockefeller credits his success to innovative business practices.

It is a common thing to hear people say that this company has crushed out its competitors. Only the uninformed could make such an assertion. It has had, and always will have, hundreds of active competitors; it has lived only because it has managed its affairs well and economically and with great vigor. . . .

I ascribe the success of the Standard Oil Company to its consistent policy of making the volume of its business large through the merit and cheapness of its products. It has spared no expense in utilizing the best and most efficient method of manufacture. It has sought for the best superintendents and workmen and paid the best wages. It has not hesitated to sacrifice old machinery and old plants for new and better ones. It has placed its manufactories at the points where they could supply markets at the least expense. It has not only

In the Gilded Age, political cartoons in newspapers and magazines played a key role in inciting public outrage against trusts and the business practices of industrialists such as Rockefeller.

Reflecting growing public outrage against John D. Rockefeller and his business practices, the January 22, 1900, edition of the Verdict *ran this political cartoon. In it Rockefeller remarks, "What a funny little government."*

The Invention of the Trust

While he managed to eliminate many of his competitors, John D. Rockefeller, like other Gilded Age industrialists, still feared the instability of competition. Seeking centralized control through consolidation, he devised the trust, in which stockholders in individual corporations turned over their stock to a small group of trustees, including Rockefeller himself, who ran the various parts of Standard Oil as one company. In return the stockholders received profits from the combination but had no direct control over the decisions of the trustees.

Other American industries copied Rockefeller's model, and trusts in beef, tobacco, and sugar soon emerged. Referring to a specific type of business organization, the term "trust," to the American public, denoted any large economic combination. Whereas the trust represented the pinnacle of modern enterprise to men like Rockefeller, to many Americans, it meant monopoly, the end of competition, and higher prices for products. Moreover, some feared that trusts placed far too much power in the hands of a few people who would inevitably abuse their power, an anonymous few who could not be held accountable.

John D. Rockefeller's business practices made him an especially notorious figure in the Gilded Age. Rockefeller did little to dispel his critics and once remarked, "The Standard Oil Company's business was that of saying nothing and sawing wood."

sought markets for its principal products, but for all possible by-products, sparing no expense in introducing them to the public in every nook and corner of the world. It has not hesitated to invest millions of dollars in methods for cheapening the gathering and distribution of oils by pipe-lines, special cars, tank-steamers, and tank-wagons.

Muckraking

Henry Demarest Lloyd provides a different interpretation of Rockefeller's success. Pioneering a new form of journalism, known as muckraking, the forerunner of today's investigative journalism, Lloyd exposed Rockefeller's underhanded— and often illegal—business practices to the nation. In this excerpt from "Story of a Great Monopoly," published in the *Atlantic Monthly* in 1881, Lloyd explored the consequences of monopolies, like Standard Oil, for average Americans.

Monopolies meant higher prices and fewer jobs, he argued. Moreover, big business, through payoffs to politicians, placed itself above the law, growing more powerful than government itself. Lloyd claimed that Standard Oil even bought off the Pennsylvania legislature to further its gains. He called upon the American people to demand that the federal government intervene to curb the power of big business. His disclosures about Standard Oil outraged the American public and helped make Rockefeller and Standard Oil synonymous with corporate greed and corruption. Lloyd's investigation and the public outcry it generated forced Congress to take action against the trusts. In 1890 Congress passed the Sherman Antitrust Act, which actually did little to eliminate trusts. Standard Oil remained intact until 1911 when the Supreme Court dissolved this infamous trust.

In the United States, in the cities as well as the country, petroleum is the general illuminator. We use more kerosene lamps than Bibles. . . . Very few of the forty millions of people in the United States who burn kerosene know that its production, manufacture, and export, its price at home and abroad, have been controlled by a single corporation—the Standard Oil Company. . . . It has refineries at Cleveland, Baltimore, and New York. Its own acid works, glue factories, hardware stores, and barrel shops supply it with all the accessories it needs in its business. It has bought land

Joseph Keppler's 1889 political cartoon "Bosses of the Senate," published in Puck, *depicts the trusts as larger than the government itself.*

at Indianapolis on which to erect the largest barrel factory in the country. It has drawn its check for $1,000,000 to suppress a rival. It buys 30,000 to 40,000 barrels of crude oil a day, at a price fixed by itself, and makes special contracts with railroads for the transportation of 13,000,000 to 14,000,000 barrels of oil a year. The four quarters of the globe are partitioned among the members of the Standard combinations. . . . Their great business capacity would have insured the managers of the Standard success, but the means by which they achieved monopoly was by conspiracy with the railroads. . . . The Standard killed its rivals, in brief, by getting the great trunk lines to refuse to give them transportation. . . . The Standard has done everything with the Pennsylvania legislature but refine it. . . . The contract is in print by which the Pennsylvania Railroad agreed with the Standard, under the name of the South Improvement Company, to double the freights on oil to everybody, but to repay the Standard one dollar for every barrel any of its competitors shipped. . . .

Hundreds and thousands of men have been ruined by these acts of the Standard and the railroads; whole communities have been rendered desperate, and the peace of Pennsylvania imperiled more than once. . . . The Pittsburg Chamber of Commerce reported

April 3, 1876, that there were twenty-one oil refineries idle in that city, owing to freight discriminations and combinations. There were $2,000,000 invested in these refineries, and if in operation they would have required the labor directly of 3,060 men, besides the much larger number of carpenters, masons, bricklayers, boiler-makers, pumpmakers, and other workingmen, who would have employment if the oil refining business were prosperous. . . .

The time has come to face the fact that the forces of capital and industry have outgrown the forces of our government. . . . Our strong men are engaged in a headlong fight for fortune, power, precedence, success. . . . The common people, the nation, must take them in hand. The people can be successful only when they are right. When monopolies succeed, the people fail; when a rich criminal escapes justice, the people are punished; when a legislature is bribed, the people are cheated. . . . The nation is the engine of the people. They must use it for their industrial life, as they used it in 1861 for their political life. The States have failed. The United States must succeed, or the people will perish.

"Survival of the Fittest"

Carnegie and other big businessmen believed that trusts and large enterprises represented the natural evolution of business. At the same time, he and other big businessmen attributed their success to their "fitness." Carnegie and many other businessmen of the Gilded Age embraced the theory of social Darwinism, a philosophy popularized in America by British theorist Herbert Spencer, who was a friend of Carnegie's. Spencer believed that the evolutionary theories of Charles Darwin could be applied to humanity. Society evolved—and inevitably improved—through a process of competition. In Spencer's terms, competition resulted in "survival of the fittest," ensuring the progress of the human race.

Not only did social Darwinism justify the massive fortunes amassed by Carnegie, Rockefeller, and others, as society's "fittest" members, it also implied that poor Americans were simply unfit, and, as such, should not be aided through charity. Moreover, social Darwinism demanded that the government not interfere with business—through legislation like the Sherman Antitrust Law—allowing it to compete in a natural way, unimpeded by regulations. In the following excerpt from "Wealth," an essay published in 1889, Carnegie

"All is well since all grows better...."
—Andrew Carnegie,
Autobiography of Andrew Carnegie, 1920

An armchair, an oven, a piano, a bicycle, and some farm tools spill out of the cornucopia of products available to American consumers through the 1897 Sears catalog.

acknowledges the widening gap between rich and poor but argues that the accumulation of extreme wealth is part of the natural evolutionary process, which, in the end, benefits all of society.

The conditions of human life have not only been changed but revolutionized within the past few hundred years. In former days there was little difference between the dwelling, dress, food, and environment of the chief and those of his retainers. . . . The contrast between the palace of the millionaire and the cottage of the laborer with us to-day measures the change which has come with civilization.

This change, however, is not to be deplored but welcomed as highly beneficial. It is well, nay, essential for the progress of the race, that the houses of some should be homes for all that is

The "cheapening of articles" for mass consumption—a positive effect of big business, according to Carnegie—seemed evident in the catalogs of mail-order houses, pioneered by Aaron Montgomery Ward in the Gilded Age. As railroads opened up new markets, especially in rural America, and factories produced goods in massive quantities, Ward founded his mail-order house in 1872. By buying items directly from manufacturers and selling his goods in massive volume, Ward managed to offer items at much lower prices than country merchants. Moreover, his catalogs offered a wide variety of goods unavailable in small country stores. His 1884 catalog offered over 10,000 items, ranging from farm equipment to clothing.

Sears, Roebuck, and Company, which started as a mail-order watch company in 1886, soon competed with Montgomery Ward for the rural market, calling its catalog "The Farmer's Friend." By 1900 Sears processed 100,000 orders a day. Mail-order houses, such as Ward and Sears, deeply damaged the sales of small-town merchants, who fought back by sponsoring bonfires of mail-order catalogs and begging their customers not to send their money off "to the Chicago millionaires." While Ward and Sears represented the evils of big business to country merchants, to countless Americans the mail-order houses offered a huge assortment of goods at affordable prices.

highest and best in literature and the arts, and for all the refinements of civilization, rather than none should be so. Much better this great irregularity than universal squalor. . . . The "good old times" were not good old times. Neither master nor servant was as well situated then as to-day. A relapse to old conditions would be disastrous to both—not the least so to him who serves—and would sweep away civilization with it. But whether the change be for good or ill, it is upon us, beyond our power to alter, and therefore to be accepted and made the best of. It is a waste of time to criticise the inevitable.

It is easy to see how the change has come. . . . In the manufacture of products we have the whole story. . . . Formerly articles were manufactured at the domestic hearth or in small shops which formed part of the household. The master and his apprentices worked side by side, the latter living with the master and therefore subject to the same conditions. . . . There was, substantially, social equality and even political equality. . . . But the inevitable result of such a mode of manufacture was crude articles at high prices. To-day the world obtains commodities of excellent quality at prices even the generation preceding this would have deemed incredible. . . . The poor enjoy what the rich could not before afford. What were the luxuries have become the necessaries of life. . . .

The price we pay for this salutary change is, no doubt, great. We assemble thousands of operatives in the factory, in the mine, in the counting-house, of whom the employer can know little or nothing and to whom the employer is little better than a myth. . . . Rigid Castes are formed, and, as usual, mutual ignorance breeds mutual distrust. . . . Under the law of competition, the employer of thousands is forced into the strictest economies, among which the rates paid to labor figure prominently, and often there is friction between the employer and the employed, between capital and labor, between rich and poor. Human society loses homogeneity.

The price which society pays for the law of competition, like the price it pays for cheap comforts and luxuries, is also great; but the advantages of this law are also greater still, for it is to this law that we owe our wonderful material development, which brings improved conditions in its train . . . and while the law may be sometimes hard for the individual, it is the best for the race, because it insures the survival of the fittest in every department. We accept and welcome, therefore, as conditions to which we must accommodate ourselves, great inequality of environment, the concentration of business, industrial, and commercial, in the

hands of a few, and the law of competition between these as being not only beneficial but essential for the future progress of the race.

Henry Demarest Lloyd questioned Carnegie's claims concerning the social benefits and progress generated by the growth of big business and competition. In this excerpt from his book, *Wealth Against Commonwealth,* published in 1899, Lloyd warned that the competitive business principles espoused by men like Carnegie and Rockefeller created a society at war with itself. An emphasis on individualism and materialism, Lloyd argued, threatens the fabric of community life.

The flames of a new economic evolution run around us, and we turn to find that competition has killed competition, that corporations are grown greater than the State and have bred individuals greater than themselves, and that the naked issue of our time is with property becoming the master instead of servant, property in many necessaries of life becoming monopoly of the necessaries of life. . . . Our industry is a fight of every man for himself. The prize we give the fittest is monopoly of the necessaries of life, and we leave these winners of the powers of life and death to wield them over us by the same "self-interest" with which they took them from us. . . .

The happiness, self-interest, or individuality of the whole is not more sacred than that of each, but it is greater. . . .

Where the self-interest of the individual is allowed to be the rule both of social and personal action, the level of all is forced down to that of the lowest. Business excuses itself for the things it does—cuts in wages, exactions in hours, tricks of competition—on the plea that the merciful are compelled to follow the cruel. . . . When the self-interest of society is made the standard, the lowest must rise to the average. The one pulls down, the other up. . . .

We are very poor. The striking feature of our economic condition is our poverty, not our wealth. We make ourselves "rich" by appropriating the property of others by methods which lessen the total property of all. . . . What we call cheapness shows

Industrialists of the Gilded Age built opulent houses to display their wealth and power. Social critic Thorstein Veblen dubbed their ostentatious displays "conspicuous consumption." The interior of Marble House, built for the Vanderbilts in 1892 at Newport, Rhode Island, contrasts sharply with the inside of a one-room working-class home in New York City.

"A man works, comes home, eats, and goes to bed, gets up, eats, and goes to work."

—Pennsylvania Steel worker, 1902 interview

itself to be unnatural fortunes for a few, monstrous luxury for them and proportionate deprivation for the people, judges debauched, trustees dishonored, Congress and State legislatures insulted and defied, when not seduced, multitudes of honest men ruined and driven to despair. . . .

If all will sacrifice themselves, none need be sacrificed. But if one may sacrifice another, all are sacrificed. That is the difference between self-interest and other interest. In industry we have been substituting all the mean passions that can set man against man in place of the irresistible power of brotherhood. To tell us of the progressive sway of brotherhood in all human affairs is the sole message of history. "Love thy neighbor as thyself" is not the phrase of a ritual sentiment for the unapplied emotion of pious hours; it is the exact formula of the force to-day operating the greatest institutions man has established. It is as secular as sacred. . . .

Responsibilities of the Rich

In an 1889 essay, Carnegie deflected some public criticism by articulating a "Gospel of Wealth." Claiming that it is a disgrace to die wealthy, Carnegie attempts to justify the massive fortunes of businessmen like himself by taking on the role of public benefactor. Rejecting outright charitable contributions, Carnegie preferred to create institutions, such as libraries, to help people help themselves. Ironically, after working exhausting 12-hour shifts in hot and dangerous conditions, few steelworkers in Carnegie's mills could take advantage of the educational opportunities available at Carnegie libraries. The following is an excerpt from Carnegie's essay.

This, then, is held to be the duty of the man of Wealth: First, to set an example of modest, unostentatious living, shunning display and extravagance; to provide moderately for the legitimate wants of those dependent upon him; and after doing so to consider all surplus revenues which come to him simply as trust funds, which he is called upon to administer and strictly bound as a matter of duty to administer in the manner, which in his judgment is best calculated to produce the most beneficial results for the community—the man of wealth thus becoming the mere agent and trustee for his poorer brethren, bringing to their service his supe-

rior wisdom, experience, and ability to administer, doing for them better than they would or could do for themselves. . . .

In bestowing charity, the main consideration should be to help those who will help themselves; to provide part of the means by which those who desire to improve may do so; to give those who desire to rise the aids by which they may rise; to assist, but rarely or never do all. Neither the individual nor the race is improved by alms-giving. . . . The best means of benefiting the community is to place within its reach the ladders upon which the aspiring can rise—parks and means of recreation, by which men are helped in body and mind; works of art, certain to give pleasure and improve the public taste, and public institutions of various kinds, which will improve the general condition of the people; in this manner returning their surplus wealth to the mass of their fellows in the forms best calculated to do them lasting good.

This is the problem of Rich and Poor to be solved. The laws of accumulation will be left free; the laws of distribution free. Individualism will continue, but the millionaire will be but a trustee for the poor; intrusted for a season with a great part of the increased wealth of the community, but administering it for the community far better than it could or would have done for itself. . . .

Attempting to live up to his own principles, Carnegie gave away more than $350 million by the time of his death in 1919—most of his fortune—while still guaranteeing that his wife and child would live in luxury. Remembering the importance of libraries in his own education, Carnegie funded more than 2,800 free libraries throughout the world. His other contributions included generous gifts to colleges and universities; pension funds for steelworkers and college professors; and an institute for international peace. Oil millionaire John D. Rockefeller gave millions of dollars away as well, establishing the University of Chicago and funding medical research.

Despite the social benefits of Carnegie and Rockefeller's acts of charity, not all Americans praised their altruism. In 1905 the Reverend Washington Gladden, along with a number of other ministers, protested the acceptance of a $100,000 contribution that Rockefeller made to the American Board of Commissioners for Foreign Missions, a Congregational group in Boston. The church, according to Gladden, should refuse "tainted money." In a letter to *The Outlook* in April 1905,

In 1890, 73 percent of the nation's wealth was held by the top 10 percent of the population. In 1990, the top 10 percent of the population accounted for 68 percent of the nation's wealth.

"Gifts of ten millions deodorize themselves."
—New York Sun, 1905

Gladden explained his position (despite his vigorous protest, the board decided to accept Rockefeller's contribution).

Mr. Rockefeller is not simply a private person. He is the representative of a great system that has become a public enemy. The organization which he represents has been and now is a gigantic oppressor of the people. . . . [It is] abundantly clear that this great fortune has been built up by the transgression and the evasion of law and by methods which are at war with the first principles of morality. Are we, as Christians, forbidden to judge this sort of thing? I rather think it is our business to be swift witnesses against it.

From Rags to Riches

Carnegie and Rockefeller captured the imaginations of many Gilded Age Americans. They symbolized the opportunity and the riches that could be made during the era. Horatio Alger wrote numerous stories for boys that stressed the importance of individual effort, enterprise, respectability, and, importantly, luck. This excerpt from *Ragged Dick,* published in 1867, tells the tale of a spunky New York City shoeshine boy and street urchin, Dick Hunter, who is befriended by a wealthy child, Frank, and his uncle, Mr. Whitney, both of whom teach Dick the secrets of success:

"Frank's been very kind to me," said Dick, who, rough street-boy as he was, had a heart easily touched by kindness, of which he had never experienced much. "He's a tip-top fellow."

"I believe he is a good boy," said Mr. Whitney. "I hope, my lad, you will prosper and rise in the world. You know in this free country poverty in early life is no bar to a man's advancement. I haven't risen very high myself," he added, with a smile, "but have met with moderate success in life; yet there was a time when I was as poor as you."

"Were you, sir?" asked Dick, eagerly.

"Yes, my boy, I have known the time when I have been obliged to go without my dinner because I didn't have enough money to pay for it."

"How did you get up in the world?" asked Dick, anxiously.

"I entered a printing-office as an apprentice and worked for some years. Then my eyes gave out and I was obliged to give that

Even children's games reflected the nation's obsession with big business and moneymaking. In 1883, at the age of 16, George S. Parker, who would eventually establish Parker Brothers, invented the Game of Banking. Several years later, the Montgomery Ward Catalog carried The Game of Moneta: or Money Makes Money, as well as the Game of Business.

up. Not knowing what else to do, I went into the country and worked on a farm. After a while I was lucky enough to invent a machine, which has brought me in a great deal of money. But there was one thing I got while I was in the printing-office which I value more than money."

"What was that, sir?"

"A taste for reading and study. During my leisure hours I improved myself by study and acquired a large part of the knowledge which I now possess. Indeed, it was one of my books that first put me on the track of the invention, which I afterwards made. So you see, my lad, that my studious habits paid me in money, as well as in another way."

"I'm awful ignorant," said Dick, soberly.

"But you are young, and, I judge, a smart boy. If you try to learn, you can, and if you ever expect to do anything in the world, you must know something of books."

"I will," said Dick, resolutely. "I ain't always goin' to black boots for a livin'."

"All labor is respectable, my lad, and you have no cause to be ashamed of any honest business; yet when you can get something to do that promises better for your future prospects, I advise you to do so. Till then earn your living in the way you are accustomed to, avoid extravagance, and save up a little money if you can."

"Thank you for your advice," said our hero. "There ain't many that takes an interest in Ragged Dick."

"So that's your name," said Mr. Whitney. "If I judge you rightly, it won't be long before you change it. Save your money, lad, buy books, and determine to be somebody, and you may yet fill an honorable position."

"I'll try," said Dick. "Good-night, sir. . . ."

"Good-by, my lad," said Mr. Whitney. "I hope to hear good accounts of you sometime. Don't forget what I have told you. Remember that your future position depends mainly upon yourself, and that it will be high or low as you choose to make it."

As the nation's factories produced a variety of goods in the Gilded Age, national advertising campaigns lured Americans—both young and old—to purchase them. This page of advertisements from Harper's Young People (1894) promoted products aimed at both young people and their parents.

Chapter Two

Immigration to a "Promised Land"

I
n the late spring of 1882 Abraham Cahan, a 22-year-old native of Vilna, Russia, arrived in Philadelphia after a 13-day crossing of the Atlantic Ocean. Jewish and a revolutionary, Cahan fled Russia in the midst of the government's massive repression of Jews that culminated in the cruel and bloody pogroms. Jews in Russia had long been legally barred from owning land and were forced to live in restricted areas, and the pogroms represented a horrific new level of oppression, as Russian soldiers marched into Jewish settlements, destroying homes, businesses, and synagogues and brutally murdering Jewish men, women, and children.

Abraham Cahan was one of approximately 2 million eastern European Jews who arrived in the United States between 1880 and World War I. Cahan made his way to New York City's Lower East Side, which during that period was a densely populated, lively neighborhood of Jewish immigrants. Like many immigrants in the Gilded Age, Cahan got his first job in one of America's rapidly expanding industries, working in a cigar factory. Taking advantage of the nation's free public school system, Cahan studied at night, learning English well enough to become an English tutor to fellow immigrants. Maintaining his involvement in radical politics, Cahan became an editor of a Jewish labor newspaper, and by 1903 served as editor of the *Jewish Daily Forward*, a newspaper of national prominence and influence, which he edited until 1946.

Even after he became a successful journalist and writer, Cahan never forgot what it was like to be an immigrant. He remembered the conflicting emotions that he and other immigrants felt as they adjusted to life

A lively, congested neighborhood, the Lower East Side of Manhattan served as the first home to many Jewish immigrants arriving in New York in the Gilded Age. Some were shocked to discover that America's streets were not literally paved with gold.

in a strange new land. Cahan spent much of his life writing about the immigrant experience, in newspaper columns, short stories, and novels, exposing native-born Americans to newcomers' struggles. Moreover, he aided the adjustment of countless fellow Jewish immigrants through a column called the "Bintel Brief" (Bundle of Letters), which, like "Dear Abby" or "Ann Landers" many years later, offered advice to those who wrote seeking guidance.

Not only part of a massive migration of eastern European Jews to the United States, Cahan was also one of more than 13 million immigrants who arrived in the United States in the Gilded Age. The United States had always been a nation of immigrants, but Gilded Age immigration was different in two ways: its enormous volume and the immigrants' region of origin. In the space of 24 years—from 1866 to 1900—more immigrants arrived in the United States than in the previous 250 years. In addition, whereas western Europeans—particularly from the British Isles, Ireland, and Scandinavia—made up the overwhelming majority of immigrants to the United States before the Civil War, eastern and southern Europeans dominated in the Gilded Age, with Italians, eastern European Jews, and Slavic peoples being the largest groups. At the same time non-European immigrants also flocked to the United States, albeit in smaller numbers than eastern and southern Europeans. Chinese and Japanese arrived on the West Coast, with Japanese immigrating to Hawaii as well; Mexicans crossed the border into California and other parts of the Southwest, such as Arizona, New Mexico, and Texas.

The volume and origins of Gilded Age immigrants created a backlash among some native-born Americans. The cultures, languages, and religions of southern and eastern Europeans seemed too different to enable them to ever become "true Americans," in the opinion of some. Because most were Roman Catholic or Jewish, arriving in an overwhelmingly Protestant nation, these immigrants were often viewed with suspicion. In Congress, colleges and universities, churches, and the popular press, native-born Americans discussed the "immigrant problem," giving rise to anti-immigrant and anti-Catholic organizations, such as the American Protective League. Moreover, Congress passed the nation's first immigration restriction law, aimed at Chinese rather than European immigrants. Once the Chinese had been welcomed; now they, more than any other immigrant group in the United States in the Gilded Age, were singled out as undesirable. In 1882, after years of anti-Chinese agitation, the Chinese became the first eth-

nic or racial group specifically barred from immigrating to the United States.

As native-born Americans fretted over the "immigrant problem," newcomers made invaluable contributions to the nation, enriching its culture and providing a cheap labor force for the expanding industrial economy. Some Gilded Age immigrants, like Abraham Cahan and other eastern European Jews, came to the United States largely to escape religious persecution; others came to work. Chronically underemployed and suffering from land shortages, Europeans responded enthusiastically to labor agents from U.S. industries, who aggressively recruited laborers, promising high wages and steady work. Railroad companies, wishing to sell lands granted them by the federal government as they built their roads, flooded Europe with flyers advertising cheap land and promising prosperity and a fresh beginning in the American West. While labor recruiters successfully encouraged immigration, letters home, written by relatives and friends in the United States, promising a better life, sealed the decision of many to risk a new life.

Chinese and Japanese laborers also sought a new beginning in the West. The Chinese, who initially labored in gold and silver mines, were recruited as railroad workers in the 1860s. The Central Pacific Railroad imported approximately 10,000 Chinese workers. Sugar plantation owners recruited Japanese men and women to labor in Hawaii, while others worked on farms on the mainland. Asian immigrants often worked dangerous and backbreaking jobs, receiving wages far lower than those paid to white laborers.

Although many immigrants came to the United States with the dream of owning land, most jobs were in cities and industrial centers. Most immigrants crowded into urban areas of the United States, creating Little Italys, Chinatowns, and other ethnic enclaves. As many arrived with paltry sums of money and few skills, they filled the ranks of unskilled labor in factories and heavy industry. Some groups, like the Italians, Greeks, and Slavs,

Immigrants disembark at Ellis Island for a new life in America. Many immigrants brought to the United States only what they could carry with them in suitcases, baskets, boxes, and sacks. In addition to clothing, immigrants often transported photographs, religious objects, and family heirlooms.

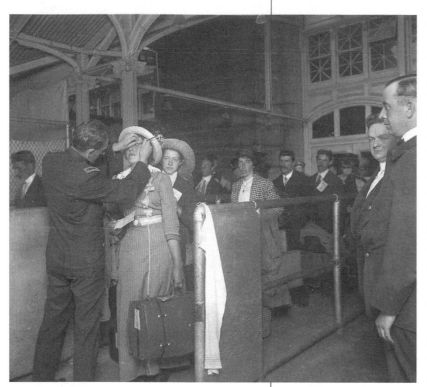

Immigrants had to undergo physical examinations in order to determine whether they were "fit" to enter the United States. At Ellis Island, officials carefully observed immigrants as they lined up for inspection, hoping to catch signs of any physical or mental problems. In this photo, medical examiners check immigrants for trachoma, an eye disease, by turning the eyelid inside out with a buttonhook, an especially painful process.

consisted mostly of young men, often referred to as "birds of passage" or "sojourners." These immigrants had planned to come to the United States only temporarily, hoping to make a lot of money and return home wealthy. Nearly 50 percent of Slavs, Italians, and Greek immigrants returned to their homelands after laboring in grueling jobs in U.S. industry. Two of every three Chinese immigrants returned as well. While many Mexicans settled permanently in the United States, others stayed only temporarily, moving back and forth across the permeable Mexican-U.S. border as their employment fluctuated.

By contrast, Abraham Cahan and his fellow Jews, as political and religious refugees, did not have the option of returning home. Unlike many other ethnic groups, Jews arrived as family units, planning to settle in the United States permanently. Moreover, they were more highly educated and skilled than many other immigrant groups. Many Jews who were tailors and seamstresses in Europe successfully transferred their skills to the United States, where they landed jobs in the garment industry, centered in New York City.

The United States proved to be the "promised land" for many immigrants in the Gilded Age, as the nation provided jobs, the chance for an education, and religious freedom, but others were left outside the "golden door." A 1790 federal law made it impossible for nonwhites to become naturalized, leaving Chinese and Japanese immigrants permanent aliens, without the rights and protections of U.S. citizens. Further, they and other nonwhite immigrants, such as Mexicans, often faced racial discrimination.

The transition from the old world to the new often proved painful and filled with tension. Letters from immigrants seeking advice from Abraham Cahan, in his "Bintel Brief" column, summed up the problems and concerns of many Gilded Age immigrants—regardless of ethnicity: How much should one give up of the old ways to become an American? Was it permissible to fall in love and marry outside of one's faith or ethnic background? How should an immigrant fight back against mistreatment and discrimination?

Arrival

In his 1917 novel *The Rise of David Levinsky*, Abraham Cahan traces the journey of David Levinsky from his days as a Talmudic scholar in Russia to his rise as a millionaire cloak manufacturer in New York City. Drawing on his own experience as an immigrant, Cahan described Levinsky's mixed emotions upon his first sighting of New York City.

The immigrant's arrival in his new home is like a second birth to him. Imagine a new-born babe in possession of a fully developed intellect. Would it ever forget its entry into the world? Neither does the immigrant ever forget his entry into a country which is, to him, a new world in the profoundest sense of the term and in which he expects to pass the rest of his life. I conjure up the

A ship's passenger list for the Iowa, which arrived in Boston from Liverpool on November 6, 1890, provides valuable information about the origin, backgrounds, destinations, and family structure of Gilded Age immigrants. Most, as this document shows, traveled in steerage, the cheapest and least desirable section of the ship, usually located below decks. Trans-Atlantic steerage was overcrowded and lacked ventilation, and tickets cost as little as $10 in the 1880s. Late-19th-century advances in technology greatly reduced the duration of the ocean voyage. In 1872, a sailing ship took 44 days on average to cross the Atlantic; by the turn of the 20th century, the slowest steamships crossed the Atlantic in 8 days.

Ellis Island

In 1892 the U.S. government opened Ellis Island in New York Harbor as the first federal immigration station. Between 1892 and 1954, when the station closed, about 80 percent of all European immigrants—an estimated 12 million people—first set foot on American soil at Ellis Island. Historians have estimated that approximately 40 percent of present-day Americans have ancestors who passed through Ellis Island.

At Ellis Island, immigrants were "processed" by officials who determined whether they were "fit" to enter the United States. Medical officers examined immigrants for diseases, physical defects, and mental illness. Then immigration inspectors peppered arrivals with questions about their place of origin, marital status, how they had paid for their passage to the United States, their plans for employment, and their destination. Processing an average of 5,000 people per day, immigration officials often felt overwhelmed and overworked, and they sometimes handled people roughly.

Most immigrants approached Ellis Island with both anticipation and dread. The island represented the final hurdle in their long journey to the United States. What if the officials rejected them? What if some family members passed the inspection and others did not? While for most immigrants Ellis Island symbolized the gateway to a new life, some experienced it as an island of heartbreak. But most managed to pass the inspection in three or four hours; only about 2 percent of those wishing to enter the United States were turned away at Ellis Island and had to return home. Those who passed inspection were free to meet friends or family, board ferries to New York or barges to railroad stations in New Jersey, and begin new lives.

For years after Ellis Island closed, it stood in disrepair. But in the mid-1980s, several of the island's buildings, including the main structure, were restored. The main building now houses the Museum of American Immigration, a monument to the millions who passed through its gates.

gorgeousness of the spectacle as it appeared to me on that clear June morning: the magnificent verdure of Staten Island, the tender blue of sea and sky, the dignified bustle of passing craft—above all, those floating, squatting, multitudinously windowed palaces which I subsequently learned to call ferries. It was all so utterly unlike anything I had ever seen or dreamed before. It unfolded itself like a divine revelation. I was in a trance or in something closely resembling one.

"This, then, is America!" I exclaimed, mutely. The notion of something enchanted which the name had always evoked in me now seemed fully borne out. . . .

My transport of admiration, however, only added to my sense of helplessness and awe. Here, on shipboard, I was sure of my shelter and food, at least. How was I going to procure my sustenance on those magic shores? I wished the remaining hour could be prolonged indefinitely.

Whereas European and Asian immigrants to the United States faced a grueling voyage across the ocean, many Mexican immigrants could make the journey to America in a matter of days, on foot or by horseback. In an interview conducted by a writer from the Federal Writers' Project in the 1930s, Juanita Hermandes Garcia described her family's trip to the United States in 1876. She and her family did not face an ocean crossing or processing at Ellis Island, but they confronted other challenges on their way to Texas. (When transcribing interviews, some writers exaggerated the dialect of the people they interviewed.)

"Me was born in old Mexico, me have 67 years," says Juanita Hermandes Garcia, of San Angelo, Texas.

"Me came with me father and mother to Texas when me have 6 years. Me family collected our possessions to make ready for transport to Texas. We put a burro to a two wheel cart and had one burro for the pack. This was one very good way to make the trip, in that time many people no have the cart. Me family transported at Del Rio, make the travel two days and make the camp for three weeks. The place make ideal for cook, scrub the clothes, rest, and make ready to continue the trip. This was free country, everything free, pecans, wood, water, wild meat; make the trip with no much money.

"Una dia (one day), heap muchos Indians make come to our camp, fell from horses, brought meat from wild animals to make

trade to me madre (my mother) for Mexican food. Me mother been make the tortillas and tamales for one whole week, to finish the trip, Indians take all and leave wild meat, she make afraid they take me.

"All of me family had plenty light complexion pero me madre y mio (except mother and I). Me father had all Spanish blood, make the home in Spain when he baby, tienen ojos asule y palo blanco (he had blue eyes and light hair). The big chief no like me father, no talk with him. They say all time, me little Indian girl, make me ride the back every day when come for trade, me make scare most to die, some day make carry way me to live with Indians. All time Indians bring presents para me. One time make bring a pair of moccasins very pretty; make the pretty little beads trim, me save this little shoes long time, they all time make give present to me, no like other ninos (little girls).

"Me family no make the know what to do, make scare of Indian make kill if leave, make kill if stay, all family almost make die of fright when see Indians. The big bunch Indians make fast ride on wild horses by our camp, make show natural born riders, we make scare and run and hide to save life. We no make the know of the harm from Indians, they make plenty scare all time, no make the fight.

"Well, me make the trip safe to this Concho County, look pretty good to me family, all people work, make plenty money to buy food. Many things make free, no need much money. We lived in a little house down by the river where we make the Santa Fe park today. We got some more scare for life, negro soldiers from Fort Concho come near our house to make practice for shooting with guns. They throw whisky and drinking bottles high in the air and shoot them in pieces before the fall on the earth. We make run, peep from little holes; they might shoot us. They no care for Mexican people, shoot Mexican as shoot animal."

Opportunity

Like Abraham Cahan, Mary Antin and her family fled Russia during the pogroms. When she was 13 years old, she and her mother and brothers and sisters reunited with her father— who had emigrated three years earlier—in Boston. Antin attended public school and went on to be a distinguished student at Boston Latin School and Barnard College. In 1912 she wrote her autobiography, *The Promised Land,* in which she exuberantly celebrated America as a land of opportunity.

In the following passage she described her Americanization process, which she compared to a "second infancy," in which, she, as a "newborn," learned the ways of a new world. As she explains, "greenhorns"—newly arrived immigrants—often received aid from more experienced immigrants in their adjustment to American life.

Now I was not exactly an infant when I was set down, on a May day some fifteen years ago, in this pleasant nursery of America. I had long since acquired the use of my faculties and had collected some bits of experience, practical and emotional, and had even learned to give an account of them. Still, I had very little perspective, and my observations and comparisons were superficial. I was too much carried away to analyze the forces that were moving me. . . . America was bewilderingly strange, unimaginably complex, delightfully unexplored. I rushed impetuously out of the cage of my provincialism and looked eagerly about the brilliant universe. . . . Plenty of maiden aunts were present during my second infancy, in the guise of immigrant officials, school-teachers, settlement workers, and sundry other unprejudiced and critical observers. . . .

Our initiation into American ways began with the first step on the new soil. My father found occasion to instruct or correct us even on the way from the pier to Wall Street, which journey we made crowded together in a rickety cab. He told us not to lean out of the windows, not to point, and explained the word "greenhorn." We did not want to be "greenhorns" and gave the strictest attention to my father's instructions. . . .

The first meal was an object lesson of much variety. My father produced several kinds of food, ready to eat, without any cooking, from little tin cans that had printing all over them. He attempted to introduce us to a queer, slippery kind of fruit, which he called a "banana," but had to give it up for the time being. After the meal, he had better luck with a curious piece of furniture on runners, which he called "rocking-chair." There were five of us newcomers, and we found five different ways of getting into the American machine of perpetual motion and as many ways of getting out. . . .

We had to visit the stores and be dressed from head to foot in American clothing; we had to learn the mysteries of the iron stove, the washboard, and the speaking-tube; we had to learn to trade with the fruit peddler through the window and not to be afraid of the policeman; and above all, we had to learn English.

The kind people who assisted us in these important matters form a group by themselves in the gallery of my friends. . . . When

I enumerate the long list of my American teachers, I must begin with those who came to us on Wall Street and taught us our first steps. To my mother, in her perplexity over the cookstove, the woman who showed her how to make the fire was an angel of deliverance. A fairy godmother to us children was she who led us to a wonderful country, called "uptown," where, in a dazzlingly beautiful palace called a "department store," we exchanged our hateful homemade European costumes, which pointed us out as "greenhorns" to the children on the street, for real American machine-made garments, and issued forth glorified in each other's eyes.

With our despised immigrant clothing we shed also our impossible Hebrew names. A committee of our friends, several years ahead of us in American experience, put their heads together and concocted American names for us all. Those of our real names that had no pleasing American equivalents they ruthlessly discarded, content if they retained the initials. My mother, possessing a name that was not easily translatable, was punished with the undignified nickname of Annie. Ftechke, Joseph, and Deborah issued as Frieda, Joseph, and Dora, respectively. As for poor me, I was simply cheated. The name they gave me was hardly new. My Hebrew name being Maryashe in full, Mashke for short, Russianized into Marya (Mar-ya), my friends said that it would be good in English as *Mary*, which was very disappointing, as I longed to possess a strange-sounding American name like the others.

I am forgetting the consolation I had, in this matter of names, from the use of my surname, which I have had no occasion to mention until now. I found on my arrival that my father was "Mr. Antin" on the slightest provocation, and not, as in Polotzk, on state occasions alone. And so I was "Mary Antin," and I felt very important to answer to such a dignified title. It was just like America that even plain people should wear their surnames on weekdays.

Like many immigrants, Mary Antin and her family were astounded that a free public education was available to all Americans, immigrant or native born. Many immigrants viewed education, as Antin explains, as the key to America's golden door.

Education was free. That subject my father had written about repeatedly, as comprising his chief hope for us children, the essence of American opportunity, the treasure that no thief could

A Mexican-American family poses in front of their modest homestead in Texas in 1880. Like the Chinese in the Gilded Age, people of Mexican descent faced discrimination because many white Americans viewed them as racially inferior.

"The Greenhorn Cousin"

Education often served as a gateway for a better job and a more comfortable life, but not all immigrant children could take advantage of educational opportunities in the United States. Low wages meant that many children had to work to support their families. Mary Antin herself was able to attend school only because her older sister, Frieda, labored in a factory. Thus while Mary celebrated the freedoms and opportunities that America offered, some immigrants sadly found their hopes for a bright future sapped by low-paying and dangerous jobs in America's shops and factories. This song, "The Greenhorn Cousin," originally appeared in a Yiddish theater production and was well-known to many Jewish immigrants.

Once a cousin came to me
Pretty as gold was she, the greenhorn,
Her cheeks were like red oranges,
Her tiny feet begging to dance.

She didn't walk, she skipped along,
She didn't talk, she sang,
Her manner was gay and cheerful,
That's how my cousin used to be.

I found a place with my neighbor,
The one who has a millinery store;
I got a job for my cousin,
Blessed be the golden land.

Since then many years have passed.
My cousin became a wreck
From many years of collecting wages
Till nothing was left of her.

Underneath her pretty blue eyes
Black lines are now drawn,
Her cheeks, once like red oranges,
Have now turned entirely green.

Today, when I meet my cousin
And ask her: "How are you, greenhorn?"
She answers with a grimace,
"To the devil with Columbus's land!"

touch, not even misfortune or poverty. It was the one thing that he was able to promise us when he sent for us; surer, safer than bread or shelter. . . .

The apex of my civic pride and personal contentment was reached on the bright September morning when I entered the public school. That day I must always remember, even if I live to be so old that I cannot tell my name. To most people their first day of school is a memorable occasion. In my case the importance of the day was a hundred times magnified, on account of the years I had waited, the road I had come, and the conscious ambitions I entertained. . . .

Father himself conducted us to school. He would not have delegated that mission to the President of the United States. He had awaited the day with impatience equal to mine, and the visions he saw as he hurried us over the sun-flecked pavements transcended all my dreams. . . .

Sacrifices

Unlike Mary Antin, who zealously shed her old name and appearance to become American, other immigrants and their American-born children retained their language and culture while making a new life. Creating insular ethnic neighborhoods, such as Little Italy and Chinatown, some immigrants found little need to learn English or assimilate American ways. Robert Ferrari, the child of Italian immigrants who arrived in New York City in the 1870s, recalls the Italian-American world of his childhood.

[D]uring my childhood and early youth the Italian had not made his way in America. My recollections go back clearly to the age of seven, when we moved to Mott Street, near what is now Chinatown, in Manhattan. . . . As a very small boy I used to accompany my mother on her shopping trips through this crowded sidewalk market, where every vendor waylaid us with loud and earnest descriptions of his offerings. With the coming of the pushcart and sidewalk market, the boundaries of the Italian community were fixed more definitely than ever. All shopping could be done within the immediate neighborhood, and my mother and her Italian neighbors, who were increasing in numbers by the month, had readily available many of the products of their native land.

The household my parents established on Mott Street was typical of those of Little Italy. We spoke only Italian in our home, ate Italian food, celebrated Italian holidays, and on Sundays entertained relatives and friends from the province of Basilicata who had followed my father and mother to America. We knew nothing of the Anglo-Saxon world which made up this country in that day. Limited transportation facilities did not encourage travel very far from home, even if the people had been so inclined, and these communities of racial blocs were somewhat isolated. . . .

Like all Italian youth of my generation, I have always been bilingual. My father of course had learned English at his work and taught himself to read the newspapers; my mother picked up some English, too, but we always spoke Italian in our home during my childhood. As soon as I started to go to school, and earlier, because my playmates were not Italian but chiefly Irish, Jewish, and English, I learned English, but at such an early age that I cannot remember acquiring a new language, different from the Italian dialect we spoke at home.

Ferrari also recalls the sacrifices of the first generation of Italian immigrants.

There was no misery in Rocca Nova to compare with that which my mother found in New York in the late 19th century. Many Italian women and children secured jobs in sweat shops near Little Italy, where unscrupulous employers exacted all they could from them for very low wages. . . .

Many of this earliest generation of Italians, and thousands who came later, sacrificed their health and even their lives in the building of America, a sacrifice for which most of them received little material reward or appreciation, either from the writers of history books or from succeeding generations who benefited from their labors. Many of this first generation returned to Italy as poor as they had left it, or remained here to live in the fast-growing slums. The death rate among them, chiefly from tuberculosis, was high.

And much more than physical strength was involved in the early Italians' contribution to America. Everything dear to them was far away, and they were exploited economically, as well as physically. Only their indomitable courage, their high hopes for the future, and their faith in this new country, now *their* country, kept them going.

"And what value there was in political freedom! Here, one was a human being. My friend Alter, who always worked hard but barely made a living and considered himself to be a failure, once said to me with a resigned smile, 'Never mind. In the old country I kept my head bowed and my back bent. Here I keep my head high and my back is straight.'"

—Abraham Cahan,
The Education of Abraham Cahan, 1926

An Immigrant's Phrase Book

From the 1850s to 1882, approximately 300,000 Chinese immigrated to the United States. Most came as "sojourners"—that is, migrants who expected to return to their homelands after making money in the United States, and thus had little incentive to learn English, shed their native garb, or learn American ways. Mostly male, they left wives and children behind, traveling thousands of miles to California, which they called "Gold Mountain," and other West Coast destinations, where they worked as miners and on the railroad. When the mining boom and railroad construction ended by the 1870s, many migrated to cities, such as San Francisco, to work as tailors, cigar makers, and domestic servants. Some operated laundries and restaurants. After the Civil War, some planters in Louisiana and Mississippi even recruited Chinese workers to replace blacks who once labored in their cotton fields. In 1875, Wong Sam and Assistants in San Francisco published *An English-Chinese Phrase Book* for Chinese immigrants. These examples provide insight into their harsh new world and ways that they tried to fight against discrimination.

The men are striking for wages.
He assaulted me without provocation.
He claimed my mine.
I will expel him if he don't leave the place.
He tries to extort money from me.
He falsely accused me of stealing his watch.
You have violated the Constitution of this
    State.
He was choked to death with a lasso, by a
    robber.
Can I sleep here tonight?
Have you any food for me?
Have you any grass for my horse?
The passage money is $50 from Hong
    Kong to California.
The United States have many immigrants.
The immigration will soon stop.

Racism

Although small in number and once highly prized as workers, the Chinese, more than any other immigrant group in the Gilded Age, became a target of discrimination, bigotry, and violence. Different racially than European immigrants and Euro-Americans, the Chinese were viewed by some native-born Americans as subhuman, as people so inferior that they were simply incapable of ever becoming Americans or good citizens. Many "old stock" Americans placed the Chinese in the same "racially inferior" category as blacks and Indians. Moreover, their dress, hairstyles, and physical appearance made them easily distinguishable. They suffered numerous violent attacks, and anti-Chinese riots erupted periodically throughout the Gilded Age.

The Chinese had already suffered economic and legal discrimination for years, when a severe economic depression in the 1870s kindled a blaze of anti-Chinese sentiment. Many white workingmen blamed the Chinese for their joblessness and for driving down the wages of native-born workers. Shouting the slogan "The Chinese Must Go," California's Workingman's Party demanded an end to Chinese immigration. By 1882 anti-Chinese sentiment had grown so great that Congress passed the Chinese Exclusion Act. The first exclusion act based on race or ethnicity in American history, the Chinese Exclusion Act was in effect until 1943. In 1876, in the midst of the economic depression, as anti-Chinese sentiment was deepening on the West Coast, Thomas Vivien wrote an article published in *Scribner's* magazine entitled "John Chinaman in San Francisco." Vivien wished to "enlighten" the rest of the nation about the Chinese "threat" to the United States. The following excerpt sums up the stereotypes and bigotry that the Chinese faced and suggests how these attitudes led to their exclusion.

Individually, John Chinaman is a clean human; collectively he is a beast. Ah Stue, the cook, keeps his coppers and pans clean and bright, washes his hands in going from dish to dish, is orderly, fresh in appearance, and ever arrayed in spotless white and blue. Follow him home, and you will find this cleanly unit become one of a herd of animals living in a state of squalor and filth, at which even a Digger Indian would shudder. Fifteen Chinamen will live, sleep, and cook, in a hovel or cellar twelve feet square, having

only a door as admitting light and air. Clouds of rancid smoke issue continually from the common chimney, window, and door, through which John and his fellows may dimly be seen crawling, cooking, smoking, and sleeping. . . .

John, as a domestic, is invaluable and a nuisance, a perfect treasure and a horror. . . . He is either passably honest, or steals everything he can lay hands on, according to his disposition. In fine, he would resemble Bridget or Pete [Irish maid and black male servant stereotypes] in many ways, were it not for that strange, impenetrable reserve, inherent with the Oriental, which is as distinctive as his expression is immobile, and which will keep John Chinaman forever an alien.

As has already been hinted, the Chinaman is not a model (American) law-abiding citizen. He gambles incessantly, smokes opium continuously, keeps his women in a state of sinful and abject bondage, and generally brings his quarrels to a conclusion by chopping his antagonist's head open. His favorite weapons of assault and battery are iron bars, butcher-knives, and cleavers ground sharp as razors. . . . To hack, to hew, to chop, and to cleave are his greatest delights when on the war-path. . . .

While immigration is the life-blood of young nations, there is such a thing as blood-poisoning, and this is frequently occasioned by the presence of some particular foreign substance. John is that substance, and is, moreover, utterly devoid of any quality of assimilation. He is a heterogeneous element, and will always remain so. Unlike the Japanese, he does not follow or care to follow our customs or our costumes; in fact he regards all western rules of life with supreme contempt. . . .

In short, the Chinese have here a power with which white labor can by no means cope, for a white man would starve on what John thrives on. Few capitalists pay their employees more than is necessary for their support, consequently, the workman who lives more cheaply is the workman who is paid more cheaply; and here it is that the Chinaman has greatly the advantage. Only by degrading white labor to a bestial scale can the two compete on equal grounds; that being impossible, the outlook for the poor white man and woman in San Francisco turns but one way. . . . one

Chinese workers played a crucial role in the successful completion of the transcontinental railroad. Making up 90 percent of the entire workforce of the Central Pacific Railroad, the Chinese worked for $31 a month (wages significantly lower than those paid to white workers) and labored in extremely perilous conditions as they built the road from Sacramento east, crossing rugged and hazardous mountains. Avalanches killed countless workers. One railroad official wrote that "many of them we did not find until the next season when the snow melted."

of these results will certainly follow: Either California will be bereft of white labor, or such an exhibition of latent hostility will occur as will somewhat startle those who pooh-pooh the possibility of collision between races arising from a struggle for employment. Either way lies a calamity. And this is no croaking, but the strong uncolored logic of observation and facts.

At the same time that the U.S. government blocked Chinese entrance to America's "golden door," newspaper owner Joseph Pulitzer, a Hungarian Jewish immigrant, appealed to the American people—including Chinese immigrants—to donate money to complete the pedestal for the Statue of Liberty, so that the United States could accept this gift from France. Saum Song Bo, a Chinese resident of New York, wrote this response to Pulitzer's request.

[T]he word liberty makes me think of the fact that this country is the land of liberty for men of all nations except the Chinese. I consider it an insult to us Chinese to call on us to contribute toward building in this land a pedestal for a statue of Liberty. That statue represents Liberty holding a torch which lights the passage of those of all nations who come into this country. But are the Chinese allowed to enjoy liberty as men of all other nationalities enjoy it? Are they allowed to go about everywhere free from the insults, abuse, assaults, wrongs and injuries from which men of other nationalities are free?

If there be a Chinaman who . . . desires to make his home in this land, and who, seeing that his countrymen demand one of their own number to be their legal adviser, representative, advocate and protector, desires to study law, can he be a lawyer? By the law of this nation, he, being a Chinaman, cannot become a citizen, and consequently cannot be a lawyer. . . .

Whether this statute against the Chinese [the Chinese Exclusion Act of 1882] or the statute of Liberty will be the more lasting monument to tell future ages of the liberty and greatness of this country, will be known only to future generations.

Liberty, we Chinese do love and adore thee; but let not those who deny thee to us make of thee a graven image, and invite us to bow down to it.

Japanese shopkeepers stand in front of their store in Honolulu. Fleeing severe economic hardship as Japan became industrialized, approximately 200,000 Japanese immigrated to Hawaii and 180,000 to the American mainland between 1885 and 1924.

Not only were Asians a target of anti-immigrant sentiment, but southern and eastern Europeans, many of whom were Roman Catholic, also were singled out by native-born Americans who opposed immigration. The American Protective Association (A.P.A.) was a secret society founded in Clinton, Iowa, in 1887, by Henry F. Bowers as an anti-Catholic, anti-immigrant organization. Members swore never to vote for a Catholic or employ one if a Protestant could be found. The A.P.A. also demanded immigration restriction. Originally gaining support in the Midwest, the association influenced a number of local elections. The A. P. A. reached its peak in 1894, during a severe economic depression, gaining national prominence with as many as half a million members. Spreading wild tales of Catholic conspiracies, the A.P.A. blamed the economic collapse on a papal plot and blamed immigrant laborers—sent by the pope, they claimed—for taking their jobs and serving as the pope's soldiers in a plan to overthrow the U.S. government. Although gaining a large membership during the Depression, the A.P.A. collapsed through internal division. The following is an excerpt from an 1896 A.P.A. publication.

WHAT ARE THE POLITICAL PRINCIPLES OF THE A.P.A.?

1st. Restriction of Immigration, so as to prevent the landing on our shores of paupers, criminals and anarchists.

2nd. Extension of the time for naturalization, to the end that foreigners may become familiar with our free institutions and our laws, before they take part in our political affairs.

3rd. Educational qualifications for every voter, to enable him to understand the duties of citizenship and not become merely a tool of politicians.

4th. One general, non-sectarian, free public school system, supported by public funds and sufficient for the primary education of all children.

5th. No public funds or public property to be used for sectarian purposes, directly or indirectly.

6th. Taxation of all property not owned and controlled by the government.

7th. All private schools, convents, nunneries, monasteries, seminaries, hospitals, asylums and

"The Pests of Our Pacific and Atlantic Coasts"
In this anti-immigration cartoon a beleaguered Uncle Sam declares to both a Chinese and an Eastern European immigrant, "There shall be no discrimination. I will shut you both out."

other educational or charitable institutions to be open to public inspection and under governmental control.

8th. No person who recognizes allegiance to any foreign of ecclesiastical potentate as superior to that of our general government, or any subdivision thereof, shall be supported for any official position whatever.

9th. American lands for actual settlers only. . . .

It is not safe to elect or appoint Roman Catholics to any important positions as servants of a free people under a republican form of government, for they are the avowed servants of a foreign despot (the Pope), and "no man can serve two masters." Suppose a Roman Catholic should be elected governor of the State of New York, he could not be inaugurated without taking the prescribed oath to support the Constitution of that State, which contains recent amendments which are radically opposed to the interests of his church, and which he in common with all members of that church were advised by their clergy to vote against, and undoubtedly did vote against. According to all Roman Catholic authorities, he cannot take such an oath without committing perjury.

Not all Americans accepted the A.P.A.'s theories concerning the immigrant and Catholic threat to the United States. "The Mischief of the A.P.A.," an editorial from the May 1896 _Century Magazine_, questions the patriotism and "Americanism" of the A.P.A.

The bigot is generally devoid of that saving sense of humor which greatly helps to make life worth living. If it were not so those secret societies, like the so-called American Protective Association, which are engaged in deadly warfare against all that is most significant and precious in American institutions, would not insist on parading themselves as "the patriotic orders." Strange patriotism is this, which begins by denying the first tenet of American liberty—freedom to worship God—and proposes to punish religious beliefs which it does not share by depriving those who hold them, not only of their political rights, but, if possible, of the means of livelihood. The very enormity of the sworn purposes of these orders seems to be what gives them their opportunity; for the majority of honorable men find themselves incapable of

The creator of this late 19th-century cartoon criticized American working-men, including the once-despised Irish, black laborers, and native-born laborers, for their participation in anti-Chinese agitation.

believing that such purposes can be cherished by civilized human beings, and therefore fail to make any effective resistance to them. Thus they have the field to themselves; and with scarcely a protest, they creep in and intrench themselves in one community after another, gathering together a large mass of the ignorant and intolerant, and by their secret methods and their compact military organization making themselves a power in the local elections. Many communities have awakened when it was too late to find the grip of these secret orders firmly fastened upon their municipal machinery. There should be no need of warning intelligent citizens against the dangers of such organizations. They are the deadly enemies of democratic institutions.

Advice

Abraham Cahan began publishing a column called "Bintel Brief" in the *Jewish Daily Forward* in 1906. In this column immigrants sought advice about a range of issues and problems. These letters, published in 1907 and 1908, provide insight into the world of Jewish immigrants and some of the problems they faced.

Worthy Editor,

I have been in America almost three years. I came from Russia where I studied at a *yeshiva*. My parents were proud and happy at the thought that I would become a rabbi. But at the age of twenty I had to go to America. Before I left I gave my father my word that I would walk the righteous path and be good and pious. But America makes one forget everything.

Here I became an operator, and at night I went to school. In a few months I entered a preparatory school, where for two subjects I had a Gentile girl as a teacher. I began to notice that the teacher paid more attention to me than to the others in the class, and in time she told me I would be better off taking private lessons from her for the same price I paid to the school.

I agreed and soon realized that her lessons with me were not ordinary. . . .

In short, I began to feel at home in her house and not only she but also her parents welcomed me warmly. I ate there often, and they also lent me money when I was in need. I used to ask myself, 'What am I doing?' but I couldn't help myself. There was a depression at the time. I had no job and had to accept their aid.

A gifted journalist, novelist, and political radical, Abraham Cahan made his Yiddish-language newspaper, the Jewish Daily Forward, an influential and powerful voice for social justice, as it helped generations of Jewish immigrants adjust to American life.

I don't know what I would have done without her help. I began to love her but with mixed feelings of respect and anguish. I was afraid to look her in the eyes. I looked at her like a Russian soldier looks at his superior officer and never imagined she thought of marrying me. . . .

Many times upon leaving her house, I would decide not to return, but my heart drew me to her, and I spent three weeks at her house. Meanwhile I received the report on my examinations, which showed that I had passed with the highest grades. I went directly to her to show her the report and she asked me what I planned to do. I answered that I didn't know yet, because I had no money for college. "That's a minor problem," she said and asked if I didn't know that she was not indifferent toward me. Then she spoke frankly of her love for me and her hope that I would love her.

"If you are not against it, my parents and I will support you while you study. The fact that I am a Gentile and you are a Jew should not bother us. We are both, first of all, human beings and we will live as such." She told me she believed all men and all nations were equal.

I was confused and I couldn't answer her immediately. . . . I do agree with her that we are first of all human beings, and she is a human being in the fullest sense of the word. She is pretty, intelligent, educated, and has a good character. But I am in despair when I think of my parents. What heartaches they will have when they learn of this!

I asked her to give me a few days to think it over. I go around confused and yet I am drawn to her. I must see her every day, but when I am there I think of my parents, and I am torn with doubt.

I wait impatiently for your answer.

Respectfully,
Skeptic from Philadelphia

Answer:

We can only say that some mixed marriages are happy, others unhappy. But then many marriages between Jew and Jew, Christian and Christian, are not successful either. It is true, however, that in some mixed marriages the differences between man and wife create unhappiness. Therefore we cannot take it upon ourselves to advise the young man regarding this marriage. This he must decide for himself.

Another letter dealt with sexual harassment at work.

Dear Editor,

I am one of those unfortunate girls thrown by fate into a dark and dismal shop, and I need your counsel.

Along with my parents, sisters, and brothers, I came from Russian Poland, where I had been well educated. But because of the terrible things going on in Russia we were forced to emigrate to America. I am now seventeen years old, but I look younger and they say I am attractive.

A relative talked us into moving to Vineland, New Jersey, and here in this small town I went to work in a shop. In this shop there is a foreman who is an exploiter, and he sets prices on the work. He figures it out so the wages are very low, he insults and reviles the workers, he fires them and then takes them back. And worse than all of this, in spite of the fact that he has a wife and several children, he often allows himself to "have fun" with some of the working girls. It was my bad luck to be one of the girls that he tried to make advances to. And woe to any girl who doesn't willingly accept them.

Though my few hard-earned dollars mean a lot to my family of eight souls, I didn't want to accept the foreman's vulgar advances. He started to pick on me, said my work was no good, and when I proved to him he was wrong, he started to shout at me in the vilest language. He insulted me in Yiddish and then in English, so the American workers could understand, too. Then, as if the Devil were after me, I ran home.

I am left without a job. Can you imagine my circumstances and that of my parents who depend on my earnings? The girls in my shop were very upset over the foreman's vulgarity, but they don't want him to throw them out, so they are afraid to be witnesses against him. What can be done about this? I beg you to answer me.

Respectfully,
A shopgirl

Answer:

Such a scoundrel should be taught a lesson that could be an example to others. The girl is advised to bring out into the open the whole story about the foreman because there in the small town it shouldn't be difficult to have him thrown out of the shop and for her to get her job back.

Chapter Three

The Sorrows of Labor

For much of her early life, Mary Harris Jones must have felt cursed with bad luck. Born in Cork, Ireland, in 1830, Jones immigrated to the United States as a child. Trained as both a teacher and dressmaker, she taught in both Monroe, Michigan and Memphis, Tennessee. In 1861 she married an iron molder, and they had four children. But only six years after her marriage, tragedy struck. A yellow fever epidemic swept though Memphis. "One by one," she recalled, "each of my four little children sickened and died." Then Jones's husband succumbed to the disease as well.

Alone and consumed with grief, Mary Harris Jones settled in Chicago, where she set up shop as a partner in a dressmaking firm. But tragedy again struck. In the Great Chicago Fire of 1871, Jones lost her shop and all of her possessions. Homeless, she camped along with fellow refugees of the fire in a Catholic church.

Near the church the Knights of Labor, a rapidly growing national labor union, held regular meetings. Jones found herself drawn to the gatherings and the union's vision of a more just and equitable society through worker cooperation and organization. During the yellow fever epidemic and her stint as a dressmaker, Jones had been struck by the growing gap between rich and poor as well as by the suffering of working people. The victims of yellow fever, she noted, "were mainly among the poor and the workers," as wealthier people could afford to flee disease-ridden Memphis or hire nurses to care for them. The poor were left to suffer and die. As a dressmaker in Chicago, Jones had seen a similar dynamic at work. She had worked for some of the city's richest families and had "ample opportunity to observe the luxury and extravagance of their lives." While "sewing for the lords and barons who lived on Lake Shore Drive," Jones "would look out of the plate glass windows and see the poor, shivering wretches, jobless and hungry, walking along the frozen lake front. The contrast

Protesting severe wage cuts, railroad workers initiated a strike that disrupted the nation for several months in the summer of 1877. Marked by riots and the destruction of railroad cars and tracks from Maryland to Ohio, the strike came to an end only after President Rutherford B. Hayes dispatched federal troops to restore order.

of their condition with that of the tropical comfort of the people for whom I sewed was painful for me."

The words she heard from the Knights of Labor inspired Jones. She dedicated her life to improving the lot of America's workers as a union organizer. Organization, Jones believed, was the only way that workers could gather strength to offset the power of their employers. Moreover, unionization was, she thought, the only way workers could achieve better pay, work shorter hours, and labor in safer working conditions.

An inspiring speaker and brilliant strategist, Jones crisscrossed the nation, rallying workers most in need of union organization. By the 1890s she worked closely with coal miners and she served as an organizer for the United Mine Workers (UMW). She was loved by the miners and despised and feared by mine owners. Her faithful and devoted followers soon dubbed her "Mother" Jones. One writer who witnessed her work firsthand recalled, "With one speech she often threw a whole community on strike, and she could keep the strikers loyal month after month on empty stomachs and behind prison bars."

Labor organizers like Mother Jones, along with the men and women she rallied into labor unions, faced formidable challenges in the Gilded Age. For the first time in its history, the United States became a nation of employees. As early as 1870 a majority of the population worked for somebody else. The age of independent, self-employed Americans was passing, as most workers labored for others, working for a wage.

In the age of big business and cutthroat industrial competition, employers often kept wages at the lowest possible level to undercut their rivals and to maximize profits. As employers adopted technological innovations, they reduced the numbers of skilled employees they needed in their factories. Unskilled laborers, if they organized into unions for better wages or conditions, could be fired and replaced easily, as desperate immigrants flooded the nation seeking jobs. Moreover state and federal governments often sided with employers in labor disputes. As Mother Jones explained, "Hand in hand with the growth of factories and the expansion of railroads, with the accumulation of capital and the rise of banks, came anti-labor legislation. Came strikes. Came violence. Came the belief in the hearts and minds of the workers that legislatures but carry out the will of the industrialists." Neither state nor federal governments recognized the right of workers to organize, and throughout the Gilded Age government officials seldom hesitated to send state militias and federal troops to quell

labor unrest. In addition, ethnic and religious differences among American workers often proved to be a barrier to labor organizing. Ethnic tensions, rivalries, and mistrust often kept workers from joining forces to work collectively for common goals.

Although organized labor could claim few victories in the Gilded Age, the efforts of organizers like Mother Jones and labor unions, such as the Knights of Labor and the UMW, reflect the fact that many American workers refused to accept passively the new industrial order. The fight of workers in the Gilded Age for just treatment and respect also reveals that from the perspective of many working men and women the period was not one of abundance and opportunity but one of scarcity, destitution, and exploitation.

Mother Jones continued to fight for America's working men and women until she was well into her 90s. She lived to be 100 years old, dying in 1930, just five years before the enactment of the Wagner Act during President Franklin Roosevelt's New Deal, which guaranteed the right of workers to organize into labor unions.

The Knights of Labor

The Noble and Holy Order of the Knights of Labor, the organization that inspired Mother Jones, was founded in Philadelphia in 1869. The Knights hoped to organize all working people into one large, national union and opened membership to all workers, regardless of color, gender, or national origin; only bankers, lawyers, professional gamblers, and liquor dealers could not join. By the mid-1880s the Knights were the largest, most inclusive labor organization in U.S. history. In January 1878 the Knights convened at Reading, Pennsylvania, established a general assembly, and adopted the following platform. Not only did the platform provide a scathing critique of industrial capitalism, it also blended concrete, short-term goals with a long-term vision of a cooperative society.

The recent alarming development and aggression of aggregated wealth, which, unless checked, will inevitably lead to the pauperization and hopeless degradation of the toiling masses, render it imperative, if we desire to enjoy the blessings of life, that a check should be placed upon its power and upon unjust accumulation, and a system adopted which will secure to the laborer the fruits of

The Knights of Labor's major emphasis on equal rights for women attracted many working women to its ranks. These women served as delegates to the 1886 Knights convention in Richmond, Virginia. Posing with a baby, they emphasized their dual role as mothers and union leaders—and that these roles did not conflict.

his toil; and as this much-desired object can only be accomplished by the thorough unification of labor and the united efforts of those who obey the divine injunction that "In the sweat of thy brow shalt thou eat bread," we have formed the Industrial Brotherhood with a view of securing the organization and direction, by co-operative effort, of the power of the industrial classes; and we submit to the world the objects sought to be accomplished by our organization, calling upon all who believe in securing "the greatest good to the greatest number" to aid and assist us:

I. To bring within the folds of organization every department of productive industry, making knowledge a standpoint for action, and industrial and moral worth, not wealth, the true standard of individual and national greatness.

II. To secure to the toilers a proper share of the wealth that they create; more of the leisure that rightfully belongs to them; more societary advantages; more of the benefits, privileges, and emoluments of the world; in a word, all those rights and privileges necessary to make them capable of enjoying, appreciating, defending and perpetuating the blessings of good government.

III. To arrive at the true condition of the producing masses in their educational, moral, and financial condition, by demanding from the various governments the establishment of Bureaus of Labor Statistics.

IV. The establishment of cooperative institutions, productive and distributive.

V. The reserving of the public lands—the heritage of the people—for the actual settler, not another acre for railroads or speculators.

VI. The abrogation of all laws that do not bear equally upon capital and labor, the removal of unjust technicalities, delays, and discriminations in the administration of justice, and the adopting of measures providing for the health and safety of those engaged in mining, manufacturing, or building pursuits.

VII. The enactment of laws to compel chartered corporations to pay their employees weekly, in full, for labor performed during the preceding week, in the lawful money of the country.

VIII. The enactment of laws giving mechanics and laborers a first lien on their work for their full wages.

IX. The abolishment of the contract system on national, state, and municipal work.

X. The substitution of arbitration for strikes, whenever and wherever employers and employees are willing to meet on equitable grounds.

XI. The prohibition of the employment of children on workshops, mines, and factories before attaining their fourteenth year.

XII. To abolish the system of letting out by contract the labor of convicts in our prisons and reformatory institutions.

XIII. To secure for both sexes equal pay for equal work.

XIV. The reduction of the hours of labor to eight per day, so that the laborers may have more time for social enjoyment and intellectual improvement and be enabled to reap the advantages conferred by the labor-saving machinery which their brains have created.

XV. To prevail upon governments to establish a purely national circulating medium, based upon the faith and resources of the nation, and issued directly to the people, without the intervention of any system of banking corporations, which money shall be a legal tender in payment of all debts, public or private.

The Haymarket Affair

At the height of its influence in 1886, the Knights of Labor boasted a membership of more than 700,000. But that year the organization suffered a major blow from which it never recovered: the Haymarket Affair. In May 1886 socialist and anarchist leaders organized a meeting in Chicago's Haymarket Square to protest the death of a striker killed at the city's International Harvester plant. A bomb thrown at a policeman set off a commotion; the police then fired into the crowd of workers attending the rally. Although the identity of the bomb-thrower was never established, seven anarchist leaders were arrested, tried, and sentenced to death, despite the lack of any evidence linking them to the crime. One of the anarchists belonged to the Knights of Labor. Notwithstanding attempts by union leadership to disavow any connection to the Haymarket riot, the Knights' reputation was ruined.

The Haymarket Affair not only hurt the Knights but in the minds of many Americans tarred all labor activists as radicals

A. W. AUNER, SONG PUBLISHER & PRINTER,
Tenth and Race Sts., Philadelphia, Pa.

KNIGHTS OF LABOR

Composed and Sung by Budd Harris.

I'll sing of an order that lately has done
Some wonderful things in our land,
Together they pull great battles have won,
A popular hard working band.
Their numbers are legion great strength they possess,
They strike good and strong for their rights,
From the North to the South from the East to the West,
God speed each Assembly of Knights.

CHORUS.

Then conquer we must,
Our cause it is just,
What power the uplifted hand,
Let each Labor Knight
Be brave in the fight,
Remember united we stand.

They ask nothing wrong you can plainly see,
All that they demand is but fair,
A lesson they'll teach with me you'll agree,
To every purse-proud millionaire.
Fair wages they want, fair wages they'll get,
Good tempered they wage all their fights,
Success to the cause may the sun never set,
On each brave Assembly of Knights.

Then conquer we must, &c.

Then fight on undaunted, you brave working men,
Down the vampires who oppress the poor,
You use noble weapons, the tongue and the pen,
Succesful you'll be I'm sure.
With hope for your watchword and truth for your shield,
Prosperity for your pathway lights,
Then let labor make proud capital yield,
God speed each Assembly of Knights.

Then conquer we must, &c.

A. W. AUNER'S
CARD and JOB PRINTING ROOMS
Tenth and Race Sts., Philadelphia. Pa.

Songs such as this were used to recruit and rally workers to the cause of organized labor and to describe the vision of the Knights of Labor.

and set off a Red scare. In the aftermath of the Haymarket Affair, journalist George Frederic Parsons wrote a piece for the *Atlantic Monthly* that reflected the fears of middle-class Americans concerning labor radicalism and the belief that workers had only themselves to blame for their troubles.

The organization of labor has hitherto been in the hands of unfit men, with too few exceptions. The leaders have been selfish, narrow-minded, or ignorant. The true way to utilize the strength of united labor is to develop the individual power of the members. By no other means have great nations been formed. An association, the effective strength of which depends on the surrender of the rights and liberties of its members, may be a dangerous instrument for the use of adventurers and demagogues, but it cannot advance the interests of the men themselves. The most urgent want of labor to-day is self-control. In this free country no man endowed with average abilities need remain all his life poor. If he has thrift, self-restraint, perseverance, he will pass from the ranks of labor to the ranks of capital. It is the saving man who becomes the capitalist—the man who has force to deny himself indulgences. What a lesson lies in the drink-bill of the American workingman, for instance! ...

At present the workingman can hardly make both ends meet. Is it not because he insists on creating capitalists out of the saloon-keepers. . . . There may be no bread at home, but there is always beer and whiskey at the bar, and the men who consider themselves the victims of circumstances or the "thralls" of capital squander their earnings, spend their savings in these dens. Can there be a serious labor question while this state of things continues? Can workingmen talk gravely of their wrongs while it is plain to all the world that if they only saved the capital they earn they would be comfortable?

Trade Unions

Even before Haymarket, the Knights had come under attack by some craft unions that opposed their strategy of organizing one big union. Craft unions, made up of skilled workers, such as cigar makers and iron puddlers (highly skilled workers who made iron bars), believed that they would lose their bargaining power—as skilled, hard-to-replace workers—by uniting with unskilled workers who had little leverage with employers. Unskilled workers easily could be replaced by the waves of desperate immigrants who provided employers with a cheap labor supply. As a result, while most Americans experienced a rising standard of living during the Gilded Age, skilled workers benefited far more than their unskilled counterparts.

In 1886 craft unions organized the American Federation of Labor (AFL). Headed by Samuel Gompers, the AFL embodied "bread and butter" unionism. Embracing the capitalist order and rejecting the long-term, utopian goals of the Knights of Labor, the AFL eschewed politics and focused only on short-term, concrete aims, such as the eight-hour day and better wages. Unlike the Knights, the AFL did not hesitate to strike to achieve its ends. Moreover, the AFL, unlike the inclusive Knights, limited its membership.

The AFL under Gompers's leadership made considerable gains for its craft-based members, and its membership grew to about 500,000 by the turn of the century. Yet the AFL represented only a fraction of American workers, as craft unions excluded women and some immigrants, whom were viewed as "cheap" competition that would lower wages and the "dignity" of the union.

Despite his rejection of radicalism and utopianism, Gompers had been well-schooled in these ideas as a cigar maker in New York City. A teenaged immigrant from England, Gompers became a cigar maker at the age of 14 and soon joined the Cigarmakers Union. In his memoirs, he described his labor education, received from his fellow cigar makers on the shop floor.

This depiction of the bombing at Haymarket Square, published in Harper's Weekly *in 1886, exacerbated the fears of many middle-class Americans that labor agitation inevitably led to chaos and violence. The drawing depicts workers shooting at police and orator Samuel Fielden rabble-rousing as the bomb exploded— neither of which occurred.*

Critics on the left attacked Samuel Gompers for the AFL's conservative goals and its exclusive membership; those on the right regarded him as a foreign-born radical whose organization would destroy individual initiative and property rights. Gompers himself remarked: "We have no ultimate ends. We are going from day to day. We are fighting only for immediate objects—objects that can be realized in a few years."

In 1873 came one of the most important changes in my life. I left my old job and found employment with David Hirsch & Company at 122 Chambers Street, then the only union shop in the city. It was also a high-class shop, where only the most skilled workmen were employed. . . . When I went to this shop, Hirsch was employing between fifty and sixty men. . . . There a new world opened to me. The cigarmakers employed at Hirsch's were practically all Germans—men of keener mentality and wider thought than any I had met before. They talked and read in German, but there was enough English spoken to enable me to understand that the trade union movement meant to those men something vastly bigger than anything I had ever conceived. Many of them were men who had learned the labor movement in Europe and who were refugees because they were active for the struggle for political as well as economic freedom.

With all the energy and confidence born of my young strength, I talked from my limited experiences. . . . On labor matters my thought was wild. I had been feeling profoundly the injustice that society meted out to wage earners. I was familiar with the vocabulary of revolutionists, but I had not yet attained a practical understanding of the scope and the power of economic organization. In truth, neither had the others. We were all groping our way, trying to develop the language, the methods, and the fundamentals of trade unionism. Some had a better understanding— fortunately they were to become my teachers. . . .

Anyone who does not know the cigarmaking trade will find it difficult to appreciate the educational value of the little forum existing in each shop. It gave education in such a way as to develop personality, for in no other place were we so wholly natural. The nature of our work developed a camaraderie of the shop such as few workers enjoy. It was a world in itself—a cosmopolitan world. Shopmates came from everywhere—some had been nearly everywhere. When they told us of strange lands and peoples, we listened eagerly. . . .

Shop life stimulated my mental development. . . . In the shop there was also reading. It was the custom of the cigarmakers to chip in to create a fund for purchasing papers, magazines, and books. Then while the rest worked, one of our members would read to us perhaps for an hour at a time, sometimes longer. . . . In fact, these discussions in the shops were more like public debating societies or what we call these days "labor forums." This practice had a great deal to do with developing the interest of cigarmakers in leading economic questions. . . .

Gompers was an eyewitness to New York's Tompkins Square Riot of 1874, in which demonstrating workers were attacked by police. He drew the following lessons from that event.

I was in no way connected with the arrangement of this demonstration and was present as an intensely interested workingman, and the import of the situation bore in upon me. As the fundamentals came to me, they became guide-posts for my understanding of the labor movement for years to come. I saw how professions of radicalism and sensationalism concentrated all of the forces of organized society against a labor movement and nullified in advance normal, necessary activity. I saw that leadership in the labor movement could be safely entrusted only to those into whose hearts and minds had been woven the experiences of earning their bread by daily labor. I saw that betterment for workingmen must come primarily through workingmen. I saw the danger of entangling alliances with intellectuals who did not understand that to experiment with the labor movement was to experiment with human life.

Industrial Unions

While Gompers and the AFL made some gains through trade unionism, other American workers attempted to organize along industrial lines; that is, they organized workers according to industry rather than trade or skill. The United Mine Workers (UMW), founded in 1890, was an industrial union known for its militancy, which often led to bitter strikes marred by violence. Mother Jones devoted most of her career to organizing for the UMW. In this excerpt from her autobiography, she described the especially difficult lot of coal miners and related the story of a successful organizing drive—won by the commitment of miners' wives—in the Pennsylvania coalfields at the turn of the century.

Before 1899 the coal fields of Pennsylvania were not organized. Immigrants poured into the country, and they worked cheap. There was always a surplus of immigrant labor, solicited in Europe by the coal companies, so as to keep wages down to barest living. Hours of work down under ground were cruelly long. Fourteen hours a day was not uncommon, thirteen, twelve. The life or limb of the miner was unprotected by any laws. Families lived in company-owned shacks that were not fit for their pigs. Children

Around 1900, the average wage for workers in manufacturing was 21.6 cents an hour, and the workweek lasted six ten-hour days. Average annual earnings were $490, with no compensation for time off.

died by the hundreds due to the ignorance and poverty of their parents. . . .

The United Mine Workers decided to organize these fields and work for human conditions for human beings. Organizers were put to work. Whenever the spirit of the men in the mines grew strong enough a strike was called.

In Arnot, Pennsylvania, a strike had been going on for four or five months. The men were becoming discouraged. . . .

Sunday afternoon I held a meeting. It was not as large a gathering as those we had later but I stirred up the poor wretches that did come.

"You've got to take the pledge," I said. "Rise and pledge to stick to your brothers and the union till the strike's won!"

The men shuffled their feet, but the women rose, their babies in their arms, and pledged themselves to see that no one went to work in the morning. . . .

The company tried to bring in the scabs. I told the men to stay home with the children for a change and let the women attend to the scabs. I organized an army of women housekeepers. On a given day they were to bring their mops and brooms, and "the army" would charge the scabs up at the mines. The general manager, the sheriff, and the corporation hirelings heard of our plans and were on hand. The day came, and the women came with the mops and brooms and pails of water.

I decided not to go up to the Drip Mouth myself, for I knew they would arrest me and that might rout the army. I selected as leader an Irish woman who had a most picturesque appearance. She had slept late and her husband had told her to hurry up and get into the army. She had grabbed a red petticoat and slipped it over a thick cotton nightgown. She wore a black stocking and a white one. She had tied a little red fringed shawl over her wild red hair. Her face was red, and her eyes were mad. I looked at her and felt she could raise a rumpus.

I said, "You lead the army up to the Drip Mouth. Take that tin dishpan you have with you and your hammer, and when the scabs and the mules come up, begin to hammer and howl. Then all of you hammer and howl and be ready to chase the scabs with your mops and brooms. Don't be afraid of anyone."

Up the mountainside, yelling and hollering, she led the women, and when the mules came up with the scabs and the coal, she began beating on the dishpan and hollering and all the army joined in with her. The sheriff tapped her on the shoulder.

'You pity yourselves, but you do not pity your brothers, or you would stand together to help one another."

—Mother Jones, 1897 speech to miners in West Virginia

"My dear lady," said he, "remember the mules. Don't frighten them."

She took the old tin pan, and she hit him with it, and she hollered, "To hell with you and the mules!"

He fell over and dropped into the creek. Then the mules began to rebel against scabbing. They bucked and kicked the scab drivers and started off for the barn. The scabs started running down the hill, followed by the army of women with their mops and pails and brooms. . . . There was a great big doctor in the crowd, a company lapdog. He had a little satchel in his hand, and he said to me, impudent like, "Mrs. Jones, I have a warrant for you."

"All right," said I. "Keep it in your pill bag until I come for it. I am going to hold a meeting now."

From that day on the women kept continual watch of the mines to see that the company did not bring in scabs. Every day women with brooms or mops in one hand and babies in the other arm wrapped in little blankets went to the mines and watched that no one went in. And all night long they kept watch. They were heroic women. In the long years to come the nation will pay them high tribute for they were fighting for the advancement of a great country. . . .

The last of February the company put up a notice that all demands were conceded. . . .

There had been no bloodshed. There had been no riots. And the victory was due to the army of women with their mops and brooms.

Women in the Work Force

The number of women in the American work force grew considerably in the Gilded Age, making up roughly 20 percent of those gainfully employed. Because of low wages of male workers and severe economic instability, many women contributed to the family economy by seeking employment. Women employed in industry concentrated in textile and garment production. Young, single women made up the bulk of the female labor force in the garment trades. Married women often took in piecework, in which they were paid by the number of garments they completed, so that they could work in their homes as they also cared for their children.

In the following passage Marie Ganz described the piecework that her mother took in after the death of Marie's father.

Danger on the Job

Industrial accidents took a devastating toll on American workers during the Gilded Age. As late as 1907, 500,000 workers were killed or injured each year. Workers in heavy industry—such as steelmaking, mining, and railroads—were especially susceptible. Approximately 2,000 coal miners died every year from mine explosions and cave-ins. In 1893 alone, 433 men died while attempting to couple railway cars. Workers had little recourse for being compensated by negligent companies. Liability laws limited the responsibility of companies to such an extent that workers rarely received restitution. While industrialized nations in western Europe, such as Germany and Great Britain, provided state-funded accident insurance for workers, the United States lagged far behind. Not until 1917, at the behest of trade unions, did workers' compensation for industrial accidents become established in all of the nation's industrial states.

Solidarity

While ethnic differences could divide workers, making it difficult to organize into unions, some managed to transcend ethnic lines and cooperate in strikes. In 1903 Mexican and Japanese farm workers in the sugar beet fields of Oxnard, California, formed the Japanese-Mexican Labor Association (JMLA) and went on strike to improve the wages of beet thinners. Their solidarity forced concessions from employers, who agreed to pay union workers $5 per acre.

After their victory, the JMLA petitioned the American Federation of Labor (AFL) to charter their organization as the Sugar Beet Farm Laborer's Union of Oxnard. But Samuel Gompers, head of the AFL, refused to charter the union unless it barred Chinese and Japanese workers. The JMLA's Mexican secretary wrote the following response to Gompers.

We beg to say in reply that our Japanese brothers here were the first to recognize the importance of cooperating and uniting in demanding a fair wage scale.... They were not only just with us, but they were generous when one of our men was murdered by hired assassins of the oppressor of labor, they gave expression to their sympathy in a very substantial form. In the past we have counseled, fought, and lived on very short rations with our Japanese brothers and toiled with them in the fields, and they have been uniformly kind and considerate. We would be false to them and to ourselves and to the cause of unionism if we now accepted privileges for ourselves which are not accorded to them.... We are going to stand by men who stood by us in the long, hard fight which ended in a victory over the enemy. We therefore respectfully petition the A.F. of L. to grant us a charter under which we can unite all the sugar beet and field laborers in Oxnard, without regard to their color or race. We will refuse any other kind of charter, except one which will wipe out race prejudice and recognize our fellow workers as being as good as ourselves.

Without the support of the AFL, the JMLA dissolved after several years.

Ganz detailed the innovative ways that she and her mother managed to make ends meet with only a tiny income.

Forty or fifty men and women sat hunched up, their heads bent low over as many foot-power sewing machines. Pale, heavy-eyed folk they were, some of whom I had seen in the streets, where their bent backs and rounded shoulders proclaimed their means of livelihood. As I recall it, the shop was about sixty feet long, twenty-five feet wide and perhaps eight feet from floor to ceiling. Besides the machine hands there were ten or twelve pressers, some women sewing by hand, three or four small boys and girls who were carrying piles of work from one part of the shop to the other, and, over all, in the centre of the room stood a man who, I immediately realized, was the boss. He did not look approachable. There was a surly expression in his eyes, and his face was cold and hard. I stood staring at him, and at last he noticed me.

"What you want?" he snarled.

It was too late to retreat. I spoke up bravely and to the point.

"Work. Work for mine mader."

"Tell her to come to-morrow."

"She won't come. She told me to get work I should take along home...."

We struck a bargain after I had explained to him the circumstances at home. He told me that my mother could get one and a half cents per skirt for sewing up bottoms by hand. I was to take a batch of skirts, and I should have to return them with the bottoms sewed before I could get more.

Forty skirts he gave me, a huge bundle, so heavy and cumbersome that I staggered under it, and it was a nerve-shaking experience carrying it down the steep stairs that hung dizzily from the outer wall. But, though my body ached under the burden, my spirits were high—higher than those heaven-aspiring steps—for an income was in sight. No longer would the fear of being put into the street keep us awake through the night. . . .

Oh, how hard mother worked at the skirts. Very late into the night she continued her sewing, and when I awoke at six in the morning every one of them was ready for me to take back to the shop before going to school. The boss was satisfied, and I carried another bundle of them home. The bundle was always twice as big as I was. Just the bundle and a pair of legs were all the neighbours could see as I passed their windows. . . . Twice every day I went to the shop to return completed skirts and to get more, and after school hours I helped my mother with the sewing. Often when

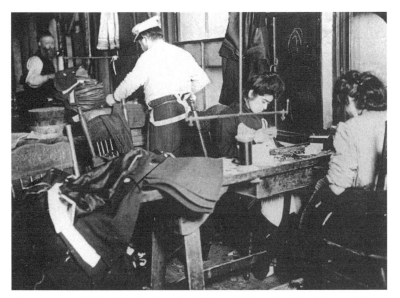

Women garment workers labor in a men's clothing factory. The supervisors, standing in the background, are men.

the sewing of the day before had been left unfinished I would get up at four o'clock in the morning, and together we would sit by candlelight hemming the wide edges of the broad skirts then in fashion. . . .

We managed to keep the home together, mother and I, though at no time did our combined earnings amount to more than ninety cents a day. Though we worked from early morning until late at night, we could earn no more. Our weekly income was about five dollars besides the four dollars a month the boarder paid. The money from the boarder was set aside to make up the rent, besides about two dollars a week from our earnings. The remaining three dollars a week had to meet all our other expenses. As a matter of fact it was only enough to pay for our food. I know just how it went, because I did the buying, and the figures were fixed firmly in my memory. For a week when we really had enough to eat our account stood as follows:

Four rolls a day (two for a penny)	$.14
Butter (one and a half pounds)	.48
Meat (half a pound a day for soup)	.49
Vegetables	.35
Milk (a quart a day)	.49
Bread (an eight-cent loaf a day)	.56
Coffee and tea	.18
Sugar	.30
TOTAL	$2.99

"A family of workers can live well, but the man with a family of small children to support, unless his wife works also, has a small chance of living properly."
—Carroll D. Wright, Chief of Bureau of Labor Statistics, Massachusetts, 1882

How were the other expenses met? I hardly know myself. As a problem in arithmetic, it was impossible to solve. According to what I had been taught at Public School No. 92, two dollars and ninety-nine cents from three dollars left one cent, no matter how often it might be figured or worried over. But I learned through hard experience that there were ways other than by arithmetic of solving that problem—ways that teacher knew nothing about. Two minus two didn't always equal nothing in the tenements. . . .

Besides food, shoes were the principal expense item. We simply had to buy a two-dollar pair sometimes, though other clothes were hardly ever bought. There was also the weekly installment of twenty-five cents to the sewing-machine man. He didn't get it every week; he thought himself lucky when he got twenty-five cents a month. Sometimes we made drastic reductions in our food purchases, sometimes—alas! I should say very often—we borrowed a dollar from a relative, sometimes we managed to hold Mr. Zalkin [the landlord] off for two or three days. We paid back the money we borrowed, but usually we borrowed a dollar somewhere else to do it. I was old enough to discover that the more intricate one's finances became the easier it was, by tangling them up a little more, to squeeze something out of nothing.

So it was that we kept our souls and bodies together.

Child Labor

In 1890 approximately 18 percent of children between the ages of 10 and 14 were employed in nonagricultural work. Employers in some industries, such as textiles, sought out child workers because they could pay them less than adults. In addition, because of mechanization, even children could run machines, and their small hands were well-suited to particular tasks in textile factories. Although several Northern states passed laws setting minimum age requirements and maximum workdays for child laborers, the laws were difficult to enforce. Moreover, the parents of working children, who depended on their children's income to support the family, often opposed such laws. Some Gilded Age reformers protested child labor, but no major improvements took place until the 1910s, when nearly every state passed minimum age and maximum hour legislation.

This article by Emma Brown, published in the *Atlantic Monthly* in 1880, points out the difficulties in enforcing child labor laws and the toll that factory work took on children.

At the start of the 20th century, one quarter of all Southern male mill workers and more than one third of all female mill workers were under 15.

Among the many excellent laws of Massachusetts there have stood for a number of years certain statutes to the effect that—

"No child, under ten years of age shall be employed in any manufacturing, mechanical, or mercantile establishment in this commonwealth.

"No child under fourteen shall be so employed except during the vacations of the public schools, unless during the year next preceding such employment he has attended some public or private school at least twenty weeks . . . .

"Every owner, superintendent, or overseer who employs or permits to be employed any child in violation of this act, and every parent or guardian who permits such employment, shall forfeit a sum of not less than twenty nor more than fifty dollars for the use of the public schools."

From these carefully worded statutes it would seem as if every precaution had been taken by the State of Massachusetts to prevent the overworking of children in the commonwealth and the neglect of their proper schooling. It is one thing, however, to make wise laws, and quite another to enforce them, as may be seen from the following statistics.

During the past year some hundred and sixty factories in the State that have been inspected give an average of only two per cent. where strict compliance was found with the enactments quoted above. In one factory the inspector was shown a file of certificates which gave the names of thirteen children employed in the mills, but no data of their ages. . . .

In still another factory, the very first child interviewed was under ten years of age; and a truant officer who visited some thirty factories in and about Boston reports that he found in every one of them children kept at work in open violation of the law. . . .

An overseer in one of the print works in the State says: "There seems to be a growing disposition on the part of parents to put their children to work before they are of the legal age, and to avoid sending them to school the length of time required by law. Scarcely a day passes but mothers come to the mills and beg us to use our influence in procuring employment for their children.". . .

"Please, sir, could Denise have a permit to stay in the mills a month longer? It's time she was in school, I know, but the father is all drawn up with rheumatis', and they've took him to the 'ospital,

Southern cotton mills were notorious for employing children, whose nimble fingers changed bobbins on textile looms.

The Modern Baron With Ancient Methods.

In this 1892 cartoon, a crate of bullets, a keg of gunpowder, a cauldron of melted pitch, and a hot-water hose in the hands of Andrew Carnegie symbolize the violence at Homestead. Carnegie's ruthless tactics at the infamous steelworks seriously damaged his reputation.

and I don't know how ever in the world we're goin' to git along if Denise has to leave the mills!"

It was all said in one breath, and the superintendent of the schools, glancing up from his books, saw a woman of thirty-five or thereabouts . . . .

He answered, not unkindly, "We cannot give any such permit. Besides, you are liable to a fine of fifty dollars, if the child is kept out of school. How old did you say she was?"

"Eleven years, sir."

"How many children have you?"

"Four, with Denise."

"Is she the eldest?"

"No, sir. I have one fourteen year old, but she's nervous and daft-like. I keep her at home to mind the baby."

"So Denise is the only one at work. Has she ever been to school?"

"Oh, yes, sir. Tell the gentleman, Denise, what reader you were in last."

"'T'was the First Reader, the primer, you know," whispered the little girl, hanging down her head.

"A child of eleven years ought to be farther advanced than that!" remarked the superintendent.

"I suppose so," acknowledged the mother, with a sigh; "but I couldn't spare her to go to school when she was a earnin' twenty cents a day."

The Homestead Lockout

The Gilded Age saw numerous strikes and many incidents of labor violence, and the Homestead Lockout of 1892 epitomized the overwhelming power of big businessmen—who had the cooperation of the state—to crush the burgeoning labor movement. The Homestead Lockout pitted one of the nation's most powerful industrialists, Andrew Carnegie, against one of the country's most successful craft unions, the Amalgamated Association of Iron and Steel Workers. Carnegie viewed the powerful union as an obstacle to efficiency and, therefore, his ability to undercut his rivals and maximize his profits. Wishing to crush the union once and for all, Carnegie and his right-hand man, Henry Clay Frick, hatched a plan. Carnegie offered a new contract to the union workers, which

would have cut their pay by as much as 26 percent. As Carnegie anticipated, the union rejected the contract.

Expecting a violent showdown, Carnegie left for Scotland, putting Frick in charge. On June 10, 1892, Frick locked out the workers, placing three miles of barbed-wire fencing around the Homestead Steelworks. A private army of Pinkerton detectives arrived on the scene to execute Carnegie's plans; Homestead workers immediately attacked them as they arrived on river barges. This 1892 drawing, "The Battle at the Landing, Homestead, Pennsylvania," depicts the exchange of gunfire between the Pinkertons, aboard the river barges, and steelworkers, which resulted in the deaths of seven workers and three Pinkertons.

At Frick's request, the governor of Pennsylvania sent 8,000 members of the state militia to restore order in Homestead and end worker resistance. Carnegie succeeded in breaking the steelworker's union once and for all; no obstacles remained to reducing wages and increasing hours, even extending the standard 12-hour shift. Another 40 years would pass before steelworkers once again organized into an effective union.

Chapter Four

The Perils
and Promise
of Urban Life

Photographer Jacob Riis captured the squalor of tenement life in Baxter Street Court in New York City around 1890. Riis wrote that "in the tenements all the influences make for evil," calling them "the nurseries of pauperism and crime" as well as "the hot-beds of epidemics that carry disease to rich and poor alike."

L ike most Americans of her generation, Jane Addams grew up in a rural community. She was born in the village of Cedarville, Illinois, in 1860. But like many young Americans who came of age after the Civil War, she realized that her future lay not in the pastoral countryside of Illinois but in one of the nation's burgeoning cities.

After graduating from Rockford Seminary, a women's college, in 1879, Addams struggled to find a meaningful career. As members of the first generation of college-educated women, Addams and others like her found their career options seriously limited. She tried medical school but dropped out after suffering health problems. Then a trip to Europe opened her eyes to the possibilities of a new career. On a tour of the East End of London, Addams witnessed what she called the "hideous human need and suffering" of that city's underprivileged. In a formative moment, she watched as "myriads of hands, empty pathetic, nerveless and workworn" clutched for rotten vegetables and fruit distributed to the poor.

Try as she might, Addams could not shake this troubling image. Though she had traveled to Europe to absorb its rich culture—its music, art, and literature—Addams found no comfort in such pursuits. Overwhelmed with a sense of "uselessness," she questioned "the assumption that the sheltered, educated girl has nothing to do with the bitter poverty and the social maladjustment which is all about her." On a second trip to Europe, Addams spent time at London's Toynbee Hall, a settlement house established by middle-class reformers to better the lot of the underclass.

As cities and their inhabitants gained influence, new words were incorporated into American English. A "hayseed" lived in the countryside. Anything old-fashioned was "country."

Inspired by her stay in London, Addams returned to the United States and set out for Chicago on a mission. Using Toynbee Hall as a model, Addams and her friend Ellen Starr purchased a dilapidated mansion in a poor, run-down section of Chicago and established the nation's first settlement house, which became known as Hull House. Settlement houses offered a plethora of programs and activities for their poor neighbors, many of whom were recent immigrants. One of Addams's first programs at Hull House introduced the neighborhood's Italian immigrants to Florentine art, but immigrant women quickly made it clear that they needed more practical assistance, particularly a kindergarten and nursery school for their children. Hull House also organized sewing and cooking classes, clubs for children, and programs and lectures by local university professors. Labor unions also met there. Addams's Hull House was replicated in numerous U.S. cities; by 1900 approximately 100 settlement houses had been established throughout the nation.

Not only did Hull House aim to better the lives of the city's poor and aid immigrants in their transition to urban life in the United States, but, in accordance with Addams's vision, it also served to reconnect the privileged with the poor. As Addams explained, the settlement was "an experimental effort to aid in the solution of the social and industrial problems which are engendered by the modern conditions of life in a great city. It is the attempt to relieve, at the same time, the overaccumulation at one end of society and the destitution at the other." The privileged and underprivileged, Addams believed, had much to learn from each other.

Cities like Jane Addams's Chicago exploded during the Gilded Age. Their rapid growth, as Addams noted, generated a profusion of problems for city dwellers, especially the poor. Between 1860, when Jane Addams was born, and 1900, when Hull House was in full operation, the urban population of the United States grew fivefold. The northeastern United States became the most urban region of the country, and the South remained the least urban, yet cities and towns of all sizes throughout the nation grew significantly during the period. Cities attracted native-born migrants from the countryside—such as Addams—as well as European immigrants who flooded urban centers seeking employment. Many African Americans also left the rural South, seeking greater opportunity in both Southern and Northern towns and cities. In Addams's Chicago, three of every four inhabitants were foreign

born or had foreign-born parents. Moreover, Chicago's black population had grown nearly tenfold—from 3,600 in 1870 to more than 30,000 by 1900.

Whereas cities offered more economic opportunities, they were also attractive because of the cultural amenities they offered, such as concert halls, museums, and theaters. Department stores, restaurants, saloons, and cafes also appealed to the urban populace during the Gilded Age. City dwellers viewed themselves as the most modern and up-to-date Americans.

Although cities represented opportunity, they were also filthy, crowded, disease-ridden, and often badly governed. Rapid population growth severely strained housing and municipal services, such as garbage collection. The construction of multifamily housing, such as tenements, attempted to relieve housing shortages. Yet tenements were usually unhealthy, dark, and dangerous firetraps. Homelessness also abounded, and children, many of whom had been abused and abandoned, were a common sight in U.S. cities.

As cities teemed with both possibilities and problems, they underwent significant physical transformations. With the introduction of electric streetcars in the 1880s came the development of "streetcar suburbs." Middle-class Americans escaped the noise,

Regional Economies

While the great metropolitan areas of New York and Chicago—with their mix of commerce, manufacturing, and banking—symbolized the Gilded Age, smaller American cities also underwent major transformations. Reflecting larger economic trends, many towns and cities specialized in manufacturing or processing particular products, many of them regional in character, for the growing national market. Denver specialized in slaughtering and packing western beef; Portland became a center for the northwestern lumber industry. Youngstown, Ohio, and Johnstown, Pennsylvania, near rich coal and coke fields, specialized in steel production. Charlotte, North Carolina, emerged as the hub of the South's cotton textile industry.

As the urban poor crowded into tenements, many members of the middle and upper classes fled cities for the suburbs to escape the squalor and problems of urban life. The advent of electric streetcars made it possible for them to live in suburban areas and commute to urban centers to work and shop.

Denver, Colorado, 1889. Although the American West usually invokes images of prairies and open plains, it was, in fact, the second most urbanized region of the nation in the Gilded Age, after the Northeast. Denver, the West's third-largest city (after San Francisco and Omaha) in the Gilded Age, tripled its population between 1880 and 1890, claiming a total of nearly 107,000 people by 1890.

dirt, and disease of cities by moving to the outskirts of urban areas and commuting to work by streetcar. The "walking city" of the preindustrial United States, where rich and poor alike lived within walking distance of shops and factories, gave way to cities increasingly partitioned by class, race, and ethnicity.

The fragmentation of U.S. cities and society deeply concerned social reformers like Jane Addams. She and others feared that the social separation and isolation of various urban groups threatened to destroy democracy in the United States. She hoped that Hull House and other settlement houses would establish an organic relationship between rich and poor, native-born and immigrant, educated and uneducated, in an attempt to reconstruct in an urban setting the connectedness of small-town America.

Just as Hull House shaped the lives of its neighborhood participants, it also transformed Addams and the many middle-class men and women who worked with her. Addams's close association with the destitute thrust her into Chicago politics. As a woman she could not vote or hold office. Nevertheless she fearlessly and relentlessly worked for better schools, housing, city services, and working conditions. Addams's work among Chicago's

poor ultimately led her to international affairs. In the aftermath of the Spanish-American War, she became an avid anti-imperialist, taking a strong stand against the United States establishing colonies abroad. During World War I, she founded the Women's International League for Peace and Freedom. In 1931, four years before her death in her beloved Chicago, Addams was awarded the Nobel Peace Prize.

More than any symbol, the teeming, bustling, ethnically and racially diverse city exemplified the United States of the Gilded Age. Full of both peril and promise, cities not only physically reconfigured the U.S. landscape but also transformed society and culture. The urbanization and suburbanization begun during the period continues to this day; in 1920, for the first time in U.S. history, more people lived in the city than the country. And although U.S. cities have changed in many ways since then, issues raised by middle-class urban reformers, such as Jane Addams, remain relevant: What, if any, responsibility do privileged Americans have for the poor? What are the best methods for reducing poverty? How can the rich and poor bridge the chasm that separates them? Can the United States be both a highly diverse and, at the same time, unified nation?

Social Activism

In her autobiography, *Twenty Years at Hull House*, published in 1910, Jane Addams discusses the evolution of her idea to found a settlement house and the challenges she faced in the early years of Hull House.

It is hard to tell just when the very simple plan which afterward developed into the Settlement began to form itself in my mind. It may have been even before I went to Europe for the second time, but I gradually became convinced that it would be a good thing to rent a house in a part of the city where many primitive and actual needs are found, in which young women who had been given over too exclusively to study might restore a balance of activity along traditional lines and learn of life from life itself. . . .

It was not until years afterward that I came upon Tolstoy's phrase, "the snare of preparation," which he insists we spread before the feet of young people, hopelessly entangling them in a curious inactivity at the very period when they are longing to construct the world anew and to conform to their own ideals. . . .

On presenting Jane Addams with the Nobel Prize for Peace in 1931, Professor Halvdan Koht stated, "Even when her views were at odds with public opinion, she never gave in, and in the end she regained the place of honor she had had before in the hearts of her people." Social critic Walter Lippman said of Addams, "she was not only good, but great."

From the first it seemed understood that we were ready to perform the humblest neighborhood services. We were asked to wash the newborn babies, and to prepare the dead for burial, to nurse the sick, and to "mind the children."

Occasionally these neighborly offices unexpectedly uncovered ugly human traits. For six weeks after an operation we kept in one of our three bedrooms a forlorn little baby who, because he was born with a cleft palate, was most unwelcome even to his mother, and we were horrified when he died a week after he was returned to his home; a little Italian bride of fifteen sought shelter with us one November evening, to escape her husband who had beaten her every night for a week when he returned home from work, because she had lost her wedding ring; two of us officiated quite alone at the birth of an illegitimate child because the doctor was late in arriving. . . .

But in spite of some untoward experiences, we were constantly impressed with the uniform kindness and courtesy we received. Perhaps these first days laid the simple human foundations which are certainly essential for continuous living among the poor: first, genuine preference for residence in an industrial quarter to any other part of the city, because it is interesting and makes the human appeal; and second, the conviction . . . that the things which make men alike are finer and better than the things that keep them apart, and that these basic likenesses, if they are properly accentuated, easily transcend the less essential differences of race, language, creed, and tradition.

With a tradition of black organization and activism, Chicago hosted the second convention of the National Association of Colored Women (NACW), held at Quinn Chapel. The NACW, founded in 1895 by elite and middle-class African-American women, addressed social reform through its local clubs. Establishing hospitals, orphanages, kindergartens, and social services for black Americans—whose needs were often ignored by white urban reformers and politicians—clubwomen played a vital role in their communities. The NACW also addressed national racial issues in the Gilded Age, especially in segregation and lynching, in which blacks (usually men) were murdered by white mobs.

The following excerpts from the minutes of the 1899 convention reveal the national scope of the black women's club movement as well as its agenda and strategies.

The emblem of the National Association of Colored Women incorporates the organization's motto "Lifting As We Climb." Made up largely of elite and middle-class women, the clubs hoped to gain respect for black women in general while improving the lot of those less fortunate than themselves.

MINUTES OF THE NATIONAL ASSOCIATION
OF COLORED WOMEN, 1899.
Chicago, Ill., August 14, 1899

MONDAY MORNING SESSION.

A large number of women assembled in Quinn Chapel, corner of 24th St. and Wabash Ave., to be present at the opening of the First Biennial Convention of the National Association of Colored Women. The meeting was called to order by the President, Mrs. Mary Church-Terrell. After singing, "Praise God from whom All Blessings Flow,." prayer was offered by 2nd Vice-President, Mrs. Lucy Thurman. . . .

Reports from the following Clubs were read by the following persons: I. B. W. Club of Chicago, Mrs. S. Taylor; Woman's Civic League, Chicago, Mrs. Minnie Roach; Ideal Club, Chicago, Mrs. Ophelia Clark; Women's Era Club, Boston, Mrs. J. St.P. Ruffin; Phillis Wheatley Club, New Orleans, Mrs. Sylvania F. Williams; Commercial Reciprocity Club, Indianapolis, Ind., Mrs. Lillian Thomas-Fox; Peoria Women's Aid, Peoria, Ill., Mrs. Sydney Wagoner; Woman's Home Improvement Club, Louisville, Ky., Mrs. Fannie B. Williams; Woman's Loyal Unions, N.Y. City, Mrs. Imogene Howard; Colterie Migratory Assembly, Memphis, Tenn., Mrs. Annie Whitlow; Sojourner Truth Club, Memphis, Tenn., Mrs. Robert Freeman. . . .

MONDAY AFTERNOON SESSION.

. . . Mrs. Harvey of Memphis, Tenn., reported for the Orphan's Home of said city, stating that twenty-five acres of land had been purchased. . . .

Mrs. Corine Brown, a woman of great worth who is noted for her success as a worker in the city of Chicago, was invited forward to be introduced to the Association. Mrs. Brown in her usual agreeable and winning way made some very choice remarks. Among other things she said that she believed that ability depended neither upon race nor upon sex. She advised work for legislation, saying the time would soon be when the two races would work together, as one cannot get along without the other. She warned the Southland to keep their children out of the factories before they are 14 years of age.

TUESDAY AFTERNOON SESSION.

Mrs. Haydee Campbell of St. Louis, Mo., was called and introduced to the Association. Her subject was "Why the National

Black Chicago

The Chicago of Jane Addams's day was a kaleidoscope of European ethnicities. But the city also had an important black community. Between 1870 and 1900, Chicago's black population exploded, from roughly 3,600 to over 30,000. Black migrants from the upper South, seeking a better life in the North, accounted for most of the city's massive black population growth.

Chicago proved to be a mixed experience for the migrants. Blacks could vote and attend school with whites—forbidden in the South—but they also faced harsh discrimination in jobs, housing, and public accommodations. In the industrial cauldron of Chicago, blacks worked chiefly in domestic and service jobs, ignored by labor organizers and social reformers alike. White Chicagoans viewed blacks as peripheral, unlike the city's European immigrants on whom Addams and many other social reformers focused.

As a separate community, Chicago's blacks established their own institutions and churches during the Gilded Age. Black Chicago boasted a plethora of women's clubs and youth organizations. Yet many black leaders clung to a vision of integration and fiercely fought racial separatism. They battled to secure their voting rights and ensure integrated schools. Moreover, they established a Vigilance Committee, which guarded against civil rights violations in Chicago.

The integrationist vision of many black Chicagoans vanished in the racially charged era of World War I. As Southern blacks flocked to Chicago to work in the city's factories and mills—with the black population reaching 109,000 by 1920—racial tensions flared. Feared by whites, blacks found themselves systematically excluded from certain neighborhoods, jobs, and even public accommodations. Whereas white European immigrants could work their way up the economic ladder and move out of the dilapidated neighborhoods if they chose, most of Chicago's blacks found themselves confined to ghettos and limited to low-paying, unskilled jobs.

The Dumb-Bell Tenement

Jacob Riis and many other urban reformers focused much of their attention on the problem of urban housing. Believing that a sound environment produced healthy children and families, urban reformers hoped to banish the evils of tenement life, as poor families huddled in crowded, dark, and badly ventilated buildings. In 1879 reformers sponsored a contest in which architects submitted designs for the best tenement that could be reasonably constructed on a city lot. Architect James E. Ware won the contest for his "dumb-bell" tenement, named for its tapered shape. Dumb-bell tenements blossomed across America's urban landscape as cheap, multifamily housing that could accommodate the booming population. But urban reformers soon criticized the shortcomings of these tenements as well, citing their dark, tiny rooms and inadequate ventilation.

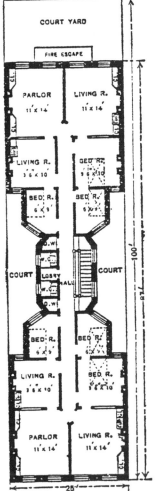

This floor plan shows how the dumb-bell tenement's shape created space for a courtyard on both sides of the building This type of tenement seemed to be a vast improvement over those built side by side, without yard space or ventilation.

Association should devise means to establish Kindergartens." Too much cannot be said of this paper. To say it was carefully prepared and well read are feeble words. . . . The subject was then open to all the delegates for general discussion. . . . Mrs. Will was present and spoke in interest of the Kindergarten. She advised working through the Legislatures of States and in that way have Kindergartens established. A motion to adjourn was carried. . . .

TUESDAY EVENING.
Mrs. Ruffin read a paper and Mr. Brown of Boston made stirring remarks concerning the Lynch Law and read resolutions which he asked all to endorse. . . . .

THURSDAY AFTERNOON SESSION
The officers had been invited by Miss Jane Addams of the Hull House to visit and to lunch. Led by Mrs. Ida B. Wells Barnett, the[y?] accordingly went forth at 12:30 P.M. . . .

FRIDAY, AUGUST 18th.
Mrs. Lottie Wilson Jackson spoke on the action taken in reference to the separate coach law. . . . It was moved and seconded that we endorse the work by Mrs. Jackson in connection with the separate coach law and give her our hearty support. Carried. . . .

Like Jane Addams, Jacob Riis was one of the Gilded Age's leading social reformers. A Danish immigrant who arrived in New York City in 1870, as a newspaper reporter, Riis became intimately acquainted with the city's teeming slums and its people. Appalled by the poverty he witnessed, Riis wrote shocking articles about the lives of slum dwellers. But more importantly, he seized upon photography as a means of revealing the urban squalor that words could scarcely describe. In 1890 Riis published his landmark work, based on his lectures, *How the Other Half Lives: Studies Among the Tenements of New York*, which combined written descriptions and photographs to tell the story of the underside of life in the United States.

Riis's observations of slum life convinced him of the importance of environment in shaping behavior. Rejecting popular assumptions that crime and poverty were the result of character defects or inherited traits, Riis argued instead that a positive environment shaped healthy, moral individuals, whereas an unhealthy environment—as found in urban slums—only encouraged destructive behavior. Riis was on

the cutting edge of thought about the links among environment, poverty, and crime, an idea that hardly seems controversial today. In an age when comfortable Americans were suspicious and disdainful of—-as well as removed from—the urban poor, Riis's startling, human portraits of slum life spurred them to consider their personal responsibility toward the less fortunate. The following excerpt from *How the Other Half Lives* focuses on the plight of poor children in New York City, many of whom lived in overcrowded and unhealthy tenements or on the streets.

The problem of the children becomes, in these swarms, to the last degree perplexing. Their very number make one stand aghast. . . . I counted the other day the little ones, up to ten years or so, in a Bayard Street tenement that for a yard has a triangular space in the centre with sides fourteen or fifteen feet long, just room enough for a row of ill-smelling closets at the base of the triangle and a hydrant at the apex. There was about as much light in this "yard" as in the average cellar. I gave up my self-imposed task in despair when I had counted one hundred and twenty-eight in forty families. . . . Bodies of drowned children turn up in the rivers . . . whom no one seems to know anything about. When last spring some workmen, while moving a pile of lumber on a North River pier, found under the last plank the body of a little lad crushed to death, no one missed a boy, though his parents afterward turned up. . . .

A little fellow who seemed clad in but a single rag was among the flotsam and jetsam stranded at Police Headquarters one day last summer. No one knew where he came from or where he belonged. The boy himself knew as little about it as anybody, and was the least anxious to have light shed on the subject after he had spent a night in the matron's nursery. . . . He sang "McGinty" all through, with Tenth Avenue variations, for the police, then settled down to the serious business of giving an account of himself. The examination went on after this fashion:

"Where do you go to church, my boy?"

"We don't have no clothes to go to church." And indeed his appearance, as he was, in the door of any New York church would have caused a sensation.

""Well, where do you go to school, then?"

"I don't go to school," with a snort of contempt.

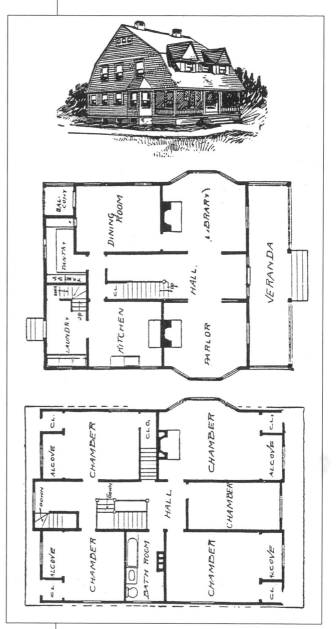

Suburbs in the Gilded Age aspired to a country ideal, promising a healthy, clean, and picturesque environment. This is an example of a suburban "country" house, from the best-selling plan books of George Palliser, whose house plans could be purchased by mail order. Unlike the dumb-bell tenement plan, this house provides for bright, airy rooms and a healthy environment.

Street Children and Orphan Trains

The predicament of urban children was of particular concern to Gilded Age reformers. In New York City alone, thousands of children—some runaways, others abandoned and neglected, still others working to support their families—roamed the streets, eking out a living by selling newspapers, matches, or their bodies. In the 1850s Charles Loring Brace, appalled by the miserable lives of the street children, formulated a plan to aid them. Rejecting workhouses and orphan asylums, Brace maintained that "the best of all asylums for the outcast child is the farmer's home. The great beauty is to get these children of unhappy future utterly out of their surroundings and to send them away to kind, Christian homes in the country."

In 1853 Brace founded the Children's Aid Society, which relocated street and orphan children to farms, mostly in the West. Boarding "orphan trains," tens of thousands of children left the congested streets of the city for new lives and families. The Children's Aid Society and the orphan trains were especially active during the Gilded Age, as the social and economic upheaval of the era took its toll on families. In the first 25 years of the Society alone, 50,000 children were relocated.

Although praised by many for aiding New York's street children, Brace and the orphan trains came under criticism, spurring an investigation in 1883. The investigation revealed that the society did not properly screen foster parents, that supervision was minimal, and that many older children had run away from their new homes. Although foster families were expected to house, feed, and educate children, some saw them only as a form of cheap labor and abused them. Despite these problems, investigators concluded that the program generally was successful in providing a new beginning for children with bleak futures in New York.

The 1883 investigation cast light on some of the problems of Brace's relocation program. The society often disregarded the rights of parents, assuming that any child on the streets was abandoned, the victim of "unfit" parents, when, in fact, some did have homes and families. Immigrant parents also often misunderstood the placement process, granting permission for their children to be taken West for what they believed was temporary work. Catholics feared that Brace's agenda included converting their children to the Protestant faith, as Catholic children were often placed in Protestant homes. In the end, although many children happily resettled in loving, supportive families, others found themselves once again exploited, mistreated, and overworked in slavelike conditions, cut off from friends and family in the East.

"Where do you buy your bread?"

"We don't buy bread; we buy beer," said the boy, and it was eventually the saloon that led the police as a landmark to his "home." It was worthy of the boy. As he had said, his only bed was a heap of dirty straw on the floor, his daily diet a crust in the morning, nothing else. . . .

Social Darwinism

Riis, Addams, and other urban social reformers faced a great deal of criticism in the Gilded Age. Some critics of social reform believed the movement was really about social control, with middle-class workers, such as Addams, forcing the urban poor, particularly immigrants, to live according to Protestant ideals, which emphasized hard work, thrift, and sobriety. Others worried that charitable efforts, such as those at Hull House, did not distinguish between the "worthy poor" and those who were simply lazy or unwilling to help themselves. Similarly, social Darwinists criticized social reformers, arguing that in aiding the poor, reformers tampered with "natural laws" of selection: the weak were meant to perish, and the strong survivors would inevitably improve the human race. William Graham Sumner, a professor of political and social science at Yale University and one of the nation's leading social Darwinists, dismissed social reform as wrongheaded, harmful to society, and a relic of a preindustrial era. This is an excerpt from *What Social Classes Owe to Each Other*, a book he published in 1883.

It is very popular to pose as a "friend of humanity," or a "friend of the working classes." . . . Anything which has a charitable sound and a kind-hearted tone generally passes without investigation, because it is disagreeable to assail it. Sermons, essays, and orations assume a conventional standpoint with regard to the poor, the weak, etc.; and it is allowed to pass as an unquestioned doctrine in regard to social classes that "the rich" ought to "care for the poor;". . .

Certain ills belong to the hardships of human life. They are natural. They are part of the struggle with Nature for existence. We cannot blame our fellow-men for our share of these. . . .

The humanitarians, philanthropists, and reformers, looking at the facts of life as they present themselves, find enough which is sad and unpromising in the condition of many members of society. They see wealth and poverty side by side. They note great

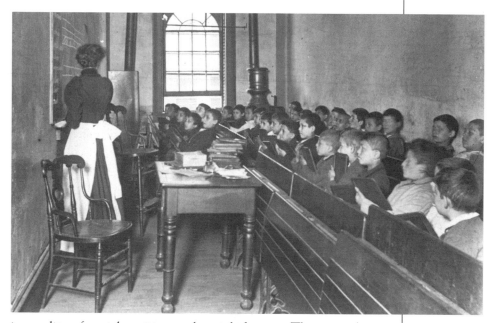

Immigrant children study at the Essex Market School in New York City, around 1890. Public schools played a crucial role in the process of "Americanizing" immigrant children. Not only did they learn English, but they also absorbed lessons in citizenship, which often stressed rejecting ethnic culture. An educator in 1906 explained: "For the immigrant children the public schools are the sluiceways into Americanism. When the stream of alien children flows through them, it will issue into the reservoirs of national life with the Old World taints filtered out, and the qualities retained that make for loyalty and good citizenship."

inequality of social position and social chances. They eagerly set about the attempt to account for what they see and to devise schemes for remedying what they do not like. In their eagerness to recommend the less fortunate classes to pity and consideration they forget all about the rights of other classes; they gloss over all the faults of the classes in question, and they exaggerate their misfortunes and their virtues. . . . When I have read certain of these discussions I have thought it must be quite disreputable to be respectable, quite dishonest to own property, quite unjust to go one's way and earn one's own living, and that the only really admirable person was the good-for-nothing. The man who by his own effort raises himself above poverty appears, in these discussions, to be of no account. The man who has done nothing to raise himself above poverty finds that the social doctors flock about him, bringing the capital which they have collected from the other class and promising the aid of the State to give him what the other had to work for. . . .

Whether social philosophers think it desirable or not, it is out of the question to go back to status or the sentimental relations which once united baron and retainer, master and servant, teacher and pupil, comrade and comrade. That we have lost some grace and elegance is undeniable. That life once held more poetry and romance is true enough. But it seems impossible that any one who has studied the matter should doubt that we have gained immeasurably and that our farther gains lie in going forward, not in going backward. . . . It follows . . . that one man, in a free state, cannot claim help from, and cannot be charged to give help to, another. . . .

Ward Bosses

Whereas urban social reformers like Addams and Riis undoubtedly helped improve the lives of poor city dwellers, the ward boss had a far greater direct impact on the poor. A ward boss was a local politician in charge of delivering votes for his party from his "ward," a section of the city. Ward bosses were vital cogs in the political machines that emerged in many American cities in the late 19th century. Political machines were a product of the growth of massive, impersonal cities that offered few social services. In return for votes, the political machines—through ward bosses—dispensed all kinds of favors to their constituents, including jobs, Christmas turkeys, food, and shelter. As William L. Riordon, a New York journalist, wrote of the ward boss, "Everybody in the district knows him. Everybody knows where to find him, and nearly everybody goes to him for assistance of one sort or another, especially the poor of the tenements." In an age of limited charities and social services, ward bosses and political machines undoubtedly alleviated the suffering of many poor city dwellers. In the following excerpt from *Plunkitt of Tammany Hall,* Riordon describes "a record of a day's work" for boss George Washington Plunkitt.

2 A.M.: Aroused from sleep by the ringing of his doorbell; went to the door and found a bartender, who asked him to go to the police station and bail out a saloonkeeper who had been arrested for violating the excise law. Furnished bail and returned to bed at three o'clock.

6 A.M.: Awakened by fire engines passing his house. Hastened to the scene of the fire, according to the custom of Tammany district leaders, to give assistance to the fire sufferers, if needed. Met several of his election district captains who are always under orders to look out for fires, which are considered great vote-getters. Found several tenants who had been burned out, took them to a hotel, supplied them with clothes, fed them, and arranged temporary quarters for them until they could rent and furnish new apartments.

8:30 A.M.: Went to the police court to look after his constituents. Found six "drunks." Secured the discharge of four by a timely word with the judge and paid the fines of two.

9 A.M.: Appeared in the Municipal District Court. Directed one of his district captains to act as counsel for a widow against

whom dispossess proceedings had been instituted and obtained an extension of time. Paid the rent of a poor family about to be dispossessed and gave them a dollar for food.

11 A. M.: At home again. Found four men waiting for him. One had been discharged by the Metropolitan Railway Company for neglect of duty, and wanted the district leader to fix things. Another wanted a job on the road. The third sought a place on the Subway and the fourth, a plumber, was looking for work with the Consolidated Gas Company. The district leader spent nearly three hours fixing things for the four men and succeeded in each case.

3 P. M.: Attended the funeral of an Italian as far as the ferry. Hurried back to make his appearance at the funeral of a Hebrew constituent. Went conspicuously to the front both in the Catholic church and the synagogue and later attended the Hebrew confirmation ceremonies in the synagogue.

7 P.M.: Went to district headquarters and presided over a meeting of election district captains. Each captain submitted a list of all the voters in his district, reported on their attitude toward Tammany, suggested who might be won over and how they could be won, told who were in need, and who were in trouble of any kind and the best way to reach them. District leader took notes and gave orders.

8 P.M.: Went to a church fair. Took chances on everything, bought ice cream for the young girls and the children. Kissed the little ones, flattered their mothers and took their fathers out for something down at the corner.

9 P.M.: At the clubhouse again. Spent $10 on tickets for a church excursion and promised a subscription for a new church bell. Bought tickets for a baseball game to be played by two nines from the district. Listened to the complaints of a dozen pushcart peddlers who said they were persecuted by the police and assured them he would go to Police Headquarters in the morning and see about it.

10:30 P.M.: Attended a Hebrew wedding reception and dance. Had previously sent a handsome wedding present to the bride.

12 P.M.: In bed.

Prohibition

For the growing middle class in the United States of the Gilded Age, home was considered to be woman's proper sphere. Middle-class women were expected to devote their lives to creating a comfortable and nurturing environment for their

In 1880 New York became the first American city to reach a population of 1 million.

Saloons

Many working-class urban residents resented the attempts by middle-class prohibitionists to ban liquor. Whereas reformers viewed the saloon as the source of family disorder, violence against women and children, and corruption, workingmen saw the saloon as a haven from their grueling jobs. Saloons served as social clubs, union halls, and even political headquarters. But prohibitionists were correct in their assessment that the nation was, in fact, saturated in alcohol. In 1898 there were 215,000 licensed liquor dealers and approximately 50,000 "blind pigs," unregulated saloons. Beer sold for a nickel, affordable even to low-wage laborers.

This 1888 photograph of the Dennis B. Nye family in their parlor in Minneapolis reflects the middle-class ideal of family life in the Gilded Age, with mother taking care of the children, father relaxing at home after a hard day's work, and children listening to their sister's piano playing.

husbands and children. Nevertheless, many women stepped outside of the domestic sphere and became involved in the political issues of the day, particularly Prohibition. A ban on the manufacture and sale of alcohol, Prohibition was one of the most important and controversial reforms of the Gilded Age. Middle-class women embraced the cause as a defense of their homes. They viewed alcohol as the root cause of many social and urban ills as well as the source of domestic violence and unstable home lives. Unable to vote, Prohibitionist women nonetheless did what they could to influence men voting to ban alcohol. Political involvement in Prohibition also led many women to fight for the right to vote. Under the leadership of Frances Willard, the Women's Christian Temperance Union, one of the nation's largest women's organizations, began to advocate woman suffrage in the late 1870s. This appeal to male voters in Mecklenburg County, North Carolina, from the Ladies Prohibitory Society of Charlotte, published in 1881, provides insight into how middle-class women justified their move from the home into the political arena.

Before another week shall pass away your votes will determine whether the traffic in intoxicants shall close forever in Mecklenburg county or not. Recognizing that our true sphere is not the

political arena or public places, but the home, the fireside, and the privacy of the domestic circle, yet we cannot be insensible to the fact that the issue of this election is freighted with vital interest to ourselves and those most dear to us.

We have, therefore, not deemed it improper to make a last appeal to the manhood of our dear old county to deliver us from the evils of the whiskey traffic.

If we are deeply moved in this matter, it is because the poisoned shafts of the great enemy of our race have entered our own hearts.

If unusual earnestness has marked our efforts in this behalf, it is because we are fully sensible that a treacherous foe stalks in our midst, ever seeking an opportunity to strike a blow at the peace and happiness of the inner circle of our homes.

Constrained by the impulse of holy love, which God has planted in the maternal bosom of animals as well as woman, we appeal to the true manhood of the men of Mecklenburg, to shield and protect the innocent boys and untried youth of our county from the baleful influence of strong drink by banishing from our midst the licensed bar. In the presence of this great question, the issue of which involves so much of happiness or woe in this sorrowing world of ours, we beseech you, men of Mecklenburg, to sink all personal differences, all objections to the law, and forgetting the bitterness and unkind feelings engendered in the heat of the campaign, let every one who seeks the good of his fellow man unite in this effort to banish from our fair land this plague of strong drink.

Brave men of Mecklenburg, it is the cry of woman, suffering woman, that bids you to the contest with the evil which has brought this suffering upon us. Be but true to yourselves and the generous emotions of your own hearts, and our appeal shall not be in vain.

The crusade against alcohol was so pervasive in the late 19th century that popular music commemorated the struggle. This song from 1875 praised "that noble band" of women willing to enter "the dens of want and shame," so that "men may not die." The chorus of the song implored, "Teach us all that woman's love, O'er earth can yet have sway."

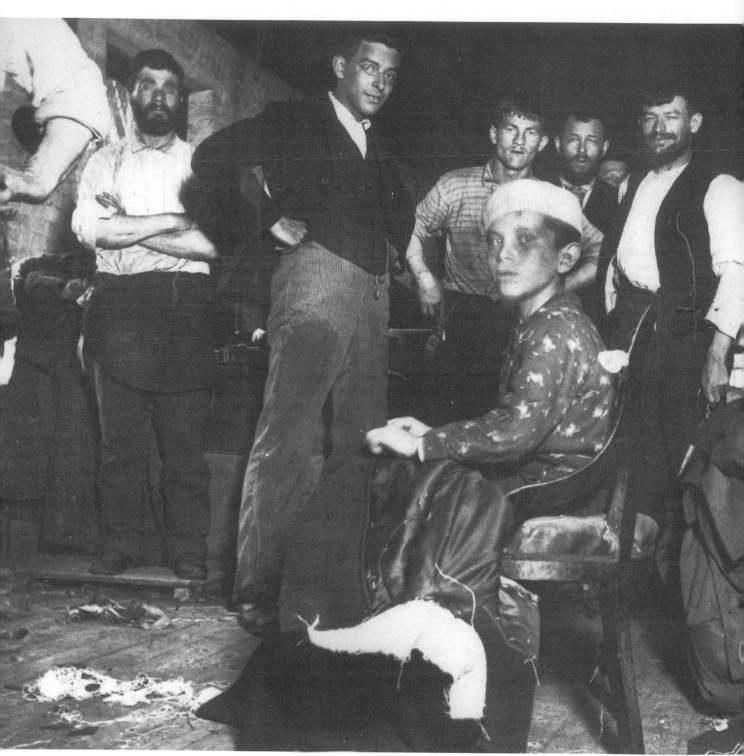

In a Sweatshop

Concerned about the exploitation of children, Riis photographed this young boy at work pulling threads in a New York City sweatshop. The boy appears to interrupt his work only long enough to look at the camera before returning to his task, for which he was probably paid by the piece. The men of the shop, towering over the boy, seem especially threatening. Riis also contrasts the ragtag, unsmiling boy with the beaming, well-dressed shop foreman, standing behind him to the left.

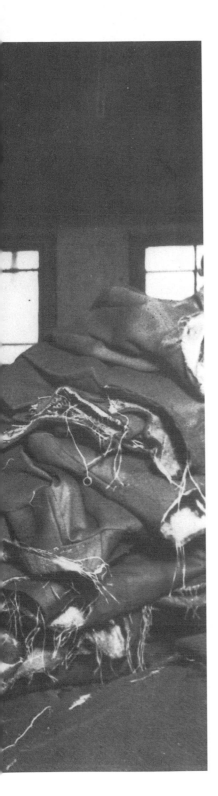

Chapter Five: Picture Essay

Jacob Riis and the Power of the Photograph

Newspaper reporter Jacob Riis knew the swarming slums of Gilded Age New York City as well as anyone. Unlike most police reporters of his day, who merely rewrote lurid pieces for the consumption of newspaper readers, Riis actually investigated the crimes he reported. His investigations gave him firsthand knowledge of the underside of New York City: a world of saloons, gambling dens, houses of prostitution, overcrowded, filthy tenements, and street children.

Riis did not flinch at the shocking world of the slums. Instead, he found himself drawn to it, to the men, women, and children who lived their lives in New York's congested, constricted neighborhoods.

An immigrant himself, Riis had arrived in New York from Denmark in 1870, and he knew what it was like to struggle. He, too, had known hunger and poverty, had been swindled, and had seen some of his dreams wither in the harsh light of the United States in the Gilded Age. As a result, he empathized with the city's poor in ways that few others did. Despite embracing some of the prejudices of native-born, middle-class Americans in his attitudes toward southern and eastern Europeans, Riis remained sympathetic to their plight. Rather than blame them for their own problems, as did most of his contemporaries, he concluded that environment played a crucial role in shaping people. In his view the key to ameliorating urban problems, such as crime and poverty, was to create a more hospitable urban set-

Danish-born Jacob Riis helped revolutionize the way that Americans thought about poverty and the urban poor: "I have aimed to tell the truth as I saw it."

ting, a more nurturing and healthy environment. But the first step, he realized, was to make the rest of society aware of the depth of New York's social problems.

As a reporter, Riis began to publish vivid stories about life in New York's slums. But words, he soon realized, proved inadequate in communicating the squalid lives of the city's poor. He recalled, "It was upon my midnight trips with the sanitary police that the wish kept cropping up in me that there were some way of putting before the people what I saw there. . . . A drawing might have done it, but it would not have been evidence of the kind I wanted."

While scanning a newspaper one morning, he spied a notice announcing a major advance in the field of photography: a new chemical made it possible to take flash photos in even the darkest rooms. Riis seized upon the idea of photographing the slums and its people about whom he had been writing. Not trained in photography, he hired two photographers but found their approach unsatisfactory. The trained professionals seemed to worry more about the technical aspects of their photographs than the subjects themselves—Riis's key concern.

"There was at last but one way out of it," Riis concluded, "namely, for me to get a camera myself." He took his camera into the slums and documented the lives of the "other half," a side of New York rarely glimpsed by its more fortunate inhabitants. An amateur, he sometimes set fires with his flashpan and once nearly blinded himself with flash powder. But his stunning photographs captured the human casualties of the Gilded Age city; the haunted faces of his subjects and their destitute surroundings could not be easily dismissed.

Riis was especially concerned with the children of the slums. A disciple of Charles Loring Brace, he made startling photographs capturing children denied a childhood, of street urchins and sweatshop workers aged by their harsh labor.

Riis made his photos into lantern slides (early projected images) to show to middle-class church groups and civic organizations, as he lectured on the lives of the urban poor. Audiences were horrified by what they saw. Some cried, others fainted. No one had ever taken photographs like these. As scholar Peter Hales explains, Riis's photos provided an "apparently irrefutable medium of proof" to buttress his demands for social reform. His photos "meant to demand of his middle-class Victorian audience a complete and active commitment to the cause of social justice and economic reform."

Lodgers in a Crowded Bayard Street Tenement—5 Cents a Spot (1890)

Riis documented cheap lodging available to those who could afford nothing more than "5 cents a spot." By packing as much as he can of the lodging room within the frame of his camera, Riis gives a sense of the crowded conditions, the lack of privacy, and the filth and clutter of the room, which includes pots and pans for cooking, trunks, dirty shoes and socks, and chamberpots. The room appears to be a breeding ground for both disease and immorality. For Americans who valued cleanliness, order, and privacy, this scene would have been especially troubling.

By 1890 Riis had translated his lectures and photographs into a book, *How the Other Half Lives: Studies Among the Tenements of New York*, which achieved instant acclaim. This pathbreaking work, like his lectures, used powerful photographs to substantiate his descriptions of tenement life. Riis's photos proved to be a mighty weapon for social reform. Because of his pioneering efforts, social reformers would use photographs to publicize the plight of those they wished to aid, and urban photographers would capture images that revealed a side of city life often hidden from middle- and upper-class observers. Through Riis's efforts, some of New York's worst tenements were destroyed, and child labor laws were enforced more effectively.

Riis aimed to provide objective evidence of the horrors of slum life, but his photographs—by nature—are not unbiased. As a social reformer seeking to shock people into action, Riis chose his subjects carefully, often posing them and arranging their surroundings for maximum impact. Artistic concerns rarely informed Riis's photographs: His social agenda did, and they should be interpreted from their partisan perspective. At the same time, they document fascinating details about slum life and dwellers, including the kinds of clothes they wore, their personal belongings, and how they furnished and arranged their homes.

A Flat in Poverty Gap, the Home of an English Coal-Heaver and His Family (c. 1890)

Jacob Riis chose subjects that would both shock and inform his audience. This photograph, capturing an impoverished immigrant family at mealtime, challenges many ideals about home that most Americans held dear. Instead of home as a comfortable haven of domesticity, this room is dark, dirty, and spare, without a single decoration or object to uplift the spirit. Plaster peels from the wall and the floors are stained. A broom on the left seems to indicate the family's desire to keep their home clean. But their surroundings are so run down that the broom seems a symbol of futility. The meager possessions of this family stand in stark contrast to the "conspicuous consumption" of more fortunate Gilded Age Americans. While the gazes of the father and the child on his lap meet our eye, drawing us into the scene, the mother and second child look away, with expressions of resignation and despair.

Minding Baby—Cherry Hill (c. 1890)

Children were one of Riis's favorite subjects. In an age in which middle and upper-class Americans celebrated childhood as an age of innocence and indulgence, Riis captured the lives of less fortunate children. In this photograph, Riis shows a child placed in charge of a small baby. The children huddle alone in a rundown room, barren except for a few basic household items. The pose of the children suggests their vulnerability; no adults are present to protect them, and they are left to fend for themselves. Their imploring eyes seem to ask us for help. Riis's photograph provokes the observer to imagine the children's impoverished lives and their bleak futures.

Katie: I Scrubs (c. 1890)

Like the children in "Minding Baby," Katie challenges widely held conventions about childhood in the Gilded Age. Riis captures a diminutive girl with the haggard face of an old woman; her passive, aged face seems incongruous with her small body. Here is a child, Riis shows us, who never experienced the joys of childhood but instead has prematurely aged as she makes her living by scrubbing. Her hands, those of a worker and not a child, seem outsized and emphasize her position as a working "woman." Photographed on the street, she seems especially alone; we are not sure whether she has a home or parents, or any adult, to care for her.

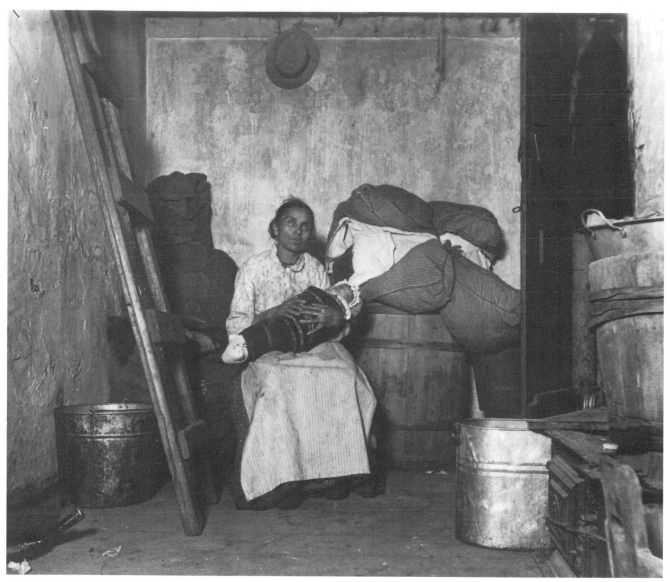

Ragpicker, Italian Mother and Her Baby (1888)

This portrait of an Italian mother and child is often cited as Jacob Riis's finest photograph. Posing the mother and child as he does, Riis alludes to Renaissance paintings depicting the Madonna and Child. Instead of the beatific smile of the Virgin Mary, this careworn Italian mother manages only an expression of grim determination. Looking up, she seems weary, her eyes hard. And rather than being surrounded by angels and adoring shepherds and kings, this mother and child are encircled instead by their few possessions, including washtubs and dirty and worn bedding. Like the broom in "A Flat in Poverty Gap," the dustpan on the left indicates the mother's wish to keep her surroundings clean; the paper next to the dustpan suggests the impossibility of doing so in her slum home. In an age when motherhood—like childhood—was often sentimentalized, this scene, like so many others that Riis photographed in New York's slums, shocked contemporary viewers by showing a domestic reality far from the Gilded Age ideal.

Bohemian Cigarmakers at Work in Their Tenement (1890)

Home had a very different purpose and function for poor immigrants, compared to the middle and upper classes. Rather than providing a sanctuary from work and the world, the home of these Bohemian cigarmakers also served as their workplace. According to Riis, who used this photograph in *How the Other Half Lives*, the husband and wife "work at the bench from six in the morning until nine at night." Working as a team to make cigars, they received $3.75 for every 1,000 cigars they made and could turn out 3,000 per week. Given Riis's concern for the children of the slums, it is not surprising that the oldest child, who is shown helping his parents, is the focal point in this photograph. He is barefoot, his feet filthy. He faces the camera, making eye contact with the viewer, looking despondent, seemingly consigned to the same future of drudgery as his parents.

Men's Lodging Room (c. 1892)

As he did in "Lodgers in a Crowded Bayard Street Tenement—'5 Cents a Spot,'" Riis captures the grim reality of cheap lodging in New York City. By centering this photo on the room's wood stove, Riis forces the viewer to seek out human forms amidst what seem at first to be inanimate objects—perhaps piles of wood like those stacked on the left side of the frame. Riis shows only one face—perhaps to remind the reader that these are indeed human beings strewn across the floor and tables and chairs. Riis might also be suggesting that this unhealthy environment reduced its human inhabitants to animals or objects. Riis clearly portrays the room as unfit for human habitation in its filth and disarray.

Chapter Six

The New South

I n June 1882, 26-six-year-old William C. Smith published the premier edition of the *Charlotte Messenger*, the North Carolina city's first black newspaper. According to Smith, the newspaper represented "an honest effort on our part to promote the moral, intellectual, and material standing of our people." Over the next several years, Smith used his newspaper to articulate his vision of a New South—a South of racial equality, a place of opportunity and advancement for all of its inhabitants, regardless of race.

Smith was a young man when he started his newspaper. Yet by the 1880s he and many Southern black men and women had already traveled a long road from slavery to freedom. Smith had been born a slave in Fayetteville, North Carolina, in 1856; he was nine years old when the Civil War ended and slavery was abolished. During Reconstruction, Smith, like many former slaves, managed to take advantage of the educational opportunities available in Freedman's Bureau schools. Like others of his generation, he learned reading and writing from Northern teachers who had come South to educate ex-slaves and help ease their transition to freedom.

Smith was such an apt student that he not only earned a teaching certificate but also learned the printing trade. He embarked on a career as a newspaperman. At the age of 18, he started his first newspaper in eastern North Carolina. But, like other young people in the Gilded Age, he migrated to the city, believing that urban life offered more to a young man or woman seeking advancement. By the early 1880s Smith had settled in Charlotte, North Carolina, a rapidly growing business and upcoming industrial center.

In 1882, when he first published the *Charlotte Messenger*, Smith and many young Southerners—both black and white—saw themselves as builders of a New South. From the ruins of the slave-holding Old

Founded in 1881, the Tuskegee Institute, Alabama, emphasized industrial training for African-American students. Tuskegee became famous under the leadership of Booker T. Washington, who believed that blacks would benefit more from learning practical trades rather than professional skills. Tuskegee's students erected their own campus buildings—even making the bricks—to learn building skills as well as self-reliance.

In 1900 approximately one out of every six Southerners lived in a village, city, or town.

William C. Smith, publisher and editor of the Charlotte Messenger, *envisioned a New South offering former slaves and their descendants equal rights and opportunities. But white supremacists, intent on keeping blacks in an inferior position, crushed that dream by enacting Jim Crow laws, denying them the right to vote, and lynching.*

South, they hoped to construct a new and better South. The New South they envisioned would be a region of prosperity, economically sound and diverse, and every bit as modern and up-to-date as the rest of the nation.

Most Southerners agreed that the Old South died in the Civil War, but they held a wide range of opinions about exactly what the New South should be. William C. Smith envisioned a New South of racial equality and justice, a world in which black men and women would have the chance to prove their worth and prosper—just like any white person. By contrast, Henry Grady, the young, white, influential editor of the *Atlanta Constitution*, imagined a New South of extensive industry and economic diversity like the North, but with blacks clearly subordinate to whites. Others, such as plantation owners, wanted a New South as similar as possible to the Old South, with themselves in control and a cheap, dependent black labor force working their fields. In the meantime, small farmers dreamed of independence, prosperity, and respect, watching in horror as the price of cotton dropped so drastically over the course of the period that it cost more to plant cotton than it could ever bring on the market. Struggles over competing visions of the New South defined the region in the Gilded Age.

With the end of Reconstruction in 1877, Southerners were left to determine the future of their region with little concern about interference from the federal government. The South, in many ways a distinctive region of the nation with a distinctive history, nonetheless followed many of the same patterns as the rest of the United States during the Gilded Age. Railroads not only bound the region together but also tied the South more tightly to the rest of the nation. The South, as did the rest of the nation, became more urbanized and industrialized. Southerners bought goods from mail-order houses like Sears, Roebuck as did other Americans, read the same magazines and books, and suffered the same economic depressions.

Yet in several crucial ways the South also remained outside the mainstream of U.S. life and differed in important ways from the rest of the nation. It remained the poorest, least urban section of the United States. Relatively few Southerners benefited from the prosperity of the Gilded Age. Henry Grady and other New South boosters did lure some Northern investors to the South to build up Southern industry. Andrew Carnegie, for example, expanded his steel empire to Birmingham, Alabama, and some New England textile magnates invested in Southern cotton mills. Yet the New South never fulfilled the industrial potential imagined by Grady

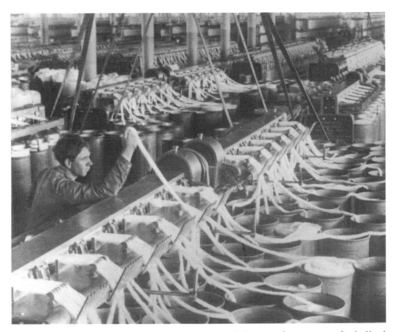

A textile worker labors in the Great Olympian Cotton Mill in Georgia in the 1880s. Textile mills in the South often attracted poor farm families, who had either lost their land or simply could not support themselves due to falling cotton prices.

and others. The region was hindered by a shortage of skilled workers, investment capital, and a lack of managerial expertise.

Moreover, few European immigrants settled in the region, and 90 percent of the nation's blacks resided there. The white South regulated racial interaction and legally separated blacks and whites by passing Jim Crow laws, which established a distinctive social system and largely defined Southern life until the Civil Rights movement dismantled them in the 1950s and 60s.

When William C. Smith started his newspaper in the 1880s, he believed that the South—even more than the North—would be a land of opportunity, especially for blacks. But before the end of the decade some ominous developments suggested otherwise. Several states had passed laws separating the races in railroad cars. Lynching, in which white mobs hanged, tortured, and mutilated blacks, mostly men, exploded in the late 1880s. White political leaders openly discussed ways to keep black men from voting, as their political activism sometimes barred white candidates from winning election.

By the 1890s Smith's vision of the New South, and that of many other black Southerners, had been destroyed. Beginning in 1890 with the state of Mississippi and ending in 1908 with Georgia, every Southern state passed laws, or added requirements—such as poll taxes and literacy tests—that kept blacks from voting. In 1896, in *Plessy v. Ferguson*, the U.S. Supreme Court upheld Louisiana's Jim Crow railroad car law, which forced blacks to sit in a separate, "colored," section, ruling seven to one that segregation did not violate

Our Opera House

"It is a source of regret to see that so many of our better class of citizens are prevented from going to operas on account of their color. Free American citizens and many of them are free born, educated and as refined as they may be, they are compelled to take back seats or none at all. . . . But think of our sitting on back seats—straight, hard benches—and in front of us a lot of rude, noisy boys. There were seats in the gallery; they are also back seats of the same class, and then we would be crowded by all manner of male and female roughs. . . . It is dangerous for a lady to wear decent dress to such a place.

"Our people are fond of amusements, and as they are becoming more intelligent, take great interest in the theatre, especially those plays which take them back to Roman history. Under the circumstances we could not advise our people to go where they must take back seats and be left at the mercy of the worst classes of both races. . . .

"We do not wish to push ourselves upon our good white friends. We only want *good* accommodations apart from noisy, bad boys and bad women, and we are willing to pay for the same. . . ."

—William C. Smith,
Charlotte Messenger, 1883

the constitutional rights of black Americans. In Smith's home state of North Carolina, racial hatred stirred up by white Democrats in a violent anti-black political campaign in 1898 led to the Wilmington Riot in November. After a white mob killed and injured 36 blacks and destroyed the office and press of black newspaperman Alexander Manly, thousands of blacks fled the city, many abandoning the South and their dream of a truly New South.

Thus for black Southerners like Smith, the Gilded Age dawned with great promise but ended with their hopes and expectations crushed. Despite the potential that Smith and others saw in the New South—the possibility that men and women of a new generation might redefine race relations and fashion a truly new society—the legacies of slavery weighed heavily, evident in white supremacy, black subordination, and economic underdevelopment that defined the region well into the 20th century.

A Sharecropper's Contract

In the aftermath of the Civil War, sharecropping emerged as a labor system negotiated between planters and former slaves. With the abolition of slavery, planters desperately needed a cheap and dependable labor force to work their fields but had little or no money to pay workers. Former slaves wishing to have their own property and to labor independently of white supervision usually lacked money to purchase land. Sharecropping allowed them to reside on and work a piece of a planter's land for a share of the yield. Planters provided seed and supplies and expected anywhere from one third to one half of the crop in return. There were many variations of sharecropping contracts. The following contract is an example of the kind of agreement reached between tenants and planters and reveals the many ways that planters maintained control over sharecroppers.

A Corrupt System

At first, sharecropping seemed to offer blacks autonomy from white supervision, the opportunity to work together as families, and a way to earn money and own land. But some planters regularly cheated sharecroppers, keeping them in debt, so that they were unable to escape the plantation or system. Sharecropping ultimately became synonymous with exploitation and corruption.

To every 30 or 35 acres, I agree to furnish the team, plow, and farming implements, except cotton planters, and I *do not* agree to furnish a cart to every cropper. The croppers are to have half of the cotton, corn, and fodder (and peas and pumpkins and potatoes if any are planted) if the following conditions are complied with, but—if not—they are to have only two-fifths (2/5). Croppers are to have no part or interest in the cotton seed raised from the crop planted and worked by them. No vine crops of any description, that is, no

These maps of the Barrow Plantation, Oglethorpe, Georgia, show the physical transformations that sharecropping brought to the plantation landscape from 1860 (left) to 1881 (right), as freed people moved out of slave quarters, beyond their former masters' view, into their own independent households.

watermelons, muskmelons, . . . squashes or anything of that kind, except peas and pumpkins, and potatoes, are to be planted in the cotton or corn. All must work under my direction. All plantation work to be done by the croppers. My part of the crop to be *housed* by them, and the fodder and oats to be hauled and put in the house. All the cotton must be topped about 1st August. . . .

For every mule or horse furnished by me there must be 1,000 good sized rails . . . hauled, and the fence repaired as far as they will go, the fence to be torn down and put up from the bottom if I so direct. All croppers to haul rails and work on fence whenever I may order. Rails to be split when I say. Each cropper to clean out every ditch in his crop, and where a ditch runs between two crop-pers, the cleaning out of that ditch is to be divided equally between them. . . . The cleaning out of all ditches must be done by the first of October. The rails must be split and the fence repaired before corn is planted. . . . .

If any cotton is planted on the land outside the plantation fence, I am to have *three fourths* of all the cotton made in those patches, that is to say, no cotton must be planted by croppers in their home patches. . . .

No cropper to work off the plantation when there is any work to be done on the land he has rented, or when his work is needed by me or other croppers. . . .

Croppers must sow & plow in oats and haul them to the crib, but *must have no part of them.* Nothing to be sold from their crops, nor fodder nor corn to be carried out of the fields until my rent is all paid, and all amounts they owe me and for which I am responsible are paid in full.

I am to gin & pack all the cotton and charge every cropper an eighteenth of his part, the cropper to furnish his part of the bagging, ties, & twine.

The sale of every cropper's part of the cotton to be made by me when and where I choose to sell, and after deducting all they owe me and all sums that I may be responsible for on their accounts, to pay them their half of the net proceeds. Work of every description, particularly the work on fences and ditches, to be done to my satisfaction, and must be done over until I am satisfied that it is done as it should be. . . .

"A Perfect Democracy"

Although most Gilded Age Southerners—black and white—remained in the countryside, the South's towns and cities—like those of the rest of the United States—experienced explosive growth, especially in the Piedmont crescent that stretched from Richmond to Atlanta. The Piedmont boasted some of the region's fastest growing cities, including Charlotte and Winston-Salem, North Carolina, and Atlanta, Georgia. Atlanta emerged as the premier city of the New South, symbolically rising from the ashes of the Civil War, when it had been burned down by Union forces, to emerge as a transportation, commercial, and industrial center.

Henry Grady, the young editor of the *Atlanta Constitution,* articulated a vision of the New South that reflected the energy and self-promotion of Atlanta and other New South cities. He envisioned a thriving New South reconciled to the North and a full participant in the prosperity of the Gilded Age. Grady made the following speech in 1886 before the

"Fellow citizens: I am not indifferent to the claims of a generous forgetfulness, but whatever else I may forget, I shall never forget the difference between those who fought for liberty and those who fought for slavery; between those who fought to save the Republic and those who fought to destroy it."

—Frederick Douglass, 1894 speech

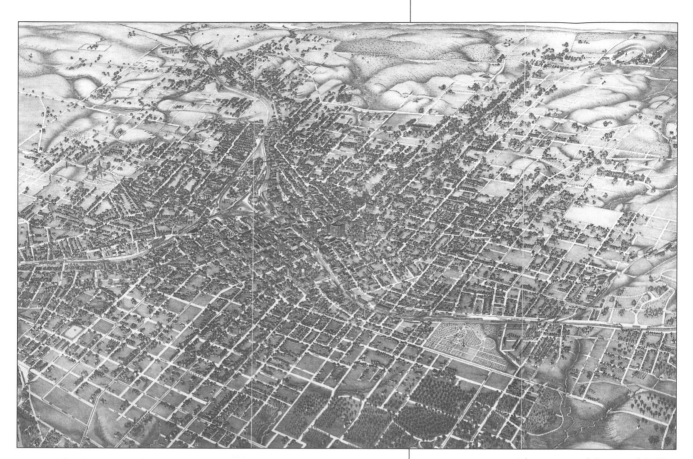

New England Society of New York, an elite social club. The speech launched him to national prominence as a spokesman for the New South.

Atlanta epitomized the spirit of the New South: an energetic, sprawling, rapidly industrializing urban center emerging from the ashes of the old Slave South.

"There was a South of slavery and secession—that South is dead. There is a South of union and freedom—that South, thank God, is living, breathing, growing every hour." These words, delivered . . . in 1866, true then and truer now, I shall make my text tonight. . . .

Dr. Talmage [an earlier speaker that evening] has drawn for you, with a master's hand, the picture of your returning armies . . . . Will you bear with me while I tell you of another army that sought its home at the close of the late war—an army that marched home in defeat and not in victory . . . .What does he find . . . when, having followed the battle-stained cross against over-whelming odds, dreading death not half so much as surrender, he reaches the home he left so prosperous and beautiful? He finds his house in ruins, his farm devastated, his slaves free, his stock killed, his barns empty, his trade destroyed, his money worthless, his social system . . . swept away. . . .

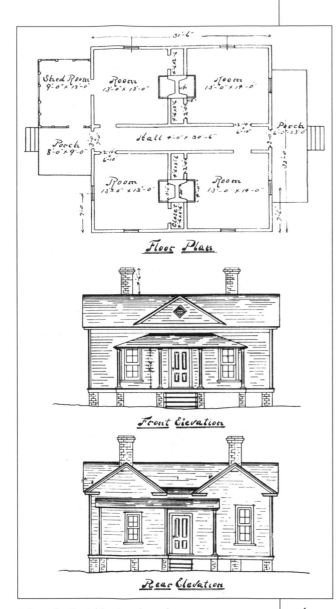

Industrialist D. A. Tompkins designed this building as a model mill worker's house. Housing like this could be found in mill villages throughout the South's textile belt.

What does he do—this hero in gray with a heart of gold? Does he sit down in sullenness and despair? Not for a day. . . . The soldiers stepped from the trenches into the furrow; women reared in luxury cut up their dresses and made breeches for their husbands and . . . gave their hands to work. . . .

But what is the sum of our work? We have found out that in the summing up the free negro counts more than he did as a slave. We have planted the schoolhouse on the hilltop and made it free to white and black. We have sowed towns and cities in the place of theories and put business above politics. . . . We have established thrift in city and country. We have fallen in love with work. . . . Above all, we know that we have achieved in these "piping times of peace" a fuller independence for the South than which our fathers sought to win in the forum by their eloquence or compel in the field by their swords. . . .

But what of the negro? Have we solved the problem he presents or progressed in honor and equity toward solution? Let the record speak to the point. No section shows a more prosperous laboring population than the negroes of the South, none in fuller sympathy with the employing and land-owning class.

But have we kept faith with you? In the fullest sense, yes. When Lee surrendered . . . the South became, and has since been, loyal to this Union. We fought hard enough to know that we were whipped and in perfect frankness accept as final the arbitrament of the sword to which we had appealed. The South found her jewel in the toad's head of defeat. The shackles that had held her in narrow limitations fell forever when the shackles of the negro slave were broken. Under the old regime the negroes were slaves to the South; the South was a slave to the system. . . .

The old South rested everything on slavery and agriculture, unconscious that these could neither give nor maintain healthy growth. The new South presents a perfect democracy, . . . a social system compact and closely knitted, less splendid on the surface, but stronger at the core—a hundred farms for every plantation, fifty homes for every palace—and a diversified industry that meets the complex needs of this complex age. . . .

This is said in no spirit of time-serving or apology. The South has nothing for which to apologize. She believes that the late struggle between the States was war and not rebellion; revolution

and not conspiracy, and that her convictions were as honest as yours. . . . The South has nothing to take back. . . .

Now, what answer has New England to this message? Will she permit the prejudice of war to remain in the hearts of the conquerors, when it has died in the hearts of the conquered? Will she transmit this prejudice to the next generation? . .

Cotton Mill Workers

Despite overall shortcomings, several New South industries prospered in the Gilded Age—cigarettes, centered in Richmond, Winston-Salem, and Durham; lumber and turpentine on the coastal plains; and textiles in the Piedmont. Rural families, squeezed by low cotton prices and the overpopulation of the countryside, left their homes in the mountains and foothills, desperately seeking economic security in the cotton mills of the Piedmont. They provided the labor force for the South's booming textile industry. But mill work was available to whites only.

Farm families were used to hard labor, but work in the cotton mills was brutal. In the 1890s workers averaged 72 hours per week. And wages were so low that entire families often worked in the mills where child labor was especially common. The following selection is an excerpt from an interview with a mill worker named Kate Brumby conducted at her home during the 1930s by the Federal Writers' Project. She first labored as a child in the South's textile mills and continued working in the mills for the rest of her life.

"Have you lived very long at the Spring Road Mill?" I asked.

"Since it were first started," Kate said. "The Brumbys was up there on opening day to help break in the machinery. Old Mr. Hall owned the Alberta Mill where we worked and he got us to move here. He wanted families that he knowed was good workers to start his new mill. . . .

"As I told you, I w'an't but nine when I went to work in the mill, and when I'd come home of a night I never felt much like learnin'. Sometimes Pa'd make me do a little spellin' but I never done so well at it. Then Pa died when I was twelve, and after that they weren't nobody to try to learn me. Ma never had a day's schoolin' in her life but she worked as hard fer her family as any woman I knowed. . . .

Mill Villages

In 1899 industrialist D. A. Tompkins, who owned several cotton mills in Charlotte, wrote *Cotton Mills, Commercial Features*, a handbook for aspiring Southern cotton mill owners. The book suggested cost-cutting measures, such as building mill villages outside of the city limits. Not only would manufacturers avoid paying city taxes, but mill workers could be kept from the "bad influences" of lawyers who might—in the case of industrial accidents—promote lawsuits that could be costly to mill owners.

Nearly all cotton mill workers resided in mill villages, constructed by mill owners, to whom they paid monthly rent. Although many mill owners, like Tompkins, boasted about the comfortable living conditions of their villages, unsanitary conditions led to regular epidemics, such as measles, which ravaged them. Mill children also commonly suffered from hookworm and pellagra, a vitamin deficiency. Poor and propertyless, mill workers also had to endure abuse from wealthier townspeople who called them "lintheads."

"This oppression of women and children is not only a shame to the State but a burning sin against God and weak humanity."

—The Reverend H. L. Atkins, on Charlotte's mill workers, 1895

"Granny died just before we moved to the mill—the Carona Cotton Mill down on the river. Ma had already got jobs fer me and her and Alice. She drawed 25 cents a day and we drawed 10 cents apiece a day. Pa stayed at home with the children. It was winter time when we first went there and we started to work by lantern light and quit by lantern light, the kerosene lanterns swinging down from the ceiling. I never seen no electric lights until we moved to Hopsonville two year later. The first mornin' I went in the mill I kept alookin' up wonderin' what on earth them things was. I walked over to the woman I was to work with and I asked her, 'What sort of bugs is them up there on the ceilin'?' That sure tickled her and she never let me forget it long as I stayed there.

"Pa died the first year we was at Hopsonville. His death was jest the beginnin' of a long, hard time. Clarence had growed big enough to go in the mill, makin' four of us to draw money. Come summer, Alice tuk the typhoid. Then Clarence. Ma had to stay outa the mill to wait on 'em. That left lone me makin' 10 cents a day fer the family to live on. But the neighbors was awful good to us, and they brought in rashins. If they hadner we woulder starved, I reckin. Alice was still awful puny when she went back to the mill. And the very day she went to work I tuk down with the fever. It was hard times fer us and hard on poor Ma.

"I must've been around fourteen when we left Hopsonville fer Alberta. But before we left Hopsonville I'd learnt that a little grit'll help a body along. I hadn't been back to work long after the typhoid when I went to my boss and done straight talkin'. 'I think I'm wurth more than 10 cents a day,' I said to him. And he raised me to 20 cents. Ma had got up to 50 cents and he raised Alice same as he did me. I was around 15 when Mr. Hall got us to move here to Spring Road to help open up. I've been here off and on ever since. I've been in this one house nigh on to 20 year. Hit oughter be mine by now."

The Rise of "Jim Crow"

Beginning in the 1880s some Southern states began to formalize and legalize racial segregation on railroad cars. In 1890 Louisiana passed a Jim Crow railroad car law, which required that blacks and whites ride separately in cars. With the support of the African-American "Citizens' Committee to Test the Constitutionality of the Separate Car Law," Homer Plessy decided to challenge the legality of this segregationist law.

"The mills are not run as charitable institutions, but to make money."

—Cotton mill owner W. S. Mallory, in response to the Reverend Atkins, 1895

He and the Committee believed that those who purchased a first-class ticket had the right to ride in the first-class car—regardless of race. Plessy boarded a train in New Orleans, taking a seat in the first-class "whites only" section of the car. The conductor asked Plessy to move to the "colored only" section of the coach. When Plessy refused, he was immediately arrested and charged with violating the state's Jim Crow Car Act of 1890.

Plessy's case made it to the U.S. Supreme Court. Although his lawyer argued that Louisiana's railroad car law violated the 14th Amendment of the Constitution, by denying Plessy equal protection under the laws, the Supreme Court found otherwise. In a seven-to-one decision, the Court upheld Louisiana's Jim Crow railroad law, sanctioning Jim Crow laws as constitutional.

Plessy v. Ferguson had profound consequences for black Americans. The decision upheld segregation—and the doctrine of "separate but equal"—as legal and constitutional for nearly 60 years, until the landmark Brown v. Board of Education of Topeka, Kansas case in 1954. Segregation applied to nearly all aspects of Southern life, including public accommodations, such as streetcars, parks, neighborhoods, and even water fountains; and—as Southern blacks could testify—separate "colored" facilities were never equal to those for "white" facilities.

Notably, all seven justices who voted against Plessy were from the North; the single dissenting justice, Justice John Marshall Harlan, was a white Southerner from Kentucky. Justice Henry Billings Brown wrote the majority opinion, an excerpt from which follows.

This case turns upon the constitutionality of an act of the general assembly of the state of Louisiana, passed in 1890, providing for separate railway carriages for the white and colored races. . . .

The constitutionality of this act is attacked upon the ground that it conflicts both with the 13th Amendment of the Constitution, abolishing slavery, and the 14th Amendment, which prohibits certain restrictive legislation on the part of the states.

1. That it does not conflict with the 13th Amendment, which abolished slavery and involuntary servitude, except as punishment for crimes, is too clear for argument. . . .

The object of the amendment was undoubtedly to enforce the absolute equality of the two races before the law, but in the nature

Unequal Education

Education proved to be far from "separate but equal" in the aftermath of the *Plessy* v. *Ferguson* decision. Local and state governments, controlled by white voters, spent little money on black schools and their pupils. In 1898, the state of Florida spent an average of $5.92 for every white student and $2.27 for each black student. In 1900, Adams County, Mississippi, spent $22.25 to educate each white child and $2.00 for each black student.

of things it could not have been intended to abolish distinctions based upon color, or to enforce social, as distinguished from political, equality, or a commingling of the two races upon terms unsatisfactory to either. . . .

So far, then, as a conflict with the 14th Amendment is concerned, the case reduces itself to the question whether the statute of Louisiana is a reasonable regulation. . . . In determining the question of reasonableness, it is at liberty to act with reference to the established usages, customs, and traditions of the people, and with a view to the promotion of their comfort, and the preservation of the public peace and good order. Gauged by this standard, we cannot say that a law which authorizes or even requires the separation of the two races in public conveyances is unreasonable or more obnoxious to the 14th Amendment than the acts of Congress requiring separate schools for colored children in the District of Columbia, the constitutionality of which does not seem to have been questioned, or the corresponding acts of state legislatures.

We consider the underlying fallacy of the plaintiff's argument to consist in the assumption that the enforced separation of the two races stamps the colored race with a badge of inferiority. If this be so, it is not by reason of anything found in the act but solely because the colored race chooses to put that construction upon it. . . . If the two races are to meet on terms of social equality, it must be the result of natural affinities, a mutual appreciation of each other's merits and a voluntary consent of individuals. . . . Legislation is powerless to eradicate racial instincts or to abolish distinctions based upon physical differences, and the attempt to do so can only result in accentuating the difficulties of the present situation. . . . If one race be inferior to the other socially, the Constitution of the United States cannot put them upon the same plane.

In his dissent, Justice Harlan argued that the Court's ruling abridged the rights guaranteed black citizens in the 13th and 14th Amendments.

In respect of civil rights, common to all citizens, the Constitution of the United States does not, I think, permit any public authority to know the race of those entitled to be protected in enjoyment of such rights. . .

In my opinion, the judgment this day rendered will, in time, prove to be quite as pernicious as the decision made by this tribunal in the Dred Scott Case. . . . The present decision, it may

well be apprehended, will not only stimulate aggressions, more or less brutal and irritating, upon the admitted rights of colored citizens, but will encourage the belief that it is possible, by means of state enactments, to defeat the beneficent purposes which the people of the United States had in view when they adopted the recent amendments to the Constitution, by one of which the blacks of this country were made citizens of the United States, and the states in which they reside and whose privileges and immunities, as citizens, the states are forbidden to abridge. Sixty million whites are in no danger from the presence here of eight million blacks. The destinies of the two races in this country are indissolubly linked together, and the interests of both require that the common government of all shall not permit the seeds of race hate to be planted under the sanction of law. What can more certainly arouse race hate, what more certainly create and perpetuate a feeling of distrust between these races, than state enactments which in fact proceed on the ground that colored citizens are so inferior and degraded that they cannot be allowed to sit in public coaches occupied by white citizens? . . .

I am of the opinion that the statute of Louisiana is inconsistent with the personal liberty of citizens, white and black, in that state, and hostile to both the spirit and letter of the Constitution of the United States.

W. F. Fonvielle was a junior at Livingstone College, in Salisbury, North Carolina, when he first experienced "Jim Crow," as he traveled to New Orleans by train in the summer of 1893. Appalled by the Jim Crow world he encountered, Fonvielle wrote an article about his experiences which was published in the *A.M.E. Zion Quarterly Review*. His article offers a rare personal perspective on the developing Jim Crow South of the 1890s, as seen through the eyes of a well-educated and sophisticated black man.

When I arrived in Spartanburg [South Carolina]—which is a pretty town—I was reminded that I was in the South by the appearance of two sign boards at the station, which told me that "This room is for colored people." "This room is for white people." I stood there and gazed at those two signs, all the time wondering what did "colored" waiting room mean? And what did "white" waiting room mean? Was one of the rooms painted in colors— done up in prismatics, just as the blue room is at the White House,

"The constituted authorities must be cheerfully and vigorously upheld. Lynching must not be tolerated in a great and civilized country like the United States. Courts, not mobs, must execute the penalties of the law. The preservation of public order, the right of discussion, the integrity of courts, and the orderly administration of justice must continue forever the rock of safety upon which our Government surely rests."
From President Wm. McKinley's message to the 56th Congress.

"Ah, Mr. Chairman, the spirit of the Republican party does not know white man or black man. All stand equal before it, as they should stand equal before the law."
From Hon. John. M. Langston's speech, 51st Congress, 2d session, January 16, 1891—page 148, Vol. 116.

27

A REPUBLICAN TEXT-BOOK FOR COLORED VOTERS.

HON. JUDSON W. LYONS
Register of the U. S. Treasury. A stalwart Republican and a worthy representative of the efficient and progressive element of the colored people.

"We made up our minds that the Fourteenth and Fifteenth Amendments to the Constitution were themselves null and void; that the acts of Congress * * * were null and void; that oaths required by such laws were null and void."
From Senator Tillman's speech in the U. S. Senate, March 23, 1900. (Democrat from South Carolina.)

Hon. W. Bourke Cochran, of New York, a leading Northern Democrat, has emphasized the above expression of Senator Tillman by advocating a repeal of the Fifteenth Amendment to the Constitution. Thus the Democratic party North and South is joining hands to disfranchise the negro.

Wash. D.C.
1900

This booklet, published by the Republican party in 1901, aimed to convince black voters of the many ways that the Republican party advocated their rights. But by 1901, support of the party was a moot point for many black Southerners, who could no longer vote due to disenfranchisement laws. Despite the claims made in this booklet, President McKinley turned a deaf ear to Southern blacks who pleaded with him to defend their voting rights.

and the other draped in white? Those signs perplexed me, for I had never seen anything like them before. Then the whole thing burst upon me at once, and I interpreted it to mean: The Negroes *must* stay in here and *not* in the other room, and the superior civilization goes where it pleases. I visited several other places in South Carolina, but nowhere else did those ominous sign boards face me. . . .

The depot at Atlanta is a dirty, smoky affair with two apartments, with sign board accompaniment, which, like its sister at Spartanburg, tells you where *you* belong. There is a restaurant attached to this building; but a Negro need not apply. If he wends his way up Wall Street for a short distance, he may purchase a ham sandwich and a piece of coconut pie and walk along the street and eat it from a paper bag. . . .

In street vernacular, Atlanta is a "mean hole." It gets on its knees, and in fact stands on its all-fours, but couldn't stand erect because it is chained down with prejudice, in fact, it would be a great city did not the monster hold it so tightly by the throat. The white citizens are not anxious for the colored citizens to ride on the street cars; and if they do ride, they like them to take back seats; and in case the car is crowded they want our women to surrender their seats to their women when they enter. A colored woman riding on one of the cars hoisted an umbrella to keep out the sunshine; a white citizen commanded her to put it down. She was not swift in executing the order, whereupon this same citizen gave her a sound thrashing and quietly sat down and read . . . . The Negroes are taxed to help keep up the city parks, but the council will not permit them nor the dogs to enter. . . .

Did you ever see a "Jim Crow" car? If you haven't, let me describe it to you. I shall speak particularly of the one in which I traveled through Alabama over the L. & N. R. R. It is a third-class car, (if there is any such thing), divided into two compartments. The end next to the baggage car is the "Crow" car, or "where de

cullard folks rides." The other end is used for a "smoker." The car behind this kitchen arrangement is the one in which the white folks lay back on cushioned seats, and . . . read the news, and enjoy the scenery. They have but one fare down there, consequently you pay as much as anybody else, notwithstanding the fact that you have to put up with this pig-sty arrangement. On the way down, very frequently, as with the case in this instance, the train stops on the way and takes on from 10 to 20 greasy, smutty railroad hands, and as they are generally colored, they come in as a matter of course and share the "Jim Crow" with you. They monopolize the seats, expectorate on the floor, crack hard jokes, smoke pipes, cigars and the modern cigarette. No matter how intelligent and refined a lady may be, she has to sit here and endure all this.

Not only did the New South enforce the daily humiliation of African Americans through Jim Crow laws, but Southern states also made it nearly impossible for black men to exercise their right to vote, which after the Civil War was supposed to have been guaranteed by the 14th and 15th Amendments to the Constitution. In 1890, Mississippi became the first Southern state to pass a disfranchisement amendment, eliminating black voters from the electorate, and by 1908 every other Southern state had implemented ways of keeping blacks from voting. The following excerpt from North Carolina's 1899 disfranchisement law mandated both a literacy test and poll tax to diminish the black vote. It also provided a "grandfather clause"—a massive loophole— that exempted males from the literacy test if they could show that they, their father, or one of their grandfathers had been qualified to vote in 1867 or before. This was a near impossibility for black voters in 1899 since in most cases they or their ancestors had been slaves. Even those who had been free or had free ancestors could not vote in North Carolina after 1835. Race is never mentioned in this law, so as not to violate the 14th and 15th Amendments explicitly.

(Sec. 4.) Every person presenting himself for registration shall be able to read and write any section of the constitution in the English language and before he shall be entitled to vote he shall have paid on or before the first day of March of the year in which

Ida B. Wells: "To Tell the Truth Freely"

Born a slave in Holly Springs, Mississippi, in 1862, Ida B. Wells grew up to become one of the nation's best-known black women. In May 1884, while traveling by train to teach in Tennessee, Wells confronted the ugly face of Jim Crow. The conductor demanded that she leave the first-class car, for which she had bought a ticket, and move to a second-class smoking car, a filthy car designated for working men and black passengers. She refused to move, and, after a physical struggle, the conductor threw her off the train. Appalled at her treatment, Wells successfully sued the Chesapeake and Ohio Railroad on the grounds that she had paid for a first-class ticket, and the railroad provided no separate and equal accommodations for blacks. She won damages of $500, but her victory was short-lived. Three years later the Tennessee Supreme Court overturned the decision.

The Tennessee Supreme Court's reversal would not be the last setback in Wells's life, and it did not stifle her fight for justice. By 1887 she became an editor and part owner of a small newspaper, the *Free Speech*, in Memphis. In 1892, three black businessmen who owned and operated a Memphis grocery store were lynched by a mob of whites. Wells concluded that the only "crime" the black men had committed was to have successfully competed against a white-owned grocery store. Revealing the truth in her newspaper, Wells soon became the target of white hysteria. While she was out of town covering a story, an angry mob wrecked her office and destroyed her printing press.

Warned that she would be killed if she returned to Memphis, Wells spent the rest of her life in the North, but she refused to be muzzled. As a writer for the *New York Age*, she crusaded against lynching in the North and abroad. Wells also urged black women to become more involved in community affairs and helped found the black clubwomen's movement, a national initiative of women dedicated to a broad agenda, including bettering housing, education, and health care in black communities as well as waging an ongoing battle against lynching, Jim Crow, and negative depictions of black women.

Wells settled in Chicago and married newspaperman Ferdinand L. Barnett. She fought against racial discrimination nationwide. In 1909, along with Jane Addams, W. E. B. Du Bois, and others, she attended a conference of the Niagara Movement, which helped lay the foundation for the National Association for the Advancement of Colored People (NAACP).

he proposes to vote his poll tax as prescribed by law for the previous year. Poll taxes shall be a lien only on assessed property, and no process shall issue to enforce the collection of the same except against assessed property.

(Sec.5) No male person who was on January one, eighteen hundred and sixty-seven, or at any time prior thereto entitled to vote under the laws of any state in the United States wherein he then resided, and no lineal descendant of any such person, shall be denied the right to register to vote at any election in this state by reason of his failure to possess the educational qualification prescribed in section four of this article: *Provided*, he shall have registered in accordance with the terms of this section prior to December one, nineteen hundred and eight. . . .

To ensure white supremacy and black subordination, some white Southerners resorted to methods outside the law. Beginning in the 1880s and continuing through the 1890s, lynchings of blacks increased dramatically. Whites often justified the brutal torture, hangings, and burnings of black men by claiming that the men had raped white women and deserved a horrible death. Ida B. Wells, a black newspaperwoman, questioned this claim. In the following excerpt from her autobiography, Wells explains how the lynchings of three black grocers opened her eyes to the truth. The grocers, Thomas Moss, Calvin McDowell, and Lee Stewart, had successfully competed with a white-owned grocery store in Memphis.

Like many another person who had read of lynching in the South, I had accepted the idea meant to be conveyed—that although lynching was irregular and contrary to law and order, unreasoning anger over the terrible crime of rape led to the lynching; that perhaps the brute deserved death anyhow and the mob was justified in taking his life.

But Thomas Moss, Calvin McDowell, and Lee Stewart had been lynched in Memphis, one of the leading cities of the South, in which no lynching had taken place before, with just as much brutality as other victims of the mob; and they had committed no crime against white women. This is what opened my eyes to what lynching really was. An excuse to get rid of Negroes who were acquiring wealth and property and thus keep the race terrorized and "keep the nigger down." I then began an investigation of every lynching I read about. I stumbled on the amazing record that

every case of rape reported in that three months became such only when it became public. . . . No torture of helpless victims by heathen savages or cruel red Indians ever exceeded the cold-blooded savagery of white devils under lynch law. None of the hideous murders by butchers of Nero to make a Roman holiday exceeded these burnings alive of black human beings. This was done by white men who controlled all the forces of law and order in their communities and who could have legally punished rapists and murderers, especially black men who had neither political power nor financial strength with which to evade any justly deserved fate.

The more I studied the situation, the more I was convinced that the Southerner had never gotten over his resentment that the Negro was no longer his plaything, his servant, and his source of income. The federal laws for Negro protection passed during Reconstruction times had been made a mockery by the white South where it had not secured their repeal. This same white South had secured political control of its several states, and as soon as white southerners came into power they began to make playthings of Negro lives and property. This still seemed not enough to "keep the nigger down."

Hence came lynch law to stifle Negro manhood. . . .

In the midst of the establishment of Jim Crow laws, disfranchisement laws, and lynchings, African Americans struggled with the question of how to halt worsening race relations. Blacks in the South embraced different strategies. Booker T. Washington rose to national prominence by articulating a strategy of economic development for blacks, who, he argued, should for the time being forgo politics and integration. His emphasis on material gain perfectly fit with the period's emphasis on economic development. A believer in self-help, Washington, born a slave in Virginia in 1856, had worked his way through Hampton Institute, a school established by Northern whites after the Civil War. He was named head of the Tuskegee Institute in Alabama in 1881. At the Atlanta Exposition in 1895, Washington made the following speech, in which he argued that blacks should not press for political or social equality but slowly gain their rights by earning the respect of white Southerners through hard work, frugality, and economic advancement.

Mr. President and Gentlemen of the Board of Directors and Citizens.

Lynching in the South increased dramatically in the early 1880s and then again around 1890, as some white Southerners attempted to assert their racial mastery over blacks.

Between 1889 and 1899 nearly 1,200 reported lynchings of African Americans occurred in the South.

Behind the Scenes

Historians have discovered that Booker T. Washington's public statements were only part of his story. Whereas publicly he seemed to accept segregation and the disfranchisement of black voters, privately he was involved in a lawsuit challenging the constitutionality of "grandfather clauses," which allowed many illiterate whites to vote yet barred all black voters because their grandfathers had not been qualified to vote.

"My experience is that there is something in human nature which always makes an individual recognize and reward merit, no matter under what colour of skin merit is found," wrote Booker T. Washington in Up from Slavery *(1901).*

One-third of the population of the South is of the Negro race. No enterprise seeking the material, civil, or moral welfare of this section can disregard this element of our population and reach the highest success. . . .

A ship lost at sea for many days suddenly sighted a friendly vessel. From the mast of the unfortunate vessel was seen a signal, "Water, water; we die of thirst!" The answer from the friendly vessel at once came back, "Cast down your bucket where you are." A second time the signal, "Water, water; send us water!" ran up from the distressed vessel, and was answered, "Cast down your bucket where you are." And a third and fourth signal for water was answered, "Cast down your bucket where you are." The captain of the distressed vessel, at last heeding the injunction, cast down his bucket, and it came up full of fresh, sparkling water from the mouth of the Amazon River. To those of my race who depend on bettering their condition in a foreign land or who underestimate the importance of cultivating friendly relations with the Southern white man, who is their next-door neighbour, I would say: "Cast down your bucket where you are"—cast it down in making friends in every manly way of the people of all races by whom we are surrounded.

Cast it down in agriculture, mechanics, in commerce, in domestic service, and in the professions. And in this connection it is well to bear in mind that whatever other sins the South may be called to bear, when it comes to business, pure and simple, it is in the South that the Negro is given a man's chance in the commercial world, and in nothing is this Exposition more eloquent than in emphasizing this chance. Our greatest danger is that in the great leap from slavery to freedom we may overlook the fact that the masses of us are to live by the productions of our hands, and fail to keep in mind that we shall prosper in proportion as we learn to dignify and glorify common labour and put brains and skill into the common occupations of life; shall prosper in proportion as we learn to draw the line between the superficial and the substantial, the ornamental gewgaws of life and the useful. No race can prosper till it learns that there is as much dignity in tilling a field as in writing a poem. It is at the bottom of life we must begin, and not at the top. Nor should we permit our grievances to overshadow our opportunities.

To those of the white race who look to the incoming of those of foreign birth and strange tongue and habits for the prosperity of the South, were I permitted I would repeat what I say to my own

race, "Cast down your bucket where you are." Cast it down among the eight millions of Negroes whose habits you know, whose fidelity and love you have tested in days when to have proved treacherous meant the ruin of your firesides. Cast down your bucket among these people who have, without strikes and labour wars, tilled your fields, cleared your forests, builded your railroads and cities, and brought forth treasures from the bowels of the earth, and helped make possible this magnificent representation of the progress of the South. Casting down your bucket among my people, helping and encouraging them as you are doing on these grounds, and to education of head, hand, and heart, you will find that they will buy your surplus land, make blossom the waste places in your fields, and run your factories. While doing this, you can be sure in the future, as in the past, that you and your families will be surrounded by the most patient, faithful, law-abiding, and unresentful people that the world has seen. . . .

Nearly sixteen millions of hands will aid you in pulling the load upward, or they will pull against you the load downward. We shall constitute one-third and more of the ignorance and crime of the South, or one-third its intelligence and progress; we shall contribute one-third to the business and industrial prosperity of the South, or we shall prove a veritable body of death, stagnating, depressing, retarding every effort to advance the body politic. . . .

The wisest among my race understand that the agitation of questions of social equality is the extremest folly, and that progress in the enjoyment of all the privileges that will come to us must be the result of severe and constant struggle rather than of artificial forcing. No race that has anything to contribute to the markets of the world is long in any degree ostracized. It is important and right that all privileges of the law be ours, but it is vastly more important that we be prepared for the exercises of these privileges. The opportunity to earn a dollar in a factory just now is worth infinitely more than the opportunity to spend a dollar in an opera-house.

In conclusion, may I repeat that nothing in thirty years has given us more hope and encouragement, and drawn us so near to you of the white race, as this opportunity offered by the Exposition; and here bending, as it were, over the altar that represents the results of the struggles of your race and mine, both starting practically empty-handed three decades ago, I pledge that in your effort to work out the great and intricate problem which God has

laid at the doors of the South, you shall have at all times the patient, sympathetic help of my race . . . .

Booker T. Washington's conservative strategy won the acclaim of many prominent white Americans, including businessmen Andrew Carnegie and John D. Rockefeller, who lavished Washington's Tuskegee Institute with financial support. But some blacks—especially in the North—questioned Washington's approach as well as his legitimacy as spokesman for the black race. W. E. B. Du Bois emerged as one of Washington's most scathing critics. Born in Great Barrington, Massachusetts, in 1868, Du Bois graduated from Fisk University in Nashville, studied at the University of Berlin, and in 1895 became the first African American to earn a doctorate at Harvard. He later helped found the National Association for the Advancement of Colored People (NAACP) in 1909. Du Bois was a professor at Atlanta University when he wrote a scathing critique of Washington titled, "Of Booker T. Washington and Others," in which Du Bois offered an alternative strategy for racial progress advocating that blacks press for the full citizenship rights granted them in the Constitution. The following is an excerpt.

Mr. Washington represents in Negro thought the old attitude of adjustment and submission; but adjustment at such a peculiar time as to make his programme unique. This is an age of unusual economic development, and Mr. Washington's programme naturally takes an economic cast, becoming a gospel of Work and Money to such an extent as apparently almost completely to overshadow the higher aims of life. Moreover, this is an age when the more advanced races are coming in closer contact with the less developed races, and the race-feeling is therefore intensified; and Mr. Washington's programme practically accepts the alleged inferiority of the Negro races. . . .

Mr. Washington distinctly asks that black people give up, at least for the present, three things—

First, political power,

Second, insistence on civil rights,

Third, higher education of Negro youth—and concentrate all their energies on industrial education, the accumulation of wealth, and the conciliation of the South. This policy has been courageously and insistently advocated for over fifteen years and has

> My Dear Mr Washington:
>   Let me heartily congratulate you upon your phenomenal success at Atlanta — it was a word fitly spoken.
>   Sincerely Yours,
>   W. E. B. Du Bois
>
> Wilberforce, 24 Sept., '95

W. E. B. Du Bois, then a professor at Wilberforce University in Ohio, initially praised Booker T. Washington's speech at the Atlanta Exposition in 1895, as this letter indicates. But both personal and ideological differences separated the two men by 1903, when Du Bois wrote his scathing attack on Washington in "The Souls of Black Folk."

been triumphant for perhaps ten years. As a result of this tender of the palm-branch, what has been the return? In these years there have occurred:

1. The disfranchisement of the Negro.

2. The legal creation of a distinct status of civil inferiority for the Negro.

3. The steady withdrawal of aid from institutions for the higher training of the Negro.

These movements are not, to be sure, direct results of Mr. Washington's teachings; but his propaganda has, without a shadow of doubt, helped their speedier accomplishment. The question then comes: Is it possible, and probable, that nine millions of men can make effective progress in economic lines if they are deprived of political rights, made a servile caste, and allowed only the most meagre chance for developing their exceptional men? If history and reason give any distinct answer to these questions, it is an emphatic *No*. And Mr. Washington thus faces the triple paradox of his career:

1. He is striving nobly to make Negro artisans business men and property-owners; but it is utterly impossible, under modern competitive methods, for workingmen and property-owners to defend their rights and exist without the right of suffrage.

2. He insists on thrift and self-respect but at the same time counsels a silent submission to civic inferiority such as is bound to sap the manhood of any race in the long run.

The Ragtime Rage

In the 1890s a new kind of music—ragtime—took the nation by storm. Featuring the syncopated rhythms integral to African music, ragtime (sometimes called "ragged" music because of its unusual beat) had its roots in the black South and was popularized by a black Southerner born in Texarkana, Scott Joplin. Joplin's mother taught him to play the banjo; his father, who had performed as a slave musician in his master's house, taught him the music of elite whites. Joplin also mastered the piano. Transposing the syncopated banjo rhythms he had learned as a child to the piano, he concocted a new kind of music. With his own band, at the age of 16, Joplin traveled across east Texas performing ragtime. By the late 1880s he made St. Louis his home base and performed extensively in the Midwest and North.

Like jazz in the 1920s and rock and roll in the 1950s, ragtime began as black music but was soon embraced by white musicians and audiences as well. Even as segregation laws separated blacks and whites in public settings in the 1890s, ragtime music—like rock and roll in the segregated South of the 1950s—crossed racial lines, a testament to the interracial nature of American culture.

3. He advocates common-school and industrial training, and depreciates institutions of higher learning; but neither the Negro common-schools, nor Tuskegee itself, could remain open a day were it not for teachers trained in Negro colleges, or trained by their graduates. . . .

It would be unjust to Mr. Washington not to acknowledge that in several instances he has opposed movements in the South which were unjust to the Negro; he sent memorials to the Louisiana and Alabama constitutional conventions, he has spoken against lynching, and in other ways has openly or silently set his influence against sinister schemes and unfortunate happenings. Notwithstanding this, it is equally true to assert that on the whole the distinct impression left by Mr. Washington's propaganda is, first, that the South is justified in its present attitude toward the Negro because of the Negro's degradation; secondly, that the prime cause of the Negro's failure to rise more quickly is his wrong education in the past; and thirdly, that his future rise depends primarily on his own efforts. Each of these propositions is a dangerous half-truth. The supplementary truths must never be lost sight of: first, slavery and race-prejudice are potent if not sufficient causes of the Negro's position; second, industrial and common-school training were necessarily slow in planting because they had to await the black teachers trained by higher institutions; . . . and, third, while it is a great truth to say that the Negro must strive and strive mightily to help himself, it is equally true that unless his striving be not simply seconded, but rather aroused and encouraged, by the initiative of the richer and wiser environing group, he cannot hope for great success.

In his failure to realize and impress this last point, Mr. Washington is especially to be criticised. His doctrine has tended to make the whites, North and South, shift the burden of the Negro problem to the Negro's shoulders and stand aside as critical and rather pessimistic spectators; when in fact the burden belongs to the nation, and the hands of none of us are clean if we bend not our energies to righting these great wrongs. . . .

The black men of America have a duty to perform, a duty stern and delicate—a forward movement to oppose a part of the work of their greatest leader. So far as Mr. Washington preaches Thrift, Patience, and Industrial Training for the masses, we must hold up his hands and strive with him, rejoicing in his honors and glorying in the strength of this Joshua called of God and of man to lead the headless host. But so far as Mr. Washington apologizes for

In 1899 Scott Joplin wrote his "Maple Leaf Rag." Named after a black social club, the song became a national hit and ragtime a national phenomenon.

injustice, North or South, does not rightly value the privilege and duty of voting, belittles the emasculating effects of caste distinctions, and opposes the higher training and ambition of our brighter minds—so far as he, the South, or the Nation, does this—we must unceasingly and firmly oppose them. By every civilized and peaceful method we must strive for the rights which the world accords to men, clinging unwaveringly to those great words which the sons of the Fathers would fain forget: "We hold these truths to be self-evident: That all men are created equal; that they are endowed by their Creator with certain unalienable rights; that among these are life, liberty, and the pursuit of happiness."

Chapter Seven

The West

These contrasting images of the Western homestead reveal the difference between a Currier and Ives ideal (above) and reality. Many settlers started out in sod houses, built of prairie earth, or dugouts, such as this Nebraska home built out of a hillside that provided natural insulation (left).

From the time of his birth in the 1830s until his tragic death in 1890, the great Hunkpapa chief Sitting Bull saw his world, and that of all the Plains Indians, overturned. At the time of Sitting Bull's birth, the Hunkpapa, one of seven tribes of Lakota people—as well as other Native Americans of the Great Plains—lived as they had for hundreds of years. Their lives were dictated by the hunt. The open plains teemed with wildlife. Deer, antelope, bear, elk, and most importantly, buffalo provided their food, clothing, and shelter. By the end of his life, Sitting Bull had been hunted down by the U.S. government and nearly all Plains Indians relegated to impoverished reservations, their lands stolen and their sources of food decimated.

Displaying qualities of bravery, spirituality, wisdom, and kindness, Sitting Bull rose to the position of a tribal chieftain in his early 20s. By the time he became a chief, he and his people—and all Plains Indians—faced a formidable challenge. The *wasichus* (white people) began to move into the West in greater numbers than ever before. Whereas Plains Indians had dealt with the occasional white trader for years, settlers in the 1850s and 1860s seemed to flood the prairies in waves, gobbling up Western lands that seemed empty in their eyes.

In 1862 the federal government encouraged migration to the West when Congress passed the Homestead Act. The act offered free land to anyone who staked a claim and lived on the land for five years. In addition, Western settlers could purchase land for only $1.25 per acre after living on the land for six months. Railroads, funded by the federal, as well as state and local governments, extended their tentacles from the East and West coasts, and accelerated migration. In 1869 the transcontinental railroad linked the nation, making the Great Plains more accessible than ever. As a result migration into the West quickened to an astonishing pace.

Sitting Bull Asks

"What treaty that the whites have kept has the red man broken? Not one. What treaty that the whites ever made with us red men have they kept? Not one. When I was a boy the Sioux owned the world. The sun rose and set on their lands. They sent 10,000 horsemen to battle. Where are the warriors to-day? Who slew them? Where are our lands? Who owns them? What white man can say I ever stole his lands or a penny of his money? Yet they say I am a thief. What white woman, however lonely, was ever when a captive insulted by me? Yet they say I am a bad Indian. What white man has ever seen me drunk? Who has ever come to me hungry and gone unfed? Who has ever seen me beat my wives or abuse my children? What law have I broken? Is it wrong for me to love my own? Is it wicked in me because my skin is red, because I am a Sioux, because I was born where my fathers lived, because I would die for my people and my country?"

—From *Life of Sitting Bull and History of the Indian Word*

Sitting Bull recognized early on the need to respect a diversity of cultures when he remarked: "If the Great Spirit had desired me to be a white man he would have made me so in the first place. He put in your heart certain wishes and plans, and in my heart he put other and different desires. It is not necessary for eagles to be crows."

With its lure of free land and the promise of a new start and greater opportunity, the West attracted a diverse group of migrants. In addition to native-born whites who abandoned the cities, villages, and farms of the East for a fresh beginning in the West, blacks from the South hoped to escape the racial discrimination and second-class citizenship that marked their lives in the South. European immigrants also found the West particularly attractive. Ethnic enclaves of Norwegians, Swedes, and Germans sprang up in the towns and villages of the prairies. Moreover, there was a large Hispanic presence in the West, as the United States, in 1848, annexed half of Mexico's territory in the aftermath of the Mexican-American War. And even though the Chinese were barred from immigrating after 1882, they contributed to a considerable Asian population in the West, supplemented by Japanese immigrants to the West Coast.

As settlers eyed Western lands and the region's rich natural resources, they increasingly viewed the Plains Indians as relics from the past who stood in the way of progress, "civilization," and the development of the West.

Sitting Bull, from the beginning, believed that Native Americans needed to resist the incursion of settlers on their lands; this, he thought, was the only way that they could preserve their culture and way of life. Some tribes—faced with the overwhelming number of settlers and tired of conflict with U.S. troops sent West to protect them—agreed to give up their lands and live on government reservations. Sitting Bull and the Hunkpapa refused to do so. "Indian wars," as whites called them, raged in the 1860s and early 1870s. The War Department deployed, on average, 16,000 soldiers in the West in an attempt to subdue "hostile" peoples like Sitting Bull and the Hunkpapa.

By the early 1870s the Indian wars seemed to quiet down. Many Americans believed that the West was now "won" and the Indian threat eliminated. But in 1873 news of the discovery of gold in the Black Hills sparked a rush of would-be millionaires to Dakota Territory. Only five years before, the government had signed a treaty promising Native Americans that the Black Hills would remain Indian territory, off-limits to whites. Greedy miners, with little regard for the treaty, swarmed into the Black Hills anyway.

Sitting Bull and his people were outraged by the miners' arrogance and blatant disregard of the treaty. The Black Hills, considered sacred by the Lakota, also served as a food store for the natives. Sitting Bull formed an alliance with the Cheyenne that bound the Hunkpapa and Cheyenne to fight the white men

who stole their precious lands. By 1876, under pressure from business interests and miners, President Ulysses S. Grant declared war on "hostiles."

In June 1876, as the U.S. Army tramped through Lakota Territory hoping to crush native resistance, Sitting Bull had a vision. He saw soldiers and horses swarming onto the plains, as abundant as grasshoppers, attacking Indian villages. But they appeared upside down on their horses, and the soldiers in the vision had no ears. Sitting Bull interpreted this vision as a sign of a great Indian victory to come.

The great victory came on June 25, 1876, when Sitting Bull and his allies, backed by the largest force of native warriors ever assembled, routed the outnumbered Seventh Cavalry, led by Gen. George Armstrong Custer, near the Little Big Horn River in southern Montana, killing every soldier of the regiment. Sitting Bull and his people escaped into Canada, as white Americans and the federal government, shocked by Custer's defeat, demanded Sitting Bull's head. Demonized in the popular press, Sitting Bull became a household name, a symbol of Indian resistance and "savagery."

After five years, in 1881, starving and without adequate clothing or shelter, Sitting Bull gave himself up to government authorities. But he insisted that he did not surrender, only that he expected the government to return him and his people to their lands in Dakota Territory, where they could live peacefully. But in the five years of his exile, Sitting Bull's world had changed dramatically. The life that he and his peoples had led in 1876 no longer existed. Railroads now laced Lakota lands, discharging thousands of migrants caught up in the Great Dakota Boom of the late 1870s. Farmsteads and small towns now dotted the prairies once roamed by the Hunkpapa.

Sitting Bull and his people had few options by 1881. They could accept reservation life or perish. Reduced to dependency at the Standing Rock Reservation, Sitting Bull occasionally escaped the monotony of the reservation by performing with Buffalo Bill's Wild West Show before Eastern audiences fascinated with the romance of the West. The once-powerful chief of the Hunkpapa was now reduced to playing an Indian for curious audiences who turned out to see the famous warrior in person.

Despite the indignities he and his people endured, Sitting Bull still exhibited the streak of resistance that had characterized his earlier life. In 1887 the federal government undertook a policy of "Americanizing" Native Americans, hoping to alleviate the "Indian problem" by integrating native peoples into mainstream society.

Ghost-Dance Songs

An Indian messiah promised the destruction of whites and a return to the Indians' lost world through ghost dancing and the chanting of songs like these, which were popular in the late 1880s and 1890s.

Comanche
We shall live again,
We shall live again.
The sun's beams are spreading out—He'e'yo'!
The sun's yellow rays are spreading out—
Ahi'ni'yo!

Sioux
This is my work—Yo'yoyo'!
All that grows upon the earth is mine—
Yo'yoyo'!
Says the Father—Yo'yoyo'!
E'ya Yo'yoyo!

Mother, come home; mother, come home.
My little brother goes about always crying,
My little brother goes about always crying.
Mother, come home; mother come home.

He! They have come back racing,
Why, they say there is to be a buffalo hunt
    over here,
Why, they say there is to be a buffalo hunt
    over here.
Make arrows! Make arrows!
Says the father, says the father.

The whole world is coming,
A nation is coming, a nation is coming,
The eagle has brought the message to the
    tribe.
Over the whole earth they are coming;
The buffalo are coming, the buffalo are coming,
The crow has brought the message to the tribe.

Most people are familiar only with the tepee of the Plains Indians; however, native peoples built many types of housing and meeting places in the West.

Blackfeet gather for a sun dance on the northern plains in 1896. They erected hundreds of tepees in large circles up to a mile in circumference.

This plan included the Dawes Act, which attempted to turn Indians into small farmers and citizens by breaking up tribal lands into 160-acre individual plots. But Sitting Bull vehemently opposed this policy and encouraged Native Americans to resist this plan.

Sitting Bull and many Plains Indians displayed another burst of resistance by 1890. Many embraced a messiah who promised that if natives danced the ghost dance, white people would be destroyed and the natives' world would be restored to what it had been before the whites came. The ghost dance swept across the prairies. It is unclear whether Sitting Bull was a follower of the messiah and ghost dance; nevertheless he encouraged his people to participate in this religious experience. Frightened government officials, who feared that the ghost dance indicated impending violence, asked Sitting Bull to call it off; he refused. Indian policemen working for the U.S. government arrested Sitting Bull in his tepee on December 14, 1890. Quickly alerted, Sitting Bull's people surrounded him, in an attempt to avert his arrest. In a flurry of shooting and fighting, Bull Head, an Indian policeman, shot and killed Sitting Bull.

Only days later, the 19th-century Indian wars ended symbolically at Wounded Knee, South Dakota. Alarmed by the news of Sitting Bull's murder, a group of several hundred Lakota, led by Big Foot, fled from their reservation. Intercepted by federal troops attempting to force them back to their reservation, approximately 200 Native Americans—mostly women, children, and the elderly—died in yet another flurry of gunfire.

This walled pueblo in Taos, New Mexico, around 1880 shows a block five stories high.

This earth lodge, which stood near Ione, California, was the site of community ceremonies.

Sitting Bull's story illustrates many of the tensions and conflicts that characterized the West in the Gilded Age. Like the South, the West remained a distinctive region even as a site of the major currents of the United States in the Gilded Age. Peopled with Native Americans, Chinese, Japanese, Hispanics, native-born whites, and a variety of European immigrants, the West was the most ethnically diverse section of the nation. Romanticized as a land of individualism, opportunity, and refuge, it also was a land of violent racial and cultural conflict and exploitation. Just as social Darwinism was used in the East to justify the economic exploitation of European immigrants and the amassing of huge fortunes, the theory was invoked to rationalize the conquering of "unfit," "primitive" natives, as the "fittest" and most "advanced" peoples continued their "inevitable" march of progress across the prairies.

Not only did Native Americans continue to lose their lands in the Gilded Age, but Hispanics in the Southwest also lost millions of acres of land through fraud and an unsympathetic legal system. When the Mexican-American War ended in 1848, thousands of Mexicans found themselves living as foreigners in their own land. With the American victory, Mexico ceded half of its territory to the United States, including what would become the states of California, New Mexico, Arizona, and Nevada. As borders drastically shifted, most Mexicans remained on their lands.

The Treaty of Guadalupe Hidalgo, which ended the Mexican-American War in 1848, promised all Mexicans who stayed in the Southwest "all the rights of citizens of the United States," including protection of their property. But in the Gilded Age, these people and their descendants lost millions of acres through deceit and

Buffalo Soldiers

Serving in the U.S. Army provided opportunity for black men in the West. Dubbed "Buffalo Soldiers" by Native Americans who likened the soldiers' short, curly hair to that of their beloved buffalo, black soldiers, like their white counterparts, participated in wars against the Indians, served as couriers, and guarded forts and Western outposts. The black Ninth and Tenth Cavalry comprised 20 percent of all U.S. Cavalry in the West.

In an era of intense racial discrimination and violence, the army provided security and a steady income. One black army chaplain encouraged recruitment by arguing that the army "is a good chance for our folks—a better chance than they have almost anywhere, much better than they have in the South." Yet even the army failed to provide a safe haven for black soldiers; they regularly faced racial attacks and indignities—even from the people they risked their lives to protect. In Jacksboro, Texas, for example, a white murdered a black soldier and then killed two more black soldiers who came to arrest him. He was then found not guilty. Blacks also were not allowed to become officers, and black regiments were issued secondhand and broken-down equipment, often cast off from white units.

Despite second-class treatment, the Buffalo Soldiers repeatedly distinguished themselves. Eleven black soldiers earned the Medal of Honor for their service in the West. Black units also had exceptionally high reenlistment rates and unusually low desertion rates, especially when compared to white units in the West.

While assigned to Fort Leavenworth, Kansas, in the early 1980s, Gen. Colin Powell became curious about the Buffalo Soldiers who had, 100 years before, served at the Kansas outpost. After researching their invaluable contributions, Powell recalled, "I believed I had a duty to those black troops who had eased my way. Building a memorial to the Buffalo Soldiers became my personal crusade. . . . Those troops had suffered second-class treatment after serving as first-class fighting men." Powell was "determined that the Buffalo Soldiers were finally going to go first class." In July 1992 thousands of people, including General Powell and a handful of elderly veteran Buffalo Soldiers, gathered at Fort Leavenworth to dedicate an 18-foot statue of a Buffalo Soldier on horseback, a permanent memorial to the black soldiers of the West.

unsympathetic courts. Mexican-owned lands were sometimes sold fraudulently or claimed by squatters, sparking years of legal battles. The burden for proving land ownership fell on Hispanic claimants, who soon found out that Spanish land grants and deeds often did not contain the precise and accurate descriptions demanded in U.S. courts as proof of legitimate titles. Moreover, courts and the state officials in charge of processing land claims, almost always Anglos, were seldom sympathetic to the cause of the Hispanic claimants. Even if Hispanic landowners successfully navigated an unsympathetic legal system, they often lost their land anyway, as they were forced to sell it to pay exorbitant legal fees.

Big business, the hallmark of the period, flourished in the West, in the form of powerful railroads, and in massive cattle and mining interests—all of which connected the regional economy to that of the East as well as the growing international economy. Technology, in the form of mechanized farm equipment like the McCormick reaper and the refrigerated railroad car, transformed the West as it did the rest of the nation. In addition, just as the nation became increasingly urban, so did the West. Despite the region's image as a land of open spaces, almost 40 percent of Westerners lived in an urban setting by 1900.

Sitting Bull and native peoples lost their world in the Gilded Age, but Native Americans did not disappear. In 1890, the year of Sitting Bull's death, only about 250,000 Native Americans remained. But 100 years later, in 1990, the federal government recognized 2 million of its citizens as Native Americans. Despite governmental policies and social and economic transformations aimed at obliterating them during the Gilded Age, Native Americans survived, their culture resilient even in a hostile era.

An Indian Victory

News of George Armstrong Custer's defeat at Little Big Horn and the demise of the entire Seventh Cavalry caught the nation by surprise. Most Americans assumed in 1876 that the Indian wars were over and the Native Americans were successfully subdued. Moreover news of Custer's crushing defeat filtered back around July 4, 1876, just as Americans celebrated the nation's centennial. The following is a comment on Little Big Horn from the July 7, 1876, *New York Times*, which stressed the "savagery" and "cunning" of "wild Indians" like Sitting Bull.

[The] overwhelming defeat of Custer's command and the butchery of this gallant commander and his men, will produce both astonishment and alarm. We have latterly fallen into the habit of regarding the Indians yet remaining in a wild or semi-subdued state as practically of very little account. It is only now and then when some such outburst . . . comes like a shock, that we realize the character of the Indian and the difficulties of the situation. Sitting Bull's band of Sioux left their reservation with hostile intent. They refused negotiations for peace. They defied the power and authority of the United States. They invited war. A force was sent against them. This force became divided, and Gen. Custer, with five companies, coming up to the main body of the Sioux, attacked them impetuously, without waiting for the support of the remainder of the column. The result was that the entire body of men, numbering between three and four hundred, and including Gen. Custer and several other commissioned officers fell into a death-trap; they were overwhelmed by superior numbers, and were all slaughtered. The precise particulars of that horrible catastrophe will never be known. There are no survivors. The course of the detachment, after it began the attack, is traced only by the bodies of the slain. How gallantly these poor fellows fought can only be surmised. The Indians carried off some of their dead and wounded; others were concealed . . . with Indian cunning, in order that the white man should not know how much damage they had suffered. . . .

. . . The Indians who have just wrought this bloody revenge are nominally on reservations. They have refused to stay there, and the expedition intended to chastise them and compel them to return has met with frightful disaster. The victory of the savages will inflame the border, and restless tribes will be impatient to share in the glory suddenly achieved by Sitting Bull and his braves. Year after year, the wild Indians have been hemmed in; they fight with no less desperation for that; and, now that we have been defeated in a considerable engagement, defensive tactics must precede the operations necessary for the chastisement of so dangerous and determined a foe.

The *New York Times* and other newspapers romanticized Custer—called "Long Hair" by Native Americans—and the Seventh Cavalry, and demonized Sitting Bull and other Native American warriors. But Two Moons, who participated in the Battle of Little Big Horn, offered a different perspective. In 1898 he told his story to a reporter from *McClure's Magazine*.

Black soldiers, serving in segregated units, played a major role in military actions in the American West. Some whites questioned the abilities of black soldiers, but Western artist Frederic Remington, who observed them in action, had nothing but praise: "As to their bravery, he wrote, "I am often asked, 'Will they fight?' That is easily answered. They have fought many, many times. . . ."

About May, when the grass was tall and the horses strong, we broke camp and started across the country to the mouth of the Tongue River. . . .

From there we all went over the divide, and camped in the valley of Little Horn. Everybody thought, "Now we are out of the white man's country. He can live there, we will live here. . . ." We were very glad to think we were far away from the white man.

I went to water my horses at the creek, and washed them off with cool water, then took a swim myself. I came back to the camp afoot. When I got near my lodge, I looked up the Little Horn towards Sitting Bull's camp. I saw a great dust rising. It looked like a whirlwind. Soon Sioux horseman came rushing into camp shouting: "Soldiers come! Plenty white soldiers." . . .

I said, "All right, I am ready."

I got on my horse, and rode out into my camp. I called out to the people all running about: "I am Two Moon, your chief. Don't run away. Stay here and fight. You must stay and fight the white soldiers. I shall stay even if I am to be killed."

I rode swiftly toward Sitting Bull's camp. There I saw the white soldiers fighting in a line [Reno's men]. Indians covered the flat. They began to drive the soldiers—all mixed up—Sioux, then soldiers, then more Sioux, and all shooting. The air was full of smoke and dust. I saw the soldiers fall back and drop into the river-bed like buffalo fleeing. They had no time to look for a crossing. The Sioux chased them up the hill, where they met more soldiers in wagons, and then messengers came saying more soldiers were going to kill the women, and the Sioux turned back. . . .

While I was sitting on my horse I saw flags come up over the hill to the east like that [he raised his finger-tips]. Then the soldiers rose all at once, all on horses, like this [he put his fingers behind each other to indicate that Custer appeared marching in columns of fours]. . . .

Then the Sioux rode up the ridge on all sides, riding very fast. The Cheyennes went up the left way. Then the shooting was quick, quick. Pop-pop-pop—very fast. Some of the soldiers were down on their knees, some standing. Officers all in front. The smoke was like a great cloud, and everywhere the Sioux went the dust rose like smoke. We circled all round him—swirling like water round a stone. We shoot, we ride fast, we shoot again. . . .

Indians keep swirling round and round, and the soldiers killed only a few. Many soldiers fell. At last all horses killed but five. Once in a while some man would break out and run toward the river, but he would fall. At last about a hundred men and five horsemen

stood on the hill all bunched together. All along the bugler kept blowing his commands. He was very brave too. Then a chief was killed. I hear it was Long Hair [Custer], I don't know . . . . One man all alone ran far down toward the river, then round up over the hill. I thought he was going to escape, but a Sioux fired and hit him in the head. He was the last man. He wore braid on his arms [sergeant].

All the soldiers were now killed, and the bodies were stripped. After that no one could tell which were officers. The bodies were left where they fell. We had no dance that night. We were sorrowful.

Next day four Sioux chiefs and two Cheyennes and I, Two Moon, went upon the battlefield to count the dead. One man carried a little bundle of sticks. When we came to dead men, we took a little stick and gave it to another man, so we counted the dead. There were 388. There were thirty-nine Sioux and seven Cheyennes killed, and about a hundred wounded. . . .

"Whitening" Indians

The eruption of Indian resistance in the mid-1870s provoked a reassessment of the U.S. government's Indian policy. Friends of the Indian, an organization of Eastern middle-class reformers, lobbied for what they believed was a more humane policy. Hoping to save Indians from what they feared would be certain extermination, reformers called for a program of assimilation, to "Americanize" them. The federal government, at the behest of reformers, established boarding schools for Indian children. Taken from reservations at an early age, Indian children were to be educated in the ways of white society. They were expected to cast off all trappings of their culture—including their long hair, clothing, language, and name—and to learn English, a trade, and white society's ways.

The process of whitening Indian children was often cruel and painful. Some resisted the process, refusing to cooperate with their teachers. Others ran away, and many died of diseases caught from whites. Zitkala-Sä (Redbird; also known as Gertrude Simmons Bonnin), was born at the Yankton, South Dakota, Sioux Agency to an Indian mother and a white father who deserted his family. She left her reservation at the age of eight for a boarding school in Indiana. A writer and activist, she returned to her home as an adult and

Educator and former military officer Richard Henry Pratt established the first Indian boarding school, the Carlisle Indian School in Pennsylvania, in 1879. It served as the model for an additional 25 government-sponsored schools established as part of the Americanization program. Pratt described the process of Americanizing native children as a means to "kill the Indian and save the man."

"Before" and "after" photos of Tom Torleno, a Navajo who attended the Carlisle Indian School in Pennsylvania. Richard Henry Pratt, head of the school, took many such photographs, which he used to garner support for his efforts. After their experience at schools like Carlisle, many Native Americans felt that they belonged in neither the native nor the white world. They faced rejection on their reservations because of their white ways and found a lack of acceptance in white society—even after the Americanization process.

Natural Resources

To many settlers, the resources of the West seemed limitless. In the Gilded Age, the buffalo (American bison) nearly became extinct. Buffalo were destroyed by hunters on shooting expeditions, who often let carcasses rot in the sun, and by soldiers, who saw its destruction as a means to exterminate Plains Indians, who depended on the animal for food, clothing, and shelter. Railroad owners also encouraged destruction of buffalo to increase agricultural production, so that farmers would buy railroad lands.

This photograph, taken in 1878, shows 40,000 buffalo hides in Rath & Wright's hide yard, Dodge City, Kansas. Historians estimate that in 1865, 10 million buffalo freely roamed the plains; by 1890, the buffalo population had been reduced to 1,000.

devoted her life to bettering the conditions of reservation Indians. She was the author of numerous essays, short stories, and musical compositions. In this excerpted article, published in the _Atlantic Monthly_ in 1900, she describes the decision to attend a boarding school and the Americanizing process she underwent.

From some of my playmates I heard that two paleface missionaries were in our village. They were from that class of white men who wore big hats and carried large hearts, they said. Running direct to my mother, I began to question her why these two strangers were among us. She told me, after I had teased much, that they had come to take away Indian boys and girls to the East. My mother did not seem to want me to talk about them.

Thus my mother discouraged my curiosity about the lands beyond our eastern horizon. . . . But on the following day the missionaries did come to our very house. . . .

Judéwin had told me of the great tree where grew red, red apples and how we could reach out our hands and pick all the red apples we could eat. I had never tasted more than a dozen red apples in my life; and when I heard of the orchards of the East, I was eager to roam among them. The missionaries smiled into my eye and patted my head. I wondered how Mother could say such hard words against them.

"Mother, ask them if little girls may have all the red apples they want, when they go East," I whispered aloud, in my excitement.

The interpreter heard me and answered: "Yes, little girl, the nice red apples are for those who pick them, and you will have a ride on the iron horse if you go with these good people."

I had never seen a train, and he knew it.

"Mother, I'm going East! I like big red apples, and I want to ride on the iron horse! Mother, say yes!" I pleaded.

My mother said nothing. The missionaries waited in silence; and my eyes began to blur with tears, though I struggled to choke them back. The corners of my mouth twitched, and my mother saw me.

"I am not ready to give you any word," she said to them. "Tomorrow I shall send you my answer by my son. . . . "

The next morning came, and my mother called me to her side. "My daughter, do you still persist in wishing to leave your mother?" she asked.

"Oh, mother, it is not that I wish to leave you, but I want to see the wonderful Eastern land," I answered.

My dear old aunt came to our house that morning, and I heard her say, "Let her try it."

I hoped that, as usual, my aunt was pleading on my side. My brother Dawee came for mother's decision. I dropped my play and crept close to my aunt.

"Yes, Dawee, my daughter, though she does not understand what it all means, is anxious to go. She will need an education when she is grown, for then there will be fewer real Dakotas, and many more palefaces. This tearing her away, so young, from her mother is necessary, if I would have her an educated woman. The palefaces, who owe us a large debt for stolen lands, have begun to pay a tardy justice in offering some education to our children. But I know my daughter must suffer keenly in this experiment. For her sake, I dread to tell you my reply to the missionaries. Go, tell them that they may take my little daughter, and that the Great Spirit shall not fail to reward them according to their hearts. . . . "

Upon her arrival to the white man's school, Zitkala-Sä found her experience to be very different from what she expected.

I had arrived in the wonderful land of rosy skies, but I was not happy, as I had thought I should be. My long travel and bewildering sights had exhausted me. I fell asleep, heaving deep, tired sobs. My tears were left to dry themselves in streaks, because neither my aunt nor my mother was near to wipe them away. . . .

Late in the morning, my friend Judéwin gave me a terrible warning. Judéwin knew a few words of English; and she had overheard the paleface woman talk about cutting our long, heavy hair. Our mothers had taught us that only unskilled warriors who were captured had their hair shingled by the enemy. Among our people, short hair was worn by mourners and shingled hair by cowards!

We discussed our fate some moments, and when Judéwin said, "We have to submit, because they are strong," I rebelled.

"No, I will not submit! I will struggle first!" I answered.

I watched my chance, and when no one noticed I disappeared. I crept up the stairs as quietly as I could in my squeaking shoes—my moccasins had been exchanged for shoes. Along the hall I passed, without knowing whither I was going. Turning aside to an

John Muir and the Conservation Movement

Naturalists such as John Muir helped spark interest in preserving what was left of the nation's precious wilderness. Muir published 300 articles and 10 major books describing his travels in the U.S. wilderness. Seizing the imagination of many Americans, his writings generated massive public support for the establishment of national parks and the conservation of America's forests. In 1892, John Muir and his supporters established the Sierra Club, which aimed, in Muir's words, to "do something for wildness and make the mountains glad." Muir helped establish Sequoia, Mount Rainier, Petrified Forest, and Grand Canyon National Parks. He also played a key role in the establishment of national forests.

Loggers showed little concern for the trees they felled, in this case, an ancient sequoia. This kind of thoughtless destruction of massive redwoods led conservationists like John Muir to demand federal action to protect some of America's ancient forests and wilderness in the 1890s.

The construction of railroads transformed the American West, discharging settlers, creating towns and villages, and linking the West to eastern markets. Here the citizens of Anthony, Kansas, celebrate the start of construction of the Kansas City, Mexico, and Orient Railroad in May 1901.

open door, I found a large room with three white beds in it. The windows were covered with dark green curtains, which made the room very dim. Thankful that no one was there, I directed my steps toward the corner farthest from the door. On my hands and knees I crawled under the bed, and cuddled myself in the dark corner.

From my hiding place I peered out, shuddering with fear whenever I heard footsteps nearby. Though in the hall loud voices were calling my name, and I knew that even Judéwin was searching for me, I did not open my mouth to answer. Then the steps were quickened and the voices became excited. The sounds came nearer and nearer. Women and girls entered the room. I held my breath, and watched them open closet doors and peep behind large trunks. Some one threw up the curtains, and the room was filled with sudden light. What caused them to stoop and look under the bed I do not know. I remember being dragged out, though I resisted by kicking and scratching wildly. In spite of myself, I was carried downstairs and tied fast in a chair.

I cried aloud, shaking my head all the while until I felt the cold blades of the scissors against my neck, and heard them gnaw off one of my thick braids. Then I lost my spirit. Since the day I was taken from my mother I had suffered extreme indignities. People had stared at me. I had been tossed about in the air like a wooden puppet. And now my long hair was shingled like a coward's! In my anguish I moaned for my mother, but no one came to comfort me. Not a soul reasoned quietly with me, as my own mother used to do; for now I was only one of many little animals driven by a herder.

Pioneers

In 1853 Phoebe Judson left her home in Ohio and traveled west to Oregon Territory with her husband. By the 1870s they had settled in the remote Nooksack Valley in Washington Territory. Judson published a memoir in 1925 titled *A Pioneer's Search for an Ideal Home.* The following excerpt reveals the chronic loneliness and special challenges faced by pioneer women.

No one but those who have spent years isolated from the outside world, debarred from frequent mail privileges, can understand the peculiar excitement produced by the arrival of long delayed mail.

When an Indian made his appearance with the much coveted treasure, some one would wind the old "ox horn," and soon I would see Mr. Judson come tumbling over the fence, for no matter how pressing the work, when the mail signal reached his ears, it was dropped right then and there. Everything else was forgotten in the intellectual enjoyment, from which we could scarcely tear ourselves away to attend to pressing duties, or to secure necessary repose. . . .

When living in our Chehalis home, I thought a mile a long distance to be separated for my nearest neighbor; but now I was twenty miles away from any white woman. I never could have endured the wearing loneliness without the diversion of our good literature. My dreams were filled with visions of old friends and visits to familiar scenes. . . .

I so often longed for the companionship of womankind that I often took my sewing and sat by old Sally's campfire, trying to imagine I was visiting some old friend, talking to her to the limited extent of my "Chinook" vocabulary and taking notes of the Indian method of family government. . . .

Annie wrote that she and her husband were going to attend the state fair at Salem, Oregon, and invited me to accompany them, which I decided to do, and visit my mother who had, after my father's death, moved to Forest Grove, Oregon, to educate her boys. . .

My heart was filled with conflicting emotions as I viewed the familiar scenes I had left so reluctantly three years before. I loved Olympia—my life there had been very pleasant. . . .

I looked across to Swantown, dear Lucretia's home. Sweet memories of bygone days were before me, mingled with dark

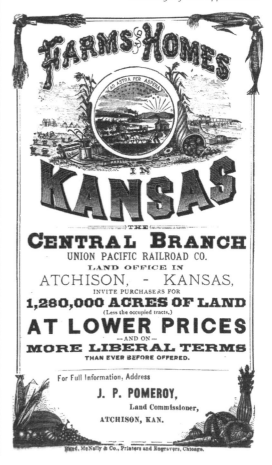

This broadside promotes railroad lands for purchase in the West. Blacks and whites alike took advantage of such opportunities.

clouds of sorrow and pain. Standing on the steamer's deck, my overcharged heart found relief in a flood of tears. With the scene of so many pleasant recollections lying before me, I realized with painful intensity the utter loneliness of my life on the river.

Western states were the first to grant women the right to vote long before women nationally gained voting rights in 1920. Wyoming Territory granted full suffrage to women in 1869 (a right preserved when the territory became a state in 1890). Colorado, Utah, and Idaho also allowed women to vote by the mid-1890s. In the following excerpt, Judson recounts how the political activism of women in Washington—as they cast their ballots for local option to shut down saloons—eventually led to their loss of the ballot.

For four years, from 1883 to 1887, the territory of Washington enjoyed impartial suffrage. I took my turn on petit and grand jury, served on election boards, walked in perfect harmony to the polls by the side of my staunch Democratic husband, and voted the Republican ticket—not feeling any more out of my sphere than when assisting my husband to develop the resources of our country.

At the polls, men were respectful; voting places were kept clean and free from loafers. The women, as a rule, allowed character, rather than party, to influence their votes. Party spirit ran high, but the women worked nobly, leaving no stone unturned, and during the four years local option carried in Lynden. It was not because of failure, by any means, that we were deprived of equal rights, for it was a grand success; in so much that a prominent politician remarked that if the women were allowed the ballot they would be compelled to nominate good, competent men for office, and so we were disenfranchised, except in menial service. . . .

Oh, yes, Uncle Sam was very liberal in allowing us equal rights with the sterner sex in taking up land, paying taxes, and sharing in their perils and labors; but when it comes to covering this fair land (which we have so dearly purchased and helped to make blossom like the rose) with licensed saloons, we have no voice in the matter. He would have us bear the disgrace, poverty, and heartrending sorrow in silent tears, without protest.

Better far a log cabin in the primeval forests, surrounded by savages and wild animals, than a palace with all its luxuries, shadowed by this dreadful "hydra-headed monster, rum."

Exodusters

In 1879 alone, roughly 6,000 Southern blacks, largely from Louisiana, Mississippi, and Texas, migrated west, to Kansas. Called Exodusters, these migrants, like their white counterparts, hoped to purchase land and own farmsteads in the West. But unlike whites they were also escaping the second-class citizenship and racial terrorism that defined their lives in the South.

In 1880 Col. Frank H. Fletcher, a representative of the Executive Committee of the Freedmen's State Central Organization, traveled to Kansas to investigate the black exodus. The following are excerpts from his report, which included these interviews with migrants Nancy Guptil, Mrs. William Ray, and Richard Coutcher. Their stories reveal how and why they left the South and provide insight into the new lives they created in the West.

Nancy Guptil: "Came from Middle Tennessee. Heard neighbors talking of Kansas two or three years. We received two or three circulars that told about Kansas. I lived with a white man who took Kansas papers. There are not many such white men in the South. I find things here a heap better than I expected. We have forty acres. We came last May. We built our house in the fall. My husband finds enough work around here to support us. We had plenty of supplies to live on through the winter. We got them by working for white neighbors. Politics never pestered us at the South, but the people took all we made. People treats us better here than they did there because they is willing to pay us what we work for. Before I came we had letters about this country from a son-in-law at Topeka. We have a prayer-meeting every Wednesday night, and every two weeks of a Sunday in my house. Am a Baptist. I wouldn't go back for nothing. . . . All my people are mighty well satisfied here." . . .

Mrs. William Ray: "Came from Texas in a wagon of our own; stopped a while at Fort Scott. We left Texas because they treated us so bad. They took out my husband's brother-in-law and shot him three times in the face. They

The Shores family of Custer County, Nebraska, pose before their sod house in the late 1880s, a proud example of strength, determination, and the fulfilled promise of a new life in the West.

As they lost ground economically, Mexican Americans saw their political influence decline in the Gilded Age. Poll taxes and other legal obstacles meant to keep black men from voting also barred Mexican-American men from voting in some states.

came after my husband one night and made him give up his pistol. They took out my aunt and cut her because she would not tell them where her son was. We have been on this place between four and five years. We have a hundred and sixty acres. My husband hires help." At this point the husband, who had been ploughing in an adjoining field with two other men, came up and continued the narration; "Last year I raised five hundred and sixty bushels of corn, fifty bushels of wheat, one hundred and sixty bushels of oats, and two hundred and fifty bushels of potatoes. . . . I have now seven horses, twenty hogs, and eight head of cattle. My children are learning to read and write. They go to the same school with the whites. We have church and Sunday-school in the schoolhouse. We are Baptists. . . . I came here with only one pair of horses and a wagon. I had no tools. I arrived in Kansas with fifty cents. I made a horse trade after I got to the State, and got fifteen dollars boot. That was my start. . . ."

Richard Coutcher: "I came from Hines County, Miss. I think we can raise as good crops here as we can down South. I have a claim of forty acres: four of us have a hundred and sixty acres. I think this is a very fine country. If colored people can only get here and get started they can do well. . . . All are well and have been lately. Those who were sick when they started have got well. Some have taken colds, but none have colds now. There is just as fine a people here, so far as I have experienced, as I could hope to see. I would not go back South unless I was forced to. . . . The colored people have got so that they are afraid for their lives to live there. They have come away from there because they can't live there. The white people have sworn they will kill the last one of us if we don't vote with them, and they are killing us so fast, I thought I would get away while I could. . . ."

Mexican Americans Fight Back

After the Mexican-American War ended, conflicts over land rights were especially fierce in New Mexico. Courts there handed over to whites four fifths (over 35 million acres) of land once owned by Mexicans or Mexican Americans. Hispanic land titles granted property to both large and small landholders; in addition, the titles granted the right to share range lands with adjacent property owners, crucial to small landholders for grazing animals. To fight this subversion of their rights, Mexican Americans formed a secret organization,

known as **Las Gorras Blancas (The White Caps). They attempted to protect their lands and traditional land rights through guerrilla warfare. They cut fences and telegraph lines, destroyed railroad ties, and set fire to ranches. The following is a platform of The White Caps, detailing their grievances concerning land claims in San Miguel County, New Mexico. It first appeared in the *Las Vegas Optic* on March 12, 1890.**

Our purpose is to protect the rights and interests of the people in general and especially those of the helpless classes.

We want the Las Vegas Grant settled to the benefit of all concerned, and this we hold is the entire community within the Grant.

We want no "land grabbers" or obstructionists of any sort to interfere.

We will watch them.

We are not down on lawyers as a class, but the usual knavery and unfair treatment of the people must be stopped.

Our judiciary hereafter must understand that we will sustain it only when "Justice" is its watchword.

We are down on race issues, and we will watch race agitators.

We favor irrigation enterprises but will fight any scheme that tends to monopolize the supply of water sources to the detriment of residents living on lands watered by the same streams.

The people are suffering from the effects of partisan "bossism," and these bosses had better quietly hold their peace. The people have been persecuted and hauled about in every which way to satisfy their caprices.

We must have a free ballot and fair court, and the will of the Majority shall be respected.

We have no grudge against any person in particular, but we are the enemies of bulldozers and tyrants.

If the old system should continue, death would be a relief to our suffering. And for our rights our lives are the least we can pledge.

If the fact that we are law-abiding citizens is questioned, come out to our houses and see the hunger and desolation we are suffering; and "this" is the result of the deceitful and corrupt methods of "bossism."

Job Status Lost

The loss of land to whites in the Southwest had dire economic and social consequences for Hispanic peoples. This chart reflects a downturn in the employment status of Texas's rural Mexican population from 1850 to 1900.

	1850	1900
Ranch/Farm Owners	34%	16%
Skilled Laborers	29%	12%
Manual Laborers	24%	67%

These miners of Mexican descent worked in Arizona. Without land, many Mexican Americans found themselves reduced to wage work, as day laborers, farm laborers, miners, and railroad workers.

Chapter Eight

The Farmers' Revolt

I n 1889 Tom Watson, a lawyer and owner of a large amount of land in Georgia, summed up the quandary of many American farmers. "We are told," he wrote, "in the splendid phraseology of silver-tongued orators from the city that our country is absolutely smothered under the plenteous flow of milk and honey of another Canaan." Yet, noted Watson, "our newspapers are absolutely crowded with advertisements of sheriff's sales." As many as 200 farms went on the auction block in a single day, as farmers lost their land to pay their debts. "There is no romance in having twenty-five per cent upon our money," Watson wearily explained, "no romance in being fleeced by a fifty per cent tariff, no romance in seeing other classes and other properties exempted from taxation, and realizing fabulous dividends upon their investments, when the lands are taxed to their uttermost dollar and farming has paid no dividend since the war."

Many Americans criticized the injustices of the Gilded Age, including urban reformers and industrial laborers who voiced their concerns about a United States that seemed increasingly removed from the principles of its founding. But the most thorough and powerful critique came not from the nation's teeming cities but from the countryside, not from urban radicals but from farmers, often considered to be among the most conservative Americans.

In the 1880s and 1890s, in response to their worsening economic condition and declining status, America's farmers mounted a nationwide political movement aimed at establishing economic justice. They argued that they, as producers, had the right to the fruits of their labor. Bankers, merchants, the railroads, and "middlemen," farmers maintained, benefited from their hard work, leaving them destitute. By organizing collectively, farmers hoped to seize the inordinate power wielded by bankers and industrialists and restore it to "the people."

Tom Watson personally experienced and witnessed a dramatic decline in the status and independence of Southern farmers. The son of a wealthy antebellum planter, Watson had seen his own family's for-

In this political cartoon from 1896, William Jennings Bryan straddles the three parties that nominated him as their candidate for President: the People's Party (Populists), the Democratic Party, and the Free Silver Party. Bryan's candidacy reflected the deep discontent of farmers and their faith in the unlimited coinage of silver as a solution to their economic problems.

The Colored Alliance of farmers aimed to alleviate problems specific to its membership, individuals and families such as these sharecroppers. In 1891 the Alliance initiated a strike of cotton pickers in an attempt to increase their wages from 50 cents to a dollar a day. Violence flared on several plantations in East Texas; 17 cotton pickers and a white plantation manager died. The strike's failure irreparably damaged the Colored Alliance in the South, as membership fell sharply.

tunes plummet dramatically after the Civil War. Though he managed to attend college for several years, establish a prosperous law practice, and eventually accumulate 3,000 acres of Georgia farmland, Watson nonetheless felt deeply troubled by the hard times he observed in the countryside. As New South cities, like Atlanta, crowed about progress and prosperity, Watson saw little but desperation and suffering among farmers.

Southern farmers, once proud and independent, found themselves entangled in the web of the crop lien system, which emerged after the Civil War. The crop lien system, in the words of one Southern historian, "converted the Southern economy into a vast pawnshop." Cash poor after the war, farmers depended upon local merchants to extend them credit for tools, seed, and fertilizer—and even food—as they planted their fields in cotton, the crop that had brought them prosperity before the war. In return, as security for the farmers' credit, merchants placed a lien on the upcoming crop. If cotton brought the anticipated price on the market, the farmer simply paid off his loan to the merchant. But cotton prices dropped precipitously after the Civil War, owing to overproduction in the South and foreign competition. Cotton brought $1 a pound after the war. In the 1880s a farmer could expect to receive nine cents a pound; by the 1890s, seven-cent cotton was the norm. Year after year—as cotton prices plunged—farmers found themselves increasingly indebted to merchants. And until he paid his debt, the farmer remained dependent upon the merchant for all of his purchases, including food and clothing. Throughout the South merchants acquired notorious reputations for gouging farmers, charging them exorbitant prices, and exploiting their suffering. Unable to pay their debts, farmers lost their land.

In the West, the farmers' situation was hardly better. Wheat prices, like those of Southern cotton, declined in the Gilded Age. While a bushel of wheat in 1866 sold for $1.45, by the mid-1880s, it sold for 80 cents and by the 1890s, 49 cents. Mechanization and the cultivation of additional Western land led to overproduction. Foreign competition also conspired to drive down prices. As

prices dropped, other costs—such as storage and transportation—remained the same or even increased. Like farmers in the South, Westerners found their hard work repaid with foreclosures and the loss of their independence. Railroads, monopolies that charged exorbitant prices to ship goods to market, bankers, who charged high interest rates for loans, and middlemen, who profited handsomely for selling farmers' products, all became the targets of frustrated Western farmers.

In both the South and West, farmers looked for answers. Something was desperately wrong. Once considered the backbone of the nation, farmers now struggled to feed and clothe their families. At the same time they saw other Americans accumulating fortunes. The United States was becoming, as politicized farmers would contend by 1896, "a nation of tramps and millionaires." And—most frustrating of all—no one beyond the countryside seemed to care. Politicians ignored farmers' pleas for reform. City people dismissed country people as "hayseeds" and "rubes," laughable and quaint, the antithesis of Gilded Age modernity and progress.

By the 1880s, when Tom Watson began to speak out about the plight of farmers and demand change, an organization known as the Farmers' Alliance was spreading like wildfire across the Cotton Belt and into the West. Started in Texas, the Alliance stressed that the only way for embattled farmers to challenge successfully the power of merchants and monopolies was to unite and work cooperatively. Farmers established cooperative stores and cotton-buying houses as well as cotton gins and warehouses. The Alliance drew on a rich tradition of farmer organizations and protest. Revitalizing the message of Greenbackers and Grangers from the 1870s, members of the Alliance railed against merchants, railroads, and bankers, whom they blamed for their problems and for depriving them of the fruits of their labor.

In addition to bettering the economic conditions of farmers, the Alliance also hoped to enrich the lives of its members, "mentally, morally, [and] socially." Mining a deep seam of bitterness toward town merchants, the Alliance in the South and West claimed 1.5 million members by 1890.

Because he was a lawyer, Tom Watson could not officially join the Alliance. Membership was limited to the "farmer and farm laborer, mechanic, country schoolteacher, country physician, or minister of the gospel." Watson later recalled, "I did not lead the Alliance. I followed the Alliance. . . . " But he also shaped the Alliance and propelled the farmers' movement into politics. While

"Each year the plunge into debt is deeper; each year the burden is heavier. The struggle is woe-begone. Cares are many, smiles are few, and the comforts of life are scantier. . . . Anxious days, sleepless nights, deep wrinkles, gray hairs, wan faces, cheerless old age, and perhaps abject poverty make up in part the melancholy story. . . . Independence! It is gone. Humiliation and dependence bow the head of the proud spirit."

—C. H. Otken, *The Ills of the South*, 1894

The Wonderful Wizard of Oz

The story upon which the classic 1939 Hollywood movie *The Wizard of Oz* is based is actually a parable about Populism. L. Frank Baum, author of *The Wonderful Wizard of Oz*, lived in South Dakota from 1887 to 1891, just as the farmers' revolt began. In 1896 he staunchly supported William Jennings Bryan for President. A few years later, wanting to fashion tales that "bear the stamp of our times and depict the progressive fairies of today," Baum tried his hand at writing children's literature. In 1900 a Chicago publisher printed *The Wonderful Wizard of Oz*.

A tornado carries Dorothy, Baum's everyperson, to Oz—a colorful, magical place, in contrast with the bleakness of Kansas. "Oz" was a well-known abbreviation for silver advocates, who called for the coinage of silver and gold in a ratio of 16 ounces (abbreviated "oz.") to 1. By destroying the Wicked Witch of the East (symbol of Eastern bankers and supporters of the gold standard), Dorothy frees the Munchkins (the common people) held in bondage by the moneyed establishment. To return to Kansas she must travel to the Emerald City (Washington, the color of money), wearing silver shoes (Hollywood would substitute ruby slippers) as she walks the yellow brick road, which represents the gold and silver monetary standard of the Populists. Dorothy, like most Americans, does not at first understand the power of her silver shoes, but, after a kiss from the Good Witch of the North (Northern voters), she travels the dangerous yellow brick road with protection.

Along her way she meets the Scarecrow (a symbol of the farmer), the Tin Woodman (the industrial worker), and the Cowardly Lion (William Jennings Bryan). The Scarecrow is convinced that he is inferior, a "hayseed" with no brain, but soon demonstrates that he indeed can think for himself. The Tin Woodman has rusted and believes that he is no longer capable of love. But he rediscovers his passion and the power of cooperation. The Cowardly Lion, who at first claws the Tin Woodman, finds that he "could make no impression on the tin," (a reference to the fact that Bryan garnered little support from industrial workers in 1896) and seems incapable of scaring anyone. But he turns out not to be cowardly at all.

technically nonpartisan, the Alliance quickly realized its political power. By 1889, in the West, some Alliance members created their own third party, the People's (Populist) Party; in the South, in 1890, the Alliance successfully elected a number of members to state legislatures and even to Congress. Watson won a seat in the House of Representatives in 1890 as an Alliance candidate.

Convinced that the two major parties would never pay attention to the needs of farmers, Watson embraced the People's Party in 1891 and started the *People's Party Paper* that year. Many white Southern Alliance members followed his lead, leaving the Democratic Party for the People's Party. He helped create strong bonds between Southern and Western Populists, and together they worked to establish a political voice for the forgotten and suffering Americans in rural areas.

Not only did Watson break ranks with the "white man's party" of the South, he also challenged racial divisions. He appealed to black farmers and tenants to join forces with white farmers and cast their lot with the People's Party. He called for a revolutionary order in the South, for an end to the race-based politics of white Democrats and black Republicans, demanding that exploited farmers—regardless of race—recognize their common interests and oppressors and work together to get what was rightly theirs. Similarly, in the West, Populists built alliances of the exploited across the color line. In New Mexico, for example, Las Gorras Blancas fused with the People's Party.

Watson's appeal provoked the anger of white Democrats. When he ran for reelection to Congress in 1892 as a Populist, Democrats stole the election through ballot-box stuffing and a campaign of fraud and terror.

Despite his defeat, Watson was heartened that year by the showing of the Populists nationally. In 1892 the Populists met in Omaha, devised a national platform, and ran their first candidate for President, Gen. James B. Weaver of Iowa. While not a very popular candidate in the South—he was a Union army veteran—Weaver nonetheless garnered more than a million votes nationwide, an auspicious national debut for the party.

As the nation plunged into a severe economic depression in 1893, the People's Party strengthened. Massive unemployment, bank failures, and countless mortgage foreclosures signaled to many Americans the need for radical change and set the stage for the crucial Presidential election of 1896.

The year 1896 found the Populists at a crossroads. The Democrats—in many states the nemesis of the Populists—nominated

William Jennings Bryan of Nebraska for the presidency. Sympathetic to the plight of farmers, Bryan advocated the free coinage of silver as a way to improve their economic plight. Farmers had long attributed many of their problems to what they believed was an inadequate money supply. As the nation grew, they argued, the money supply had not kept pace, leading to falling prices and tight credit. Both the Northern and Southern Alliances had called for the coining of silver and a rejection of the strict gold standard to remedy the situation; however, the silver issue had always been far more popular in the West than in the South.

Some Populists argued that the party should support Bryan; endorsing the Democrat could mean electing a compassionate President in touch with the needs of farmers. Tom Watson, however, and other Populists disagreed. By supporting Bryan and adopting silver coinage as its platform, the party would compromise its cherished ideals, be swallowed up, and lose its identity. Muckraker Henry Demarest Lloyd, famous for his attack on Rockefeller and Standard Oil, and a staunch Populist, summed up the dilemma of the Populists in 1896: "If we fuse, we are sunk; if we don't fuse, all the silver men we have will leave us for more powerful Democrats."

In the end the Populists cast their lot with Bryan. However, they also ran Tom Watson as their Vice Presidential candidate. Bryan, with his own Democratic running mate, Arthur Sewall of Maine, awkwardly ignored Watson as he crisscrossed the country campaigning. Despite the alliance of Populists and Democrats, Bryan lost overwhelmingly to Republican William McKinley.

Although the Populist Party managed to survive the crushing defeat of 1896, the party was a shadow of its former self. Tom Watson retreated to his rural Georgia home, heartbroken over the demise of the farmers' revolt. Watson immersed himself in writing and his law practice. Embittered and disillusioned, the one-time advocate of interracial political alliances and reform spent the last decade of his life as a race-baiting, anti-Semitic, anti-Catholic journalist who helped reestablish the Ku Klux Klan in Georgia in 1915. Watson died in 1922, in the midst of the Klan's nationwide resurgence.

Despite the demise of the People's Party, many reforms it advocated—rejected by critics as too radical in the 1890s—were taken up by Progressive reformers and enacted in the early 20th century. The Populist demand that the federal government intervene on behalf of the common person to offset powerful business interests gained widespread support under the Progressives; specific proposals, such

Brother farmers let us hold on to our organization, for if we fail this time, the farmers' doom is fixed, the merchants will then have us where they will hold us forever. The merchants are laughing, but it is only from their lips out, it don't come from the heart at all. Brethren, have you thought of it; when we farmers are in the fields working hard in the summer, with the drops of sweat falling from our brow, go to the village and see the merchants sitting around the store doors with their linen shirts and black neckties on, waiting for us to bring in our first bale of cotton.

—"A Member of the Davidson Bethel Alliance (North Carolina)" in a letter to the *Progressive Farmer,* 1888

A Dull, Gray World

This excerpt from the opening paragraphs of *The Wonderful Wizard of Oz* vividly depicts the merciless, colorless lives of Western farm people.

Dorothy lived in the midst of the great Kansas prairies, with Uncle Henry, who was a farmer, Aunt Em, who was the farmer's wife. Their house was small, for the lumber to build it had to be carried by wagon many miles. . . .

When Dorothy stood in the doorway and looked around, she could see nothing but the great gray prairie on every side. Not a tree nor a house broke the broad sweep of flat country that reached to the edge of the sky in all directions. The sun had baked the plowed land into a gray mass, with little cracks running through it. Even the grass was not green, for the sun had burned the tops of the long blades until they were the same gray color to be seen everywhere. Once the house had been painted, but the sun blistered the paint and the rains washed it away, and now the house was as dull and gray as everything else.

When Aunt Em came there to live she was a young, pretty wife. The sun and wind had changed her, too. They had taken the sparkle from her eyes and left them a sober gray; they had taken the red from her cheeks and lips, and they were gray also. She was thin and gaunt, and never smiled now. When Dorothy, who was an orphan, first came to her, Aunt Em had been so startled by the child's laughter that she would scream and press her hand upon her heart whenever Dorothy's merry voice reached her ears; and she still looked at the little girl with wonder that she could find anything to laugh at.

as a graduated federal income tax and the direct election of senators, were also enacted within the next 20 years.

Farmers' Alliances

Stressing self-improvement, morality, and neighborliness, the Farmers' Alliance provided a much-needed sense of community for isolated, embattled farm men and women. Meetings and encampments often took on a religious tone as people gathered to hear lectures, enjoy entertainment, and visit with neighbors, seeking salvation from their problems in the policies of the Alliance. Lectures were especially important in explaining to farmers the sources of the agricultural crisis and providing specific proposals for change through cooperation. In 1890 the Farmers' Alliance held a national meeting at Ocala, Florida, and expressed the following demands.

1.a. We demand the abolition of national banks.

  b. We demand that the government shall establish sub-treasuries or depositories in the several states, which shall loan money direct to the people at a low rate of interest, not to exceed two per cent per annum, on nonperishable farm products, and also upon real estate, with proper limitations upon the quantity of land and amount of money.

  c. We demand that the amount of the circulating medium be speedily increased to not less than $50 per capita.

2. We demand that Congress shall pass such laws as will effectually prevent the dealing in futures of all agricultural and mechanical productions; providing a stringent system of procedure in trials that will secure the prompt conviction and imposing such penalties as shall secure the most perfect compliance with the law.

3. We condemn the silver bill recently passed by Congress [The Sherman Silver Purchase Act], and demand in lieu thereof the free and unlimited coinage of silver.

4. We demand the passage of laws prohibiting alien ownership of land and that Congress take prompt action to devise some plan to obtain all lands now owned by aliens and foreign syndicates; and that all lands now held by railroads and other corporations in excess of such as is actually used and needed by them be reclaimed by the government and held for actual settlers only.

In this illustration for The Wonderful Wizard of Oz, *Dorothy scolds the Cowardly Lion, representing William Jennings Bryan, who overcomes his fear while travelling down the yellow brick road and comes to protect the weaker creatures in "a grand old forest."*

5. Believing in the doctrine of equal rights to all and special privileges to none, we demand—

    a. That our national legislation shall be so framed in the future as not to build up one industry at the expense of another.

    b. We further demand a removal of the existing heavy tariff tax from the necessities of life, that the poor of our land must have.

    c. We further demand a just and equitable system of graduated tax on incomes.

    d. We believe that the money of the country should be kept as much as possible in the hands of the people, and hence we demand that all national and state revenues shall be limited to necessary expenses of the government economically and honestly administered.

"Raise Less Corn and More Hell"

The most prominent female member of the Farmers' Alliance, and later a Populist, was Mary Elizabeth Lease. Lease was famous for her challenge to prairie farmers to "raise less corn and more hell." Born Mary Elizabeth Clyens to Irish parents in Pennsylvania in 1850, she made her way to Kansas in 1871, seeking better wages as a teacher. There she married druggist Charles L. Lease. They later moved to Texas, where she became active in the Women's Christian Temperance Union. Returning to Kansas, she devoted herself to the fight for woman suffrage and became a professional lecturer. She also joined the Knights of Labor at the height of its popularity in 1886. Lease eventually devoted herself almost entirely to the Farmers' Alliance, in which, as a woman, she was treated as an equal. She soon emerged as one of the Kansas Alliance's most popular speakers and campaigned incessantly for Alliance candidates in state elections.

Standing almost six feet tall, she spoke passionately on behalf of the nation's downtrodden farmers and challenged them to unite to improve their condition. Her legendary speeches could mesmerize an audience for two or three hours. By 1890 she backed the Populist Party and traveled in the West and South, stirring up support for the third party. "Let the old political parties know that the raid is over," she exhorted, "and that monopolies, trusts, and combines shall be relegated to Hades."

Lease received a great deal of criticism from her political opponents. Questioning her femininity, detractors described her as "raw-boned" and "ugly as a mud hen." Her views were described as "un-American and villainous." But such criticism only made her more heroic in the eyes of her Populist supporters.

As the Populists surged as a national party in the 1890s, Lease was in the center of the whirlwind. Even though as a woman she could not vote for President, she seconded the Presidential nominations of both Weaver in 1892 and Bryan in 1896 at the national Populist conventions. And she made thousands of speeches in support of the party's Presidential candidates, sometimes speaking as many as eight times a day.

As the People's Party declined after 1896, Lease left Kansas and settled in New York. Like her Southern counterpart, Tom Watson, she was embittered by the party's collapse and, by 1900, wrote articles denouncing both Bryan and the Populists. But she never cut her ties with the countryside, spending the last years of her life on a farm in upstate New York.

6. We demand the most rigid, honest, and just state and national government control and supervision of the means of public transportation, and if this control and supervision does not remove the abuse now existing, we demand the government ownership of such means of communication and transportation.

7. We demand that the Congress of the United States submit an amendment to the Constitution providing for the election of United States Senators by the direct vote of the people of each state.

Women played a particularly important role in the Alliance, making up about one fourth of the membership. Treated as equals in an age of second-class citizenship for women, female members of the Alliance held office, served as lecturers, and wrote innumerable columns and letters for Alliance newspapers. The following article by Annie L. Diggs, published in the *Arena* in July 1892, explains the appeal of the Farmers' Alliance to farm women and their many contributions to the movement.

The women prominent in the great farmer manifesto of this present time were long preparing for their part; not consciously, not by any manner of means even divining that there would be a part to play. In the many thousands of isolated farm homes the early morning, the noonday, and the evening-time work went on with a dreary monotony which resulted in that startling report of the physicians that American farms were recruiting stations from whence more women went to insane asylums than from any other walk in life.

Farm life for women is a treadmill. The eternal climb must be kept up though the altitude never heightens. For more than a quarter of a century these churning, washing, ironing, baking, darning, sewing, cooking, scrubbing, drudging women, whose toilsome, dreary lives were unrelieved by the slight incident or by-play of town life, felt that their treadmills slipped cogs. Climb as they would, they slipped down two steps while they climbed one. They were not keeping pace with the women of the towns and cities. The industry which once led in the march toward independence and prosperity, was steadily falling behind as to remuneration. Something was wrong. . . .

Politics for the farmer had been recreation, relaxation, or even exhilaration, according to the varying degree of his interest, or of

honor flatteringly bestowed by town committeemen upon a "solid yeoman" at caucus or convention. . . .

But the farmers' wives participated in no such ecstasies. Hence for them no blinding party ties. And therefore when investigation turned on the light, the women spoke right out in meeting, demanding explanation for the non-appearance of the home market for the farm products, which their good husbands had been prophesying and promising would follow the upbuilding of protected industries. These women in the Alliance, grown apt in keeping close accounts from long economy, cast eyes over the long account of promises of officials managing public business, and said, "Promise and performance do not balance." "Of what value are convention honors, or even elected eloquence in national Capitol, if homelessness must be our children's heritage?" . . .

Strangely enough, the women of the South, where women, and men's thought about women, are most conservative, were first to go into the Alliance, and in many instances were most clear of thought and vigorous of speech. Though never venturing upon the platform, they contributed much to the inspiration and tenacity of the Alliance.

In several states, notably Texas, Georgia, Michigan, California, Colorado, and Nebraska, women have been useful and prominent in the farmer movement, which indeed is now widened and blended with the cause of labor other than that of the farm.

Kansas, however, furnished by far the largest quota of active, aggressive women, inasmuch as Kansas was the theatre where the initial act of the great labor drama was played. . . .

The great political victory of the people of Kansas would not have been won without the help of the women of the Alliance. Women who never dreamed of becoming public speakers, grew eloquent in their zeal and fervor. Farmers' wives and daughters rose earlier and worked later to gain time to cook the picnic dinners, to paint the mottos on the banners, to practice with the glee clubs, to march in procession. . . .

Kansas politics was no longer a "dirty pool." That marvelous campaign was a great thrilling crusade. It was religious to the core. Instinctively the women knew that the salvation of their homes, and more even, the salvation of the republic, depended upon the outcome of that test struggle. Every word, every thought, every act, was a prayer for victory, and for the triumph of right. Victory was compelled to come.

Narrow ignoramuses long ago stumbled upon the truth. "The home is woman's sphere." Ignoramus said, "Women should cook

"You may call me an anarchist, a socialist, or a communist, I care not, but I hold to the theory that if one man has not enough to eat three times a day and another man has $25 million, that last man has something that belongs to the first."

—Mary Elizabeth Lease,
1891 speech

William Allen White, a vociferous opponent of the Populist movement who once called Mary Elizabeth Lease a "harpy," wrote upon her death: "She was an honest, competent woman who felt deeply and wielded great power unselfishly. Peace to her ashes."

and gossip, and rock cradles, and darn socks"—merely these and nothing more. Whereas the whole truth is, women should watch and work in all things which shape and mould the home, whether "money," "land," or "transportation." So now Alliance women look at politics and trace the swift relation to the home—their special sphere. They say, "Our homes are threatened by the dirty pool. The pool must go."

Before this question of the salvation of the imperilled homes of the nation, all other questions, whether of "prohibition" or "suffrage," pale into relative inconsequence. . . . Upon such great ethical foundation is the labor movement of to-day building itself. How could women do otherwise than be in and of it?

African-American farmers and tenants, squeezed in the same economic vise as white farmers, also found the Farmers' Alliance especially attractive. Barred from membership in the Southern Alliance, which admitted only whites, black farmers formed their own organization, the Colored Farmers' Alliance, as a separate but parallel organization that espoused the same principles as the white Farmers' Alliance. By 1890 the Colored Farmers' Alliance claimed more than a million members. Some whites viewed the Colored Alliance with trepidation, fearing any organization that might mobilize blacks to political action and challenge the status quo. The following editorial and letter on July 10, 1888, to the *Progressive Farmer,* the official newspaper of the North Carolina Farmers' Alliance, reflects white concerns about the Colored Farmers' Alliance as well as the ambivalent attitude of the white Alliance toward its black counterpart.

It has been said, heretofore, that no one but white men were allowed to join the Alliance concern. How is it now about organizing negroes?

For our esteemed contemporary the *Democrat,* we refer him to Section 1, Article IV of the Constitution of the Alliance *concern.*

Section 1. No person shall be admitted as a member unless he has been a citizen of the State of North Carolina for six months past, and not then unless he be a farmer, farm laborer, mechanic, country schoolteacher, country physician, or a minister of the gospel, be of good moral character, believe in the existence of a Supreme Being, be of industrious habits, is a white person and over the age of sixteen years. . . .

We repeat what "has been said heretofore that no one but white people are allowed to join (our) Alliance *concern.* . . . "

We understand that the negroes in Louisiana, Texas, and Mississippi have an organization regularly chartered and, which, in its general features, is somewhat similar to the Farmers' Alliance, and that this organization is rapidly spreading among the negroes of the South. We learn that it is being introduced into this State.

But it is a separate and distinct organization from *our* "Alliance concern." It is a different *"concern"* altogether, but if it shall make them more industrious, more frugal, more reliable, more thoughtful, more faithful, and a better people and better citizens, our *"concern"* and all other good people will bid them God-speed.

In response, J. J. Rogers, a member of the Colored Alliance, wrote this letter, which was published in the *Progressive Farmer* on July 31, 1888. In it, he explained his organization's purpose and pointed out that it posed no threat to the South's racial hierarchy.

The article in your paper of last week . . . explains itself to some extent, especially with your information but not fully. The features you speak of as possibly or probably existing need confirmation. If you will allow me space. . . . The colored Farmers' Alliance is a separate and distinct organization from the white Alliance. It is regularly chartered, and according to its Constitution is composed of colored members alone. Its principal objects are: to educate the colored race, to make them more industrious, more frugal, more reliable, more thoughtful, more faithful, better people, better citizens, and to better their condition financially. . . .

It is true that the colored Alliance is organized with good intentions and with the hope of accomplishing much good to the race for which it is organized. And, too, if kept separate as it is organized, and only *aided* by the members of the white Alliance and all other good people, it will work out great good to both white and colored.

The Populist Party

The Populist Party met on July 4, 1892, in Omaha, Nebraska, to nominate its first candidate for President, James B. Weaver. Mary Elizabeth Lease seconded his nomination. The party also adopted the following platform. The preamble,

It is quite true that society cannot be maintained without food-producers. Neither can it be maintained without millers and butchers and grocers and cooks and the whole round of purveyors and workers. Nor can American agriculture be carried on without the help of wheelwrights and blacksmiths and tailors and milliners and others who work in the service of civilization. . . .

The fact that those in one industry outnumber those in another does not give them a greater claim to consideration. A farmer is not a farmer because farming is the basis of society; he is a farmer because his circumstances, his tastes, or his capacity indicates that farming is the business or the labor by which he can best make his way in the world. If his neighbor selects another occupation, he follows it without the least obligation to do more for the farmer, nor need the farmer do more for him than ordinary business considerations suggest. Both are free men, and both are entitled to what they can fairly get in the struggle for existence. If either has made a mistake, he suffers the consequences. . . . The shiftless and the incompetent fail in farming as they fail elsewhere, but thrift and industry and intelligent adjustment to conditions succeed there, perhaps to a less degree, but with more certainty, than elsewhere. It is a question, not of class, but personal equation. . . .

—George E. Waring, Jr.
North American Review, 1891

This diagram from Tom Watson's People's Party Paper graphically displayed the worsening plight of Southern cotton farmers as cotton prices dropped from 1870 to 1894. In 1870, a farmer earned $120 from a single bale of cotton; by 1894 he needed to sell 4.8 bales to make the same profit.

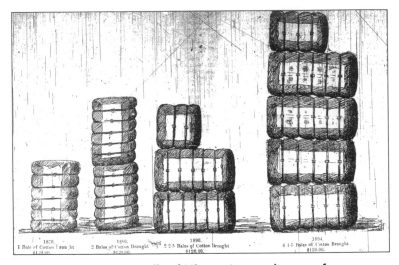

1870.
1 Bale of Cotton Brought
$120.00.

1880.
2 Bales of Cotton Brought
$120.00.

1890.
2 2-5 Bales of Cotton Brought
$120.00.

1894.
4 1-5 Bales of Cotton Brought
$120.00.

written by Ignatius Donnelly of Minnesota, remains one of the most powerful and eloquent critiques of the United States in the Gilded Age. In it, Donnelly calls for a regeneration of the corrupt nation through cooperation and use of the power of the federal government on behalf of the people. The following is an excerpt of the party platform as published in Tom Watson's *People's Party Paper* in August 1892.

Assembled upon the one hundred and sixteenth anniversary of the declaration of independence, the People's Party of America, in their first national convention, invoking upon their action the blessing of the Almighty God, put forth in the name of the people of this country, the following preamble and declaration of principles:

The conditions which surround us best justify our co-operation; we meet in the midst of a nation brought to the verge of moral, political and material ruin. Corruption dominates the ballot box, legislatures, congress, and touches even the ermine of the bench.

The people are demoralized. . . . Newspapers are largely subsidized or muzzled; public opinion silenced; business prostrated; our homes covered with mortgages; labor impoverished; and the land concentrating in the hands of capitalists. The urban workmen are denied the right of organization for self-protection; imported pauperized labor beats down their wages. . . . The fruits of the toil of millions are boldly stolen to build up colossal fortunes for a few, unprecedented in the history of mankind; and the possessors of these in turn despise the republic and endanger liberty. From the same prolific womb of governmental injustice, we breed two great classes—tramps and millionaires. . . .

We have witnessed for more than a quarter of a century the

Mr. Weaver is the candidate of the People's Party for President. It mattered very little what candidate was nominated by the convention at Omaha after the adoption of the platform with its extraordinary preamble. That strange document put the People's Party on the same level with the "third parties" of the past and made it impossible for it to win support from sane and sober men. It made ridiculous its claim of carrying States and getting Electoral votes. On such a platform it can carry no State whose population is not made up of "cranks." We do not believe there is any State peopled with believers in these wild vagaries. . . . On such a platform a man of standing and character would be made ridiculous and would lose the respect of all men of sense. His acceptance of its declarations would be evidence of an impaired intellect and a loss of moral sense and self-respect. . . .

The proposed remedies for the alleged evils are as crazy as the statement of the evils. . . .

—*New York Times*, July 5, 1892

struggles of two great political parties for power and plunder, while grievous wrongs have been inflicted upon the suffering people. We charge that the controlling influence dominating both these parties has permitted the existing dreadful conditions to develop without serious effort to prevent or restrain them. Neither do they now promise us any substantial reform. They have agreed together to ignore in the coming campaign every issue but one. They propose to drown out the cries of the plundered people with the uproar of a sham battle over the tariff, so that capitalists, corporations, national banks, rings, trusts, watered stock, demonetization of silver and the oppression of the usurers may all be lost sight of. They propose to sacrifice our homes, lives and children on the altar of mammon; to destroy the multitude in order to secure corruption funds from millionaires. . . .

We pledge ourselves that if given power we will labor to correct these evils by wise and reasonable legislation in accordance with the terms of our platform. . . .

We declare, therefore:

1. That the union of the Labor forces of the United States this day consummated shall be permanent and perpetual. May its spirit enter into all hearts for the salvation of the republic and the uplifting of mankind.

2. Wealth belongs to him who creates it, and every dollar taken from industry without an equivalent is robbery. "If any will not work, neither shall he eat." The interests of rural and civic labor are the same; their enemies are identical.

3. We believe that the time has come when railroad corporations will either own the people or the people must own the railroads. . . .

We demand a national currency, safe sound and flexible, issued by the general governments only, a full legal tender for all debts, public and private, and that without the use of banking corporations; a just, equitable and efficient means of distribution direct to the people at a tax not to exceed 2 percent per annum be provided as set forth in the sub-treasury plan of the Farmers' Alliance, or some better system. . . .

We demand the free and unlimited coinage of silver and gold at the present legal ratio of 16 to 1.

We demand that the amount of the circulating medium be speedily increased to not less than fifty dollars per capita.

We demand a graduated income tax.

We believe that the money of the country should be kept as much as possible in the hands of the people, and hence we

"Leaving the Party"

Leaving the Democratic or Republican Party for the Populist Party was often an agonizing decision. Political parties were an important source of identity for men in the Gilded Age, and party loyalty was considered to be a positive masculine trait. Moreover, in the South, the Democratic Party was traditionally the white man's party. To leave the party not only meant being branded a "race traitor," but many white Southerners also feared that a third party would split the ranks of white voters and open up the way for black Republicans to be elected and rule the South. The following Populist song "Leaving the Party" explains why—despite tradition and previous loyalty—many turned their backs on the "old party."

I've worked for my old party,
I've toiled for many an hour,
I used to say we'd have good times
Whenever we got in power;
But now I've been taught better,
They've but increased the fetter,
They've broken every promise,
And I will go.

I'm going to leave the party,
I'll stay with it no longer.
I'll help the money power to overthrow,
I'll join the People's Party,
Support it true and hearty,
It labors for the people,
And I will, too.

Old party politicians
Are faithless, drunk or sober;
It took them nearly thirty years
To learn the war is over.
They rave about the tariff,
But little do they care if
They only get the offices,
High or low.

They both submit to Wall street,
And do just as they plan it.
And then aver they had no hand
In bringing on a panic.
No cash in circulation,
And still they tell the nation
The law which made the money
Must be no more.

They work so well together,
We're going now to leave them.
There's nothing the old parties have
That ever can retrieve them.
The court house rings control them
Their party leaders sold them
They're rotten to the core,
We'll let them go.

Why does a Southern Democrat leave his party and come to ours? Because his industrial condition is pitiably bad; because he struggles against a system of laws which have almost filled him with despair, because he is told that he is without clothing because he produces too much cotton and without food because he is too plentiful, because he sees everybody growing rich off the products of labor except the laborer, because the millionaires who manage the Democratic Party have contemptuously ignored his plea for a redress of grievances and have nothing to say to him beyond the cheerful advice to "work harder and live closer."

—Tom Watson, "The Negro Question in the South," 1892

demand, that all state and national revenues shall be limited to the necessary expenses of the government economically and honestly administered. . . .

Transportation being a means of exchange and a public necessity, the government should own and operate the railroads in the interest of the people. The telegraph and the telephone, like the postal system, being a necessity for the transmission of news, should be owned and operated by the government in the interest of the people.

The land, including all the natural sources of wealth, is the heritage of all the people and should not be monopolized for speculative purposes, and alien ownership of land should be prohibited. All lands now held by railroads and other corporations in excess of their actual needs, and all lands now owned by aliens should be reclaimed by the government and held for actual settlers only.

Populist Tom Watson suggested a new answer to the perennial "Negro Question" of the Gilded Age South. In this controversial piece he demanded a rejection of race-based politics, which divided black and white farmers, and forcefully argued instead the common economic concerns that bound black and white farmers in a struggle against exploitation.

The white people of the South will never support the Republican Party. This much is certain. The black people of the South will never support the Democratic Party. This is equally certain.

Hence, at the very beginning, we are met by the necessity of new political alliances. As long as the whites remain solidly Democratic, the blacks will remain solidly Republican.

As long as there was no choice, except as between the Democrats and the Republicans, the situation of the two races was bound to be one of antagonism. . . .

The two races can never act together permanently, harmoniously, beneficially, till each race demonstrates to the other a readiness to leave old party affiliations and to form new ones, based upon the profound conviction that, in acting together, both races are seeking new laws which will benefit both. On no other basis under heaven can the "Negro Question" be solved.

Now, suppose the colored man were educated upon these questions just as the whites have been; suppose he were shown that his poverty and distress came from the same source as ours; suppose

we should convince him that our platform principles assure him an escape from the ills he now suffers and guarantee him the fair measure of prosperity his labor entitles him to receive—would he not act just as the white Democrat who joined us did? . . .

Now let us illustrate: Suppose two tenants on my farm; one of them white, the other black. They cultivate their crops precisely by the same conditions. Their labors, discouragements, burdens, grievances are the same.

The white tenant is driven by cruel necessity to examine into the causes of his continued destitution. He reaches certain conclusions which are not complimentary to either of the old parties. He leaves the Democracy in angry disgust. He joins the People's Party. Why? Simply because its platform recognizes that he is badly treated and proposes to fight his battle. Necessity drives him from the old party, and hope leads him into the new. . . .

Now go back to the colored tenant. His surroundings being the same and his interests the same, why is it impossible for him to reach the same conclusions? Why is it unnatural for him to go into the new party at the same time and with the same motives?

Cannot these two men act together in peace when the ballot of one is a vital benefit to the other? Will not political friendship be born of the necessity and the hope which is common to both? Will not race bitterness disappear before this common suffering and this mutual desire to escape it? Will not each of these citizens feel more kindly for the other when the vote of each defends the home of both? If the white man becomes convinced that the Democratic Party has played upon his prejudices and has used his quiescence to the benefit of interests adverse to his own, will he not despise the leaders who seek to perpetuate the system? . . .

The question of social equality does not enter into the calculation at all. That is a thing each citizen decides for himself. . . .

The conclusion then, seems to me to be this: the crushing burdens which now oppress both races in the South will cause each to make an effort to cast them off. They will see a similarity of cause and a similarity of remedy. They will recognize that each should help the other in the work of repealing bad laws and enacting good ones. They will become political allies, and neither can injure the other without weakening both. It will be to the interest of both that each should have justice. And on these broad lines of mutual interest, mutual forbearance, and mutual support the present will be made the stepping-stone to future peace and prosperity.

Woman Suffrage

Populists in the West enthusiastically supported the right of women to vote. Populist state conventions in Idaho, Kansas, Oregon, South Dakota, and Washington included woman suffrage in their party platforms. As Populists were elected to state legislatures, they attempted to pass measures granting the vote to women. But in every state except Colorado, which passed woman suffrage in 1893, Republican and Democratic legislators stymied the efforts of Populists to give women the vote.

Election 1896

William Jennings Bryan of Nebraska was a staunch Silverite, who believed that the farmers' economic problems could be solved with an unlimited coinage of silver to expand the money supply. Sympathetic to the plight of America's farmers, he won the nomination for President on the Democratic ticket in 1896. Two weeks later, the Populists met to nominate their Presidential ticket. After fervent debate, the Populists chose to back Bryan, forming an alliance with the Democrats, but ran their own candidate for Vice President, Tom Watson.

Bryan won the Democratic nomination after giving a stirring address, known as "The Cross of Gold Speech," named after a famous line in the speech. The following is an excerpt, in which Bryan passionately defends downtrodden Westerners and farmers against those in the party who viewed Bryan and the Silverite Democrats as dangerous.

Ah, my friends, we say not one word against those who live upon the Atlantic coast, but the hardy pioneers who have braved all the dangers of the wilderness, who have made the desert to blossom as the rose—the pioneers away out there (pointing to the West), who rear their children near to Nature's heart, where they can mingle their voices with the voices of the birds—out there where they have erected schoolhouses for the education of their young, churches where they praise their Creator, and cemeteries where rest the ashes of their dead—these people, we say, are as deserving of the consideration of our party as any people in this country. It is for these that we speak. We do not come as aggressors. Our war is not a war of conquest; we are fighting in the defense of our homes, our families, and posterity. We have petitioned, and our petitions have been scorned; we have entreated, and our entreaties have been disregarded; we have begged, and they have mocked when our calamity came. We beg no longer; we entreat no more; we petition no more. We defy them. . . .

They tell us that this platform was made to catch votes. We reply to them that changing conditions make new issues; that the principles upon which Democracy rests are as everlasting as the hills, but that they must be applied to new conditions as they arise. Conditions have arisen, and we are here to meet these conditions. . . .

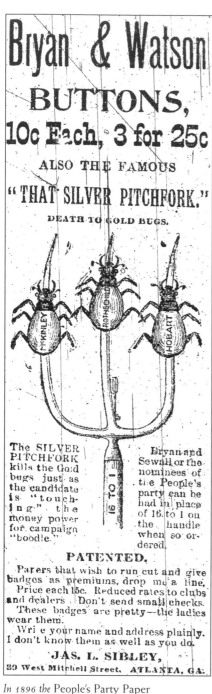

In 1896 the People's Party Paper *offered these Bryan and Watson campaign buttons for a dime, showing "goldbugs," including McKinley, skewered on a farmer's silver pitchfork.*

And now, my friends, let me come to the paramount issue. If they ask us why it is that we say more on the money question than we say upon the tariff question, I reply that, if protection has slain its thousands, the gold standard has slain tens of thousands. If they ask us why we do not embody in our platform all the things that we believe in, we reply that when we have restored the money of the Constitution all other necessary reforms will be possible; but that until this is done there is no other reform that can be accomplished. . . .

We go forth confident that we shall win. Why? Because upon the paramount issue of this campaign there is not a spot of ground upon which the enemy will dare to challenge battle. . . .

You come to us and tell us that the great cities are in favor of the gold standard; we reply that the great cities rest upon our broad and fertile prairies. Burn down your cities and leave our farms, and your cities will spring up again as if by magic; but destroy our farms and the grass will grow in the streets of every city in the country.

My friends, we declare that this nation is able to legislate for its own people on every question, without waiting for the aid or consent of any other nation on earth; and upon that issue we expect to carry every State in the Union. . . . It is the issue of 1776 over again. Our ancestors, when but three millions in number, had the courage to declare their political independence of every other nation; shall we, their descendants, when we have grown to seventy millions, declare that we are less independent than our forefathers? No, my friends, that will never be the verdict of our people. Therefore, we care not upon what lines the battle is fought. If they say bimetallism is good, but that we cannot have it until other nations help us, we reply that, instead of having a gold standard because England has, we will restore bimetallism, and then let England have bimetallism because the United States has it. If they dare to come out in the open field and defend the gold standard as a good thing, we will fight them to the uttermost. Having behind us the producing masses of this nation and the world, supported by the commercial interests, the laboring interests, and the toilers everywhere, we will answer their demand for a gold standard by saying to them: "You shall not press down upon the brow of labor this crown of thorns, you shall not crucify mankind upon a cross of gold."

Despite the confusion and the painful splits within the Populist Party, the Presidential election of 1896 still stands as

one of the most significant in U.S. history, a contest of two distinctive visions for the nation. William Jennings Bryan, Democrat/Populist candidate, represented the rural population of farmers and small towns. Republican candidate William McKinley, a former congressman and governor of Ohio, represented the interests of big business and industry. Backed by many of the nation's banks, businessmen, and industrialists, McKinley and the Republicans spent as much as $7 million on the campaign. "Dollar Mark" Hanna, a Cleveland industrialist and chairman of the Republican National Committee, raised millions from fellow moneyed men who feared Bryan and the Silverite challenge. John D. Rockefeller's Standard Oil alone contributed $250,000 to McKinley's campaign.

The campaign, according to journalist William Allen White, "took the form of religious frenzy." Bryan launched the first modern Presidential campaign, crisscrossing the country by train. He logged more than 18,000 miles, delivering approximately 600 speeches, sometimes making as many as 20 per day. In the meantime McKinley conducted a traditional campaign, sitting on his front porch in Canton, Ohio, meeting with his powerful supporters and promising them stability and prosperity. Republicans branded Bryan a dangerous revolutionary whose silver scheme would sabotage American prosperity.

McKinley defeated Bryan by more than 600,000 popular votes and overwhelmingly carried the electoral vote, 271 to 176, the most lopsided election since 1872. Nearly all of Bryan's support came from the South and West. Despite its platform of reform, neither Democrats nor Populists managed to build bridges with industrial workers or small farmers in the Northeast; the silver issue simply did not appeal to them as much as McKinley's promise of a "full dinner pail."

The 1896 Presidential election provided endless fodder for political cartoonists. The first cartoon was titled "Political Pirates." This anti-Bryan, anti-Populist cartoon depicts the Populist and Silverite "pirates" taking over the Democratic Party ship. Bryan plays the fiddle while populist organizer Mary Elizabeth Lease appears on the right. She seems to be using her hands to keep the pirates—Populists, who have "hijacked" the Democratic ship—under control. The cartoonist is probably suggesting that the Populist pirates may not

be controllable, and that the alliance between the Populists and Democrats is tenuous and temporary.

This anti-McKinley cartoon entitled "A Man of Mark" shows Republican candidate William McKinley under the thumb of millionaire industrialist Mark Hanna.

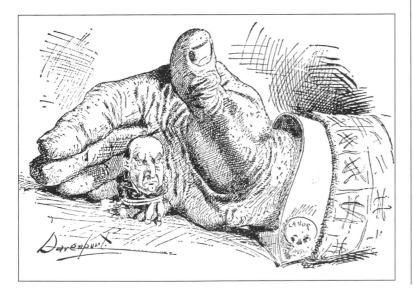

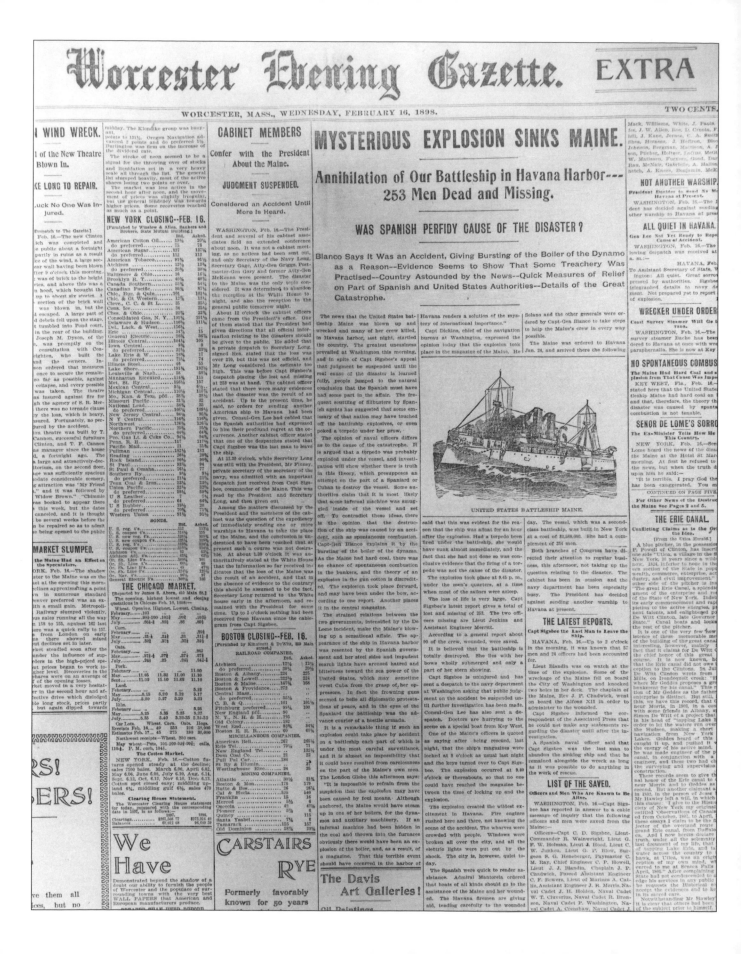

MYSTERIOUS EXPLOSION SINKS MAINE.

Annihilation of Our Battleship in Havana Harbor--- 253 Men Dead and Missing.

WAS SPANISH PERFIDY CAUSE OF THE DISASTER?

Blanco Says It Was an Accident, Giving Bursting of the Boiler of the Dynamo as a Reason--Evidence Seems to Show That Some Treachery Was Practised--Country Astounded by the News--Quick Measures of Relief on Part of Spanish and United States Authorities--Details of the Great Catastrophe.

The news that the United States battleship Maine was blown up and wrecked and many of her crew killed, in Havana harbor, last night, startled the country. The greatest uneasiness prevailed at Washington this morning, and in spite of Capt Sigsbee's appeal that judgment be suspended until the real cause of the disaster is learned fully, people jumped to the natural conclusion that the Spanish must have had some part in the affair. The frequent scuttling of filibusters by Spanish agents has suggested that some emissary of that nation may have touched off the battleship explosives, or even poked a torpedo under her prow.

The opinion of naval officers differs as to the cause of the catastrophe. It is argued that a torpedo was probably exploded under the vessel, and investigation will show whether there is truth in this theory, which presupposes an attempt on the part of a Spaniard or Cuban to destroy the vessel. Some authorities claim that it is most likely that some infernal machine was smuggled inside of the vessel and set off. To contradict these ideas, there is the opinion that the destruction of the ship was caused by an accident, such as spontaneous combustion. Capt-Gen Blanco explains it by the bursting of the boiler of the dynamo. As the Maine had hard coal, there was no chance of spontaneous combustion in the bunkers, and the theory of an explosion in the gun cotton is discredited. The explosion took place forward, and may have been under the bow, according to one report. Another places it in the central magazine.

The strained relations between the two governments, intensified by the De Lome incident, make the Maine's blowing up a sensational affair. The appearance of the ship in Havana harbor was resented by the Spanish government and her steel sides and impudent search lights have aroused hatred and bitterness toward the sea power of the United States, which may sometime wrest Cuba from the grasp of her oppressors. In fact the frowning guns seemed to belie all diplomatic protestations of peace, and in the eyes of the Spaniard the battleship was the advance courier of a hostile armada.

It is a remarkable thing if such an explosion could take place by accident on a battleship each part of which is under the most careful surveillance, and it is almost an impossibility that it could have resulted from carelessness on the part of the Maine's own men. The London Globe this afternoon says:

"It is impossible to refrain from the suspicion that the explosion may have been caused by foul means. Although anchored, the Maine would have steam up in one of her boilers, for the dynamos and auxiliary machinery. If an infernal machine has been hidden in the coal and thrown into the furnaces obviously there would have been an explosion of the boiler, and, as a result of a magazine. That this terrible event should have occurred in the harbor of

Havana renders a solution of the mystery of international importance."

Capt Dickins, chief of the navigation bureau at Washington, expressed the opinion today that the explosion took place in the magazine of the Maine. He said that this was evident for the reason that the ship was afloat for an hour after the explosion. Had a torpedo been fired under the battleship, she would have sunk almost immediately, and the fact that she had not done so was conclusive evidence that the firing of a torpedo was not the cause of the disaster.

The explosion took place at 9.45 p. m., under the men's quarters, at a time when most of the sailors were asleep.

The loss of life is very large. Capt Sigsbee's latest report gives a total of lost and missing of 253. The two officers missing are Lieut Jenkins and Assistant Engineer Merritt.

According to a general report about 90 of the crew, wounded, were saved.

It is believed that the battleship is totally destroyed. She lies with her bows wholly submerged and only a part of her stern showing.

Capt Sigsbee is uninjured and has sent a despatch to the navy department at Washington asking that public judgment on the accident be suspended until further investigation has been made. Consul-Gen Lee has also sent a despatch. Doctors are hurrying to the scene on a special boat from Key West.

One of the Maine's officers is quoted as saying after being rescued, last night, that the ship's magazines were locked at 8 o'clock as usual last night and the keys turned over to Capt Sigsbee. The explosion occurred at 9.40 o'clock or thereabouts, so that no one could have reached the magazine between the time of locking up and the explosion.

The explosion created the wildest excitement in Havana. Fire engines rushed here and there, not knowing the scene of the accident. The wharves were crowded with people. Windows were broken all over the city, and all the electric lights were put out by the shock. The city is, however, quiet today.

The Spanish were quick to render assistance. Admiral Manterola ordered that boats of all kinds should go to the assistance of the Maine and her wounded. The Havana firemen are giving aid, tending carefully to the wounded.

Solano and the other generals were ordered by Capt-Gen Blanco to take steps to help the Maine's crew in every way possible.

The Maine was ordered to Havana Jan. 24, and arrived there the following day. The vessel, which was a second-class battleship, was built in New York at a cost of $2,558,000. She had a complement of 354 men.

Both branches of Congress have directed their attention to regular business, this afternoon, not taking up the question relating to the disaster. The matter has been in session and the navy department has been especially busy. The President has decided against sending another warship to Havana at present.

THE LATEST REPORTS.

Capt Sigsbee the Last Man to Leave the Ship.

HAVANA, Feb. 16.--Up to 2 o'clock in the morning, it was known that 57 men and 24 officers had been accounted for.

Lieut Blandin was on watch at the time of the explosion. Some of the wreckage of the Maine fell on board the City of Washington and knocked two holes in her deck. The chaplain of the Maine, Rev J. P. Chadwick, went on board the Alfonso XII in order to administer to the wounded.

Capt Sigsbee informed the correspondent of the Associated Press that he could not make any statements regarding the disaster until after the investigation.

A Spanish naval officer said that Capt Sigsbee was the last man to abandon the sinking ship and that he remained alongside the wreck as long as it was possible to do anything in the work of rescue.

LIST OF THE SAVED.

Officers and Men Who Are Known to Be Alive.

WASHINGTON, Feb. 16.--Capt Sigsbee has reported in answer to a cable message of inquiry that the following officers and men were saved from the Maine:--

Officers--Capt C. D. Sigsbee, Lieut-Commander R. Wainwright, Lieut G. F. W. Holman, Lieut J. Hood, Lieut C. W. Junken, Lieut G. P. Blow, Lieut G. G. Henebergar, Paymaster C. M. Ray, Chief Engineer C. P. Howell, Lieut J. J. Blandin, Chaplain J. P. Chadwick, Passed Assistant Engineer C. F. Bowers, Lieut of Marines A. Catlin, Assistant Engineer J. R. Morris, Naval Cadet J. H. Holden, Naval Cadet W. T. Cluverius, Naval Cadet R. Bronson, Naval Cadet P. Washington, Naval Cadet A. Crenshaw, Naval Cadet J.

Column 1

...N WIND WRECK.

...1 of the New Theatre Blown In.

...KE LONG TO REPAIR.

...Luck No One Was Injured.

[Despatch to The Gazette.]

...Feb. 16.--The new Clinton ...ich was completed and ...e public about a fortnight ...partly in ruins as a result ...ce of the wind, a large section ...ear wall having been blown ...fter 9 o'clock this morning. ...was of brick to the height ...ries, and above this was a ...n hood, which brought the ...up to about six stories. A ...section of the brick wall ...d escaped. A large part of ...d debris fell upon the stage, ...t tumbled into Pond court. ...in the rear of the building. ...Joseph M. Dyson, of the ...e, was promptly on the ...consultation with Con-...eighton, who built the ...and the owners. In-...son ordered that insurance ...once to secure the remain-...es far as possible, against ...collapse, and every possible ...was taken. The theatre ...as insured against fire for ...the agency of S. R. Mer-...there was no tornado clause ...y the loss, which is heavy, ...sured. Fortunately, as per-...pared by the accident.

...n theatre was built by T. ...Cannon, successful furniture ...Clinton, and T. F. Cannon ...as manager since the house ...d, a fortnight ago. It ...a large and attractively-dec-...atorium, on the second floor, ...age was sufficiently spacious ...odate considerable scenery. ...g attraction was "My Friend ..." and it was followed by ...Widow Brown." "Chimmie ...was booked to appear there ...this week, but the dates ...canceled, and it is thought ...be several weeks before the ...n be repaired so as to admit ...being opened to the public

MARKET SLUMPED.

the Maine Had an Effect on the Speculators.

...YORK, Feb. 16.--The shadow ...ster to the Maine was on the ...ket at the opening this morn-...clines approaching a point ...n in numerous financial ...enver preferred was an ex-...ith a small gain. Metropoli-...Railway slumped violently. ...us sales running all the way ...n 158 to 155, against 162 last ...ere was a quick rally to 157. ...s from London on early ...un there showed mixed ...rket declines set in later. ...rket steadied soon after the ...under the influence of sup-...rders in the high-priced spec-...ut prices began to work to-...lower level. Recoveries in the ...shares were on an average of ...of the opening losses. ...rket moved on a very hesitat-...er in the second hour and af-...fective drive which dislodged ...ble long stock, prices partly ...but again dipped towards

...ve them all ...ces, but no

Column 2

...bidday. The Klondike group was buoyant, ...points to 151½. Oregon Navigation advanced 2 points and do preferred 1½. Burlington was firm on the increase of the dividend rate.

The stroke of noon seemed to be a signal for the throwing over of stocks and liquidation set in a very heavy scale all through the list. The general list slumped heavily, most of the active shares losing two points or over.

The market was less active in the second hour after noon, and the movement of prices was slightly irregular, but the general tendency was towards higher prices. Some recoveries reached as much as a point.

NEW YORK CLOSING--FEB. 16.

[Furnished by Winslow & Allen, Bankers and Brokers, State Mutual Building.]

	Bid.	Asked.
American Cotton Oil	19¾	20¼
do preferred	75	78
American Sugar	137	137¼
do preferred	112	113
American Tobacco	91½	91½
Atchison	12½	13¾
do preferred	30½	30¾
Baltimore & Ohio	16	16½
Brooklyn R. T.	46½	46¾
Canada Southern	51¾	54¾
Canadian Pacific	86½	87¼
Chic., Bur. & Quin	101	101¼
Chic. & Gt. Western	13½	13½
Cleve., C. C. & St L.	35	36½
Cons. Ice	25	25¾
Ches. & Ohio	21½	22½
Consolidated Gas, N. Y.	191¼	191½
Delaware & Hudson	110½	111½
Del., Lack. & West.	156½	
Erie	14¼	15
General Electric	34½	36½
Illinois Central	104½	105
Iowa Central	8½	9
do preferred	34½	35
Lake Erie & W	15½	17
do preferred	73½	74
Illinois Steel		65
Lake Shore	191¼	192½
Louisville & Nash	55½	55¾
Manhattan Elevated	114½	115
Met. St. Ry.	156½	157
Mexican Central	8½	6½
Michigan Central	110½	111½
Mo., Kan. & Tex. pfd.	33½	33½
Missouri Pacific	31½	32
National Lead	34½	35
do preferred	105¼	105½
New Jersey Central	94½	95
N Y Central	115½	116½
Northwest	126¾	126½
Northern Pacific	25¾	25¾
do preferred	64¾	64¾
Peo. Gas Lt. & Coke Co.	94½	94¾
Penn. R.	117	117½
Pacific Mail	31¾	31¾
Pullman	182½	183
Reading	20½	20½
Rock Island	90½	90½
St Paul	92¾	94
St Paul & Omaha	76½	77
Southern Ry	8½	9½
do preferred	31½	31½
Tenn Coal & Iron	23½	23¾
Union Pacific	22½	22¾
do preferred	59½	59¾
U S Leather	5¾	6¼
do preferred	64	64¾
U S Rubber	7¾	8¾
do preferred	39½	39¾
Western Union	91½	91½

BONDS.

	Bid.	Asked.
U. S. reg. 4's	...½	...½
U. S. coupon 4's	111½	111¼
U. S. new 4's	123½	123¼
U. S. new coupon 4's	123½	123¼
U. S. reg. 3's	111½	111½
U. S. coupon 3's	112	112½
Atchison 4's	82½	83
Atchison Adj. 4's	73	73½
So. Ry. 5's	93½	94
Or. S. Line 6's	111½	
Or. S. Line 5's	112½	
Or. Nav. 4's	100½	
Or. Nav. 4's		
General Electric 5's	92½	

THE CHICAGO MARKET.

[Reported by James S. Aborn, 415 Main St.]
The opening, highest lowest and closing quotations in Chicago Feb. 16, 1898:--
Wheat, Corn, Oats, Pork.

	Opening.	Highest.	Lowest.	Closing.
February	.103			
May	.102½	.100½	.100	.100½
July	.90½-8	.90½	.90½	.90½

Corn.

February				.30½
May	.31½	.31½	.31½	.31½-2
July	.33½	.33½	.33¼	.33¼

Oats.

February				..½
May	.27½-½	.27½	.27½	.27½
July	.24½	.25	.24½	.24½

Pork.

February				11.00
May	11.85	11.92	11.80	11.80
July	11.09	11.10	11.08	11.10

Lard.

February				..½
May	6.15	6.30	6.12	6.17
July	5.27	5.27	5.20	5.25

Ribs.

February				..½
May	5.35	5.35	5.35	5.35
July	5.35	5.40	5.35-35	5.32-35

Car Lots.   Wheat. Corn. Oats. Hogs.
Receipts Feb. 16... 253   138 36,000
Estimates Feb. 17... 45   273   130 20,000
Northwest receipts--Wheat, 250 cars.
May wheat--Puts, 101-100-99½-99½; calls, 130¼. P. M. curb, 100½.

The Cotton Market.

NEW YORK, Feb. 16.--Cotton futures opened steady at the close. Sales 7100 bales. March 6.00, April 6.02, May 6.06, June 6.08, July 6.10, Aug. 6.14, Sept. 6.13, Oct. 6.13, Nov. 6.10, Dec. 6.13. Cotton spot closed easy; middling uplands 6½, middling gulf 6½, sales 470 bales.

Clearing House Statement.

The Worcester Clearing House statement for today, compared with the corresponding date in 1897, is as follows:--
	1898.	1897.
Clearings	$297,580 77	$273,301 49
Balances	68,612 08	96,640 29

Column 3

CABINET MEMBERS

Confer with the President About the Maine.

JUDGMENT SUSPENDED.

Considered an Accident Until More Is Heard.

WASHINGTON, Feb. 16.--The President and several of his cabinet associates held an extended conference about noon. It was not a cabinet meeting, as no notices had been sent out, and only Secretary of the Navy Long, Secretary Gage, Atty-Gen Griggs, Postmaster-Gen Gary and former Atty-Gen McKenna were present. The disaster to the Maine was the only topic considered. It was determined to abandon the reception at the White House tonight, and also the reception to the general public tomorrow night.

About 12 o'clock the cabinet officers came from the President's office. One of them stated that the President had given directions that all official information relating to the disasters should be given to the public. He added that a private despatch to Secretary Long, signed Hea, stated that the loss was over 270, but this was not official, and Mr Long considered the estimate too high. This was before Capt Sigsbee's despatch placing the lost and missing at 253 was at hand. The cabinet officer stated that there were many evidences that the disaster was the result of an accident. Up to the present time, he said, no orders for sending another American ship to Havana had been given. Consul-Gen Lee had cabled that the Spanish authorities had expressed to him their profound regret at the occurrence. Another cabinet officer stated that one of the despatches stated that Capt Sigsbee was the last man to leave the ship.

At 12.30 o'clock, while Secretary Long was still with the President, Mr Finney, private secretary of the secretary of the navy, was admitted with an important despatch just received from Capt Sigsbee, commander of the Maine. This was read by the President and Secretary Long, and then given out.

Among the matters discussed by the President and the members of the cabinet was the question of the expediency of immediately sending one or more warships to Havana to take the place of the Maine, and the conclusion is understood to have been reached that at present such a course was not desirable. At about 1.30 o'clock it was authoritatively stated or received indicates that the loss of the Maine was the result of an accident, and that in the absence of evidence to the contrary this should be assumed to be the fact. Secretary Long returned to the White house early in the afternoon, and remained with the President for some time. Up to 2 o'clock nothing had been received from Havana since the cablegram from Capt Sigsbee.

BOSTON CLOSING--FEB. 16.

[Furnished by Kimberly & DeWitt, 359 Main street.]

RAILROAD COMPANIES.
	Bid.	Asked.
Atchison	12½	12¾
do preferred	30½	30½
Boston & Albany	224	225
Boston & Lowell	235	234
Boston & Maine	167½	168
Boston & Providence	272	
Central Mass.		45
do preferred	85½	
C. B. & Q	101	101¼
Fitchburg preferred	93¾	100
New England pfd	90	
N. Y., N. H. & H.	195	
Old Colony	192	
West End	83¾	84¾
Boston E. R. R.	60½	60½

MISCELLANEOUS COMPANIES.
American Bell	267	268½
Erie Tel	78½	71
New England Tel	112½	113¼
Dom Coal Co	21	22
Pull Pal Car		172
St Ry & Illumin		27
Westinghouse Elec	34	35

MINING COMPANIES.
Atlantic	30½	30½
Boston & Mon	178	179
Butte & Bos	6½	6½
Cal & Hecla	325	540
Franklin	15	16
Merced		7
Osceola	81	47½
Pioneer	8½	9
Quincy		115
Santa Ysabel	1½	2
Tamarack	155	157
Old Dominion	28½	29½

We Have

Demonstrated beyond the shadow of a doubt our ability to furnish the people of Worcester and the populace of surrounding towns with the very best WALL PAPERS that American and European manufacturers produce.

CARSTAIRS RYE

Formerly favorably known for 50 years

The Davis Art Galleries!

Column 5 (right)

Mack, Williams, White, J. Paus..., J. W. Alden, Roy D. Cronin, F..., bill, J. Kane, Jerees, C. A. Smit..., Shea, Hornes, J. Haffron, Bloo..., Johnson, Bergman, Mathisen, A...., son, Pulcino, Hohner, Julius McG..., W. Mathisen, Furness, Good, Dar..., Rao, McNair, Gabrielle, A. Hallom...

NOT ANOTHER WARSHIP.

President Decides to Send No More Havana at Present.

WASHINGTON, Feb. 16.--The President has decided against sending another warship to Havana at present.

ALL QUIET IN HAVANA.

Gen Lee Not Yet Ready to Report Cause of Accident.

WASHINGTON, Feb. 16.--The following despatch was received at ... a. m.:--

HAVANA, Feb...

To Assistant Secretary of State, Washington: All quiet. Great sorrow expressed by authorities. Sigsbee telegraphed details to navy department. Not prepared yet to report of explosion.

WRECKER UNDER ORDERS

Coast Survey Steamer Will Go to Havana.

WASHINGTON, Feb. 16.--The coast survey steamer Bache has been ordered to Havana at once with wrecking paraphernalia. She is now at Key...

NO SPONTANEOUS COMBUS...

The Maine Had Hard Coal and an Explosion from That Cause Was Impossible.

KEY WEST, Fla., Feb. 16.--It is stated here that the United States battleship Maine had hard coal on board and that, therefore, the theory that the disaster was caused by spontaneous combustion is not tenable.

SENOR DE LOME'S SORROW

The Ex-Minister Tells How He Heard This Country.

NEW YORK, Feb. 16.--Senor De Lome heard the news of the disaster to the Maine at the Hotel St Marc this morning. At first he refused to discuss the news, but when the truth of it was pressed upon him he said:--

"It is terrible. I pray God the news has been exaggerated. You m...

CONTINUED ON PAGE FIVE.

For Other News of the Destruction of the Maine See Pages 2 and 5.

THE ERIE CANAL.

Conflicting Claims as to the Origin of the Idea.

[From the Utica Herald.]

A blue pitcher, in the possession of P. Powell of Clinton, has inscribed on one side "Utica, a village in the State of New York, 30 years since a wilderness, 1824, inferior to none in the western section of the State in population, wealth, commerce, enterprise, industry, and civil improvement," The other side of the pitcher is the greatest Erie Canal, a splendid monument of the enterprise and energy of the State of New York. Indeed the early commencement and rapid completion of the active energies, patient talents, and enlightened policy of De Witt Clinton, late Governor of State." Canal boats and locks decorate the rest of the pitcher.

It is one of the very few relics in existence of these memorials of the building of the great canal interesting, however, inspiring the fact that it claims for De Witt Clinton the chief honor of the great course. It is now known, however, that the Erie canal did not owe its inception to the Clintons. In July, De Witt Clinton wrote from Mills, on Irondequoit creek: "At where Mr Geddes proposes a great embankment he his canal." There is distinct. But still, this, we have this record, that from near Morris, in 1801, in a conversation with some friends in Albany, at Simon De Witt of a project that in his head of "tapping Lake E... order to let the waters run over the Hudson, making a short navigation from New York L... Geddes heard of this caught it up, and passed it for the energy of his active mind... he was made engineer of the ... canal, in conjunction with ... engineer, and these two had ... the surveying and supervision ... construction.

These records seem to give ... nal honor of the Erie canal to ... now Morris and to Geddes ... record. But another claimant ... in 1822, in the person of Jesse ... Mr Hawley left it will, in which ... this claim "I give to the Histo... city of New York my original ... entitled 'Observations of Cana...' ed from October, 1807, to April, ... these essays I claim to be the first ... jector of the internal route ... grand Erie canal, from Buffalo ... on. And I now herein declare... truth, under all the solemnity... last document of my life, that ... of tapping Lake Erie, and the ... water across the country to ... hawk, at Utica, as an original... ception of my own mind, we... curred to me at Senica Falls ... April, 1807." After complaining ... State had not condescended to ... edge his services in any public ... he requests the Historical Society ... accept the evidences and to ... in the sacred care.

Notwithstanding Mr Hawley ... it is clear that others had hint... of the subject prior to himself...

Chapter Nine

The United States Builds an Empire

In late February 1898, Assistant Secretary of the Navy Theodore Roosevelt felt restless and frustrated. Ten days before, on February 15, the American battleship *Maine* exploded in the harbor of Havana, Cuba, killing 260 men aboard. Roosevelt, like many startled Americans, blamed the disaster on Spain, calling the explosion "an act of dirty treachery on the part of the Spanish." Cuban revolutionaries had been locked in a bitter struggle for independence from Spain, a nation unwilling to cede the last significant possession of its once great empire. For three years Spain had responded with the brutal repression of Cuban rebels. Most Americans sympathized with the plight of the Cuban revolutionaries, comparing it to their own fight for independence from Great Britain. Moreover, American businessmen had invested $50 million in Cuba, much of it in the island's sugar industry. In addition, newspaper rivals William Randolph Hearst and Joseph Pulitzer provoked widespread public sympathy for the Cubans, publishing sensational stories about Spanish atrocities, each attempting to outdo the other.

To the chagrin of Roosevelt, President William McKinley insisted on maintaining a neutral position. Despite massive public pressure to intervene on behalf of the Cuban revolutionaries and to retaliate for the explosion of the *Maine*, McKinley hesitated. A veteran of the Civil War, McKinley told an aide, "I have been through one war. I have seen the dead piled up, and I do not want to see another."

Theodore Roosevelt, a child during the Civil War, severely criticized the President, declaring that McKinley had "no more backbone than a chocolate eclair." For years Roosevelt had happily anticipated an American war, especially one that would expand the nation's global power. To Roosevelt and many other men of his generation, war

provided a long-awaited sense of fulfillment. Deeply influenced by social Darwinism and careful observation of the growing world empires of Great Britain, Germany, and Japan, Roosevelt and many of his compatriots believed that without a willingness to compete and fight with other nations to build an empire, the United States would decline. Additionally, by the 1890s, Roosevelt and many other social critics believed that Americans seemed to be getting "soft" and "over-civilized," and the country might be deteriorating. They stressed strenuous activity to counter this apparent degeneration. Roosevelt argued that "if we lose the virile, manly qualities and sink into a nation of mere hucksters, putting gain above everything to mere ease of life; then we shall indeed reach a condition worse than that of the ancient civilizations in the years of their decay."

War with Spain would not only provide an antidote to a U.S. decline but would also firmly establish the young nation as a world power. In the aftermath of the *Maine* disaster, Roosevelt pleaded for war. He even suggested that McKinley refuse to have the explosion investigated just in case the Spanish were not responsible. In the meantime, in April 1898, the Spanish, fearful of the growing belligerence of the United States, announced a cease-fire and sent a message to the State Department in which Spain, for all intents and purposes, surrendered. The United States would be allowed to determine the terms of the settlement, and Cuba would be granted independence.

Unfortunately Spain's offer came too late. The following day President McKinley asked Congress's approval to commit U.S. troops to Cuba. Having managed to resist public pressure for two months after the *Maine* disaster, McKinley, fearing disastrous elections in the fall, finally bowed to the overwhelming outcry for war. He also succumbed to pressure from business interests seeking a quick end to the conflict in Cuba. McKinley and Congress chose to engage in a war rather than pursue the peaceful settlement at hand.

Theodore Roosevelt enthusiastically jumped at the chance to go to war, an opportunity for which he had been preparing his entire life. He later admitted, "I now know that I would have turned from my wife's deathbed to have answered the call." Roosevelt organized the First Volunteer Cavalry Regiment, soon to be known as the "Rough Riders," made up of several hundred cowboys—and even some Indians—from the West, several New York City policemen, and Ivy League athletes. The Rough Riders and other American soldiers embarked for Cuba in mid-June 1898.

In Cuba Theodore Roosevelt would win his long-sought military honor. He led the Rough Riders, who were on foot, along with several black cavalry units, to glory near San Juan Hill in Santiago in July 1898. The Rough Riders' exploits were reported widely in the American press. Not humbled by the experience of combat, Roosevelt bragged that he had "doubled up" a Spaniard and enthusiastically guided visitors after the battle to "look at those damned Spanish dead."

The Spanish-American War ended on August 12, 1898, less than four months after it began. Though nearly 275,000 Americans served during the war, only 379 died in battle; however, an additional 5,462 perished from tropical diseases and eating rancid meat.

On one hand, the episode to many Americans did indeed seem to be, in the words of U.S. Ambassador to Great Britain John Hay, "a splendid little war." A dramatic show of U.S. might, the war provided a stunning debut for the nation as a world power. But the war, on the other hand, created a troubling new issue: What should the United States do with the empire it won from Spain? While the conflict was ostensibly about Cuban liberation—which the United States had promised even before entering the war—the victor proved unwilling to liberate Cuba immediately or completely. A U.S. military government ruled Cuba for several years. Then the Platt Amendment, passed by Congress in 1901 and added as an appendix to the new Cuban constitution, restricted Cuba's freedom in several ways: the United States maintained the right to intervene to preserve Cuban independence and required Cuba to sell or lease land for use as U.S. naval stations and coaling bases.

The treaty with Spain also ceded to the United States the former Spanish possessions of Puerto Rico and Guam as well as the Philippines. Puerto Rico, valuable as an American outpost in the Caribbean, and Guam, strategically located in the Pacific, are still U.S. possessions. Their ambiguous and often complicated relationships with the United States are still a source of political controversy.

Theodore Roosevelt and his volunteer regiment, the Rough Riders, became instant American heroes in July 1898 after the American press publicized their charge up Kettle Hill, as part of the battle for nearby San Juan Hill in the Spanish-American War. Roosevelt called the battle "the great day of my life."

Reconciliation

The Spanish-American War provided the first opportunity since the Civil War for Northerners and Southerners to fight side by side as a united nation. The first soldier to die in battle was a white Southerner, Worth Bagley of North Carolina. Both Northern and Southern newspapers extolled Bagley's death as a symbol of a reconciled nation.

The Philippines—on the other side of the globe—did not even enter in the debate over war with Spain in the spring of 1898. But these islands would become one of the war's most troubling and divisive legacies—largely because of the actions of Roosevelt. Ten days after the *Maine* blew up in Havana harbor, Assistant Secretary of the Navy Roosevelt sent a telegram to Commodore George Dewey in Hong Kong, ordering him to engage the Spanish in the Philippines if and when the United States declared war on Spain. In a typically bold and independent move, Roosevelt sent these orders without consulting his boss, the secretary of the navy—who had taken the day off— or the President. In late April, after the United States declared war on Spain, Dewey's fleet destroyed the Spanish fleet in Manila Bay; by mid-August, with the aid of Filipino rebels who, like their Cuban counterparts, sought independence from Spain, American forces entered Manila, just after the United States agreed to an armistice with Spain.

Even though President McKinley admitted that initially he could not even find the Philippines on a map, he concluded that the islands should be made a colony of the United States. He justified the colonization of the Philippines with an elaborate rationale that combined the "responsibility" and "Christian duty" of the United States with economic self-interest. While Spanish negotiators protested that U.S. forces did not even enter Manila until after Spain had surrendered, McKinley stood firm. Attempting to placate the Spanish, U.S. negotiators offered them $20 million in compensation as part of the final settlement.

The value of the Philippines as an American colony seemed clear to expansionists such as McKinley and Roosevelt. The islands provided a base of operations in the Pacific and access to new markets for American goods—a special concern after the disastrous depression of the 1890s. In addition the acquisition of this strategically located colony also enhanced the position of the United States as a world power. Other Americans, however, were deeply troubled by the idea of the United States having colonies. How could a nation, they asked, founded on ideals of independence and self-determination become an imperial power without undermining its own principles? Why did the United States free Cuba but maintain a colonial grip on the Philippines? What were the financial and moral costs of maintaining an empire on the other side of the world?

After bitter debate the Senate ratified a treaty with Spain in 1899 that imposed colonial status on the Philippines. But the

United States was already enmeshed in an ugly war with Filipinos who, under the leadership of Emilio Aguinaldo, fought to free themselves of American domination. This war of attrition, which lasted for four years and cost well over 100,000 lives, symbolized the steep price of empire building.

Theodore Roosevelt used the Spanish-American War as a springboard to an illustrious career largely devoted to the expansion of U.S. global power. His highly publicized exploits as a Rough Rider and war hero led him to the governorship of New York and eventually to the Vice Presidency and Presidency of the United States. As President, Roosevelt's philosophy, "Speak softly and carry a big stick," defined the nation's new role as "the world's policeman," establishing at the dawn of the 20th century a commitment to interventionism with which Americans still struggle.

The Spanish-American War

In his autobiography, Theodore Roosevelt explained his enthusiastic support for the war with Spain.

Soon after I began work as Assistant Secretary of the Navy, I became convinced that the war would come. The revolt in Cuba had dragged its weary length until conditions had become so dreadful as to be a standing disgrace to us for permitting them to exist. There is much that I sincerely admire about the Spanish character; and there are few men for whom I have felt greater respect than for certain gentlemen of Spain whom I have known. But Spain attempted to govern her colonies on archaic principles which rendered her control of them incompatible with the advance of humanity and intolerable to the conscience of mankind. In 1898 the so-called war in Cuba had dragged along for years with unspeakable horror, degradation, and misery. It was not "war" at all, but murderous oppression. Cuba was devastated.

During those years, while we continued at "peace," several hundred times as many lives were lost, lives of men, women, and children, as were lost during the three months' "war" which put an end to this slaughter and opened a career of peaceful progress to the Cubans. Yet there were misguided professional philanthropists who cared so much more for names than for facts that they preferred a "peace" of continuous murder to a "war" which stopped the murder and brought real peace. Spain's humiliation was certain, anyhow; indeed, it was more certain without war than with it, for

Theodore Roosevelt poses before a globe, symbolically representing his—and America's—entry upon the world stage by the turn of the century.

she could not permanently keep the island, and she minded yield-ing to the Cubans more than yielding to us. Our own direct inter-ests were great, because of the Cuban tobacco and sugar, and especially because of Cuba's relation to the projected Isthmian canal. But even greater were our interests from the standpoint of humanity. Cuba was at our very doors. It was a dreadful thing for us to sit supinely and watch her death agony. It was our duty, even more from the standpoint of National honor than from the stand-point of National interest, to stop the devastation and destruction. Because of these considerations I favored war; and to-day, when in retrospect it is easier to see things clearly, there are few humane and honorable men who do not believe that the war was both just and necessary.

Many African Americans supported U.S. intervention to lib-erate Cuba. They identified the Cuban struggle against Spain as the fight of people of color against white European domi-nation. Some black Americans even viewed Cuba as a racial utopia, especially when compared to the South in the 1890s, and they dreamed of emigrating to a free Cuba. Others, how-ever, questioned whether—in an age of deteriorating race relations in the United States—blacks should fight for a gov-ernment that seemed unconcerned about their rights as citi-zens. The Reverend H. H. Proctor delivered this sermon in Atlanta on May 1, 1898, soon after the United States declared war on Spain. He responds to black critics of the war and encourages African Americans to seize the opportunity it might afford to improve their status at home.

Let me state plainly the position I take. In answering the question what attitude the Negro should take in this crisis, I say it should be that of loyalty to the Stars and Stripes. . . .

It is said that this is a white man's war, and, therefore, let the white fight it out. I reject the conclusion because I cannot accept the premise. This is not a white man's war; it is the nation's war. . . . If you say this is a white man's war, then you are bound to accept the doctrine that this is a white man's country. If it is a white man's country, then the black man has no place in it, and consequently no rights that a white man is bound to respect. This is God's coun-try, and it belongs to the people in it, be they black or white, red or yellow.

It is said that we are wrongly treated and therefore should sulk in our tents. I admit that we are wronged. God knows that. Call

over the catalogue of wrongs and which if them are we not heir to? But in my mind this constitutes a reason why we should be loyal. If in this critical hour we should be disloyal, would that not serve as a justification in the eyes of our enemies for all the wrongs inflicted upon us? "We told you these people were unworthy of better treatment," would be the cry. On the other hand, have we not fine opportunity to show the world that we deserve better than we receive? And would not such action tell on public sentiment in the future? . . .

It is said that we have fought for this country, and it treats us no better now; let the white man fight it out themselves. It is true we have fought in every war; but has the motive of our action been beyond cavil? Is it not said that we fought in 1776 with the hope of freedom? In 1812 under the inspiration of the lash? In 1863 under the impulse of emancipation? . . For the first time in our American experience we should fight, not as slaves, not as freed men, but as freemen. . . .

The real reason why the duty of the hour demands our loyalty is in this. Our country is engaged in a righteous war. It is a war for larger liberty. The freedom of manhood, the purity of womanhood, the future of childhood—these are in the womb of this struggle. It is an appeal to the highest sentiments. Our country is responding to the call. We are a real part of this country, and nothing that concerns her is without interest to us. We are not Afro-Americans, but Americans to the manor born. There should be no hyphen in American citizenship. If we do not co-operate with our country in this humanitarian movement, will it not indicate that we have not caught the American spirit? Will it not show that those finer feelings and nobler instincts that move others, that are moving this whole nation, do not appeal to us? I know there are no people richer in feeling and finer in instincts than the culture of the race I speak to tonight. The remembrance of our sad past and the Mighty Hand that delivered us but adds to our natural fitness to sympathize with the people of Cuba and their struggle to throw off the yoke that galls and dash in pieces the cup that is bitter.

We must not overlook our splendid opportunities in this crisis . . . . Shall we nurse our wrongs, treasure our resentments, exercise our vengeance, and thus lose our venture? I cannot believe that we shall permit our grievance to overshadow our opportunities. . . .

As the United States and Spain negotiated a treaty with Spain in the fall of 1898, Sen. Albert J. Beveridge, along with many

Black Soldiers in the Spanish-American War

Although African Americans debated whether they should support the war with Spain, more than 10,000 black men volunteered for military service, and 5 were awarded the Medal of Honor. Among the first troops to be mobilized for the war were the Buffalo Soldiers stationed in the western United States.

Participation in the war did not shield black soldiers from racial incidents and second-class treatment. In early June 1898, as black and white troops assembled in Tampa, preparing to embark for Cuba, a riot broke out when some intoxicated white soldiers grabbed a two-year-old black child from his mother and held him up for target practice. One white soldier shot a bullet through the child's sleeve. Black soldiers of the 24th and 25th Infantries, already frustrated and angry over their treatment in the Jim Crow South, responded by clashing with white civilians and soldiers.

At San Juan Hill, the battle that catapulted Theodore Roosevelt and the Rough Riders to national fame, the Buffalo Soldiers played a key role. One Rough Rider stated, "If it had not been for the Negro cavalry the Rough Riders would have been exterminated." Roosevelt himself initially acknowledged the valor of the black soldiers. But they never received the same publicity as the Rough Riders. Moreover, several years later, the black cavalrymen suffered further humiliation when Roosevelt, as President, denied that black troops had played any part in saving his regiment in Cuba.

Mexican-American Support

Like black Americans, Mexican Americans were divided over impending war with Spain. Some Spanish-language newspaper editors openly supported Spain; others warned Cubans of American designs to dominate their country. But most Mexican Americans supported the United States once war was declared. Hundreds of Mexican-American men served in the war, among them Maximiliano Luna of New Mexico, a member of the Rough Riders.

Albert Beveridge, senator from Indiana from 1899 to 1911, became a key spokesperson for American imperialism after he gave his speech "The March of the Flag" in September 1898, to kick off his campaign for the Senate. The speech, enthusiastically cheered by those who first heard it, was widely published and was one of the best-known orations of the era.

Americans, enthusiastically embraced the idea of an American empire as the fulfillment of the nation's God-given destiny. While the United States—on the eve of war with Spain—passed the Teller Amendment, denying any claims to Cuba and promising Cuban independence, it was not bound by any promises of freedom for the Philippines and other Spanish possessions taken in the war. In this speech, first given before a political gathering in Indianapolis in September 1898, a month after the end of the Spanish-American War, Beveridge spells out justifications for and visions of an American empire with the Philippines as its centerpiece.

Fellow Citizens: It is a noble land that God has given us; a land that can feed and clothe the world; a land whose coast lines would inclose half the country of Europe; a land set like a sentinel between the two imperial oceans of the globe, a greater England with a nobler destiny. It is a mighty people that He has planted on this soil; a people sprung from the most masterful blood of history; a people perpetually revitalized by the virile, man-producing working folk of all the earth; a people imperial by virtue of their power, by right of their institutions, by authority of their heaven-directed purposes—the propagandists and not the misers of liberty. It is a glorious history our God has bestowed upon His chosen people; a history whose keynote was struck by the Liberty Bell; a history heroic with faith in our mission and our future; a history of statesmen who flung the boundaries of the republic out in unexplored lands and savage wildernesses; a history of soldiers who carried the flag across the blazing deserts and through the ranks of hostile mountains, even to the gates of sunset; a history of a multiplying people who overran a continent in half a century; a history of prophets who saw the consequences of evils inherited from the past, and of martyrs who died to save us from them; a history divinely logical, in the process of whose tremendous reasoning we find ourselves today.

Therefore, in this campaign, the question is larger than a party question. It is an American question. It is a world question. Shall the American people continue their resistless march toward the commercial supremacy of the world? Shall free institutions broaden their blessed reign as the children of liberty wax in strength, until the empire of our principles is established over the hearts of all mankind?

Have we no mission to perform, no duty to discharge to our fellow men? Has the Almighty Father endowed us with gifts

beyond our deserts and marked us as the people of His peculiar favor, merely to rot in our own selfishness, as men and nations must who take cowardice for their companion and self for their deity—as China has, as India has, as Egypt has?

Shall we be as the man who had one talent and hid it, or as he who had ten talents and used them until they grew to riches? And shall we reap the reward that awaits on our discharge of our high duty as the sovereign power of earth; shall we occupy new markets for what our farmers raise, new markets for what our factories make, new markets for what our merchants sell—aye, and, please God, new markets for what our ships shall carry? . . .

What are the great facts of this administration? Not a failure of revenue; not a perpetual battle between the executive and legislative departments of government. . . .

But a war has marked it, the most holy ever waged by one nation against another—a war of civilization, a war for a permanent peace, a war which, under God, although we knew it not, swung open to the republic the portals of the commerce of the world. And the first question you must answer with your vote is whether you indorse that war. . . .

And the burning question of this campaign is, whether the American people will accept the gifts of events; whether they will rise as lofts their soaring destiny; whether they will proceed upon the lines of national development surveyed by the statesmen of our past; or whether, for the first time, the American people doubt their mission, question fate, prove apostate to the spirit of their race, and halt the ceaseless march of free institutions.

The opposition tells us that we ought not to govern a people without their consent. I answer: The rule of liberty, that all just government derives its authority from the consent of the governed, applies only to those who are capable of self-government. I answer: We govern the Indians without their consent, we govern our children without their consent. I answer: How do you assume that our government would be without their consent? Would not the people of the Philippines prefer the just, humane, civilizing government of this republic to the savage, bloody rule of pillage and extortion from which we have rescued them? . . .

And, regardless of this formula of words, made only for enlightened, self-governing peoples, do we owe no duty to the world? Shall we turn these people back to the reeking hands from which we have taken them? Shall we abandon them to their fate, with the wolves of conquest all about them—with Germany, Russia, France, even Japan, hungering for them? Shall we save

Puerto Rico: A Legacy of American Empire

Unlike Cuba and the Philippines, which eventually became free of U.S. control, Puerto Rico remains bound to the United States as a commonwealth—neither independent nor fully integrated as a state. U.S. military forces invaded Puerto Rico in July 1898, during the Spanish-American War. After Spain ceded Puerto Rico, along with Cuba, Guam, and the Philippines, American military authorities ruled Puerto Rico for 18 months, until May 1900. At that time, the U.S. government replaced military rule with a civilian government, dominated by Washington appointees. Unhappy with their lack of political power and U.S. control, many Puerto Ricans petitioned for statehood or some form of self-rule.

In 1917, with passage of the Jones Act, Congress granted Puerto Ricans U.S. citizenship—but not full political rights. The island's government continued to consist largely of Washington appointees, and the U.S. President retained ultimate veto power over legislation.

Control of Puerto Rico by the United States spawned a vigorous independence movement that escalated in the 1930s and 40s. In 1947, in response to unrest in Puerto Rico, Congress passed an amendment to the Jones Act, granting Puerto Ricans permission to elect their government and appoint department heads. In 1948 Luís Muñoz Marín became the first elected governor in Puerto Rico's history. Despite the U.S. government's concessions, the Puerto Rican nationalist movement continued to grow. In 1952 the United States granted Puerto Rico commonwealth status, and Puerto Rico adopted a new constitution. Commonwealth status provided a final measure of internal self-government. It also stipulated that Puerto Rican laws must be consistent with the U.S. Constitution. Puerto Rico immediately adopted its own flag (long a symbol of Puerto Rican nationalism) and its own national anthem.

When Puerto Rico became a commonwealth in 1952, Governor Muñoz Marín suggested that this status was not permanent but a pause on the road to either statehood or independence—a matter that Puerto Ricans would decide. But nearly half a century later, Puerto Rico remains a commonwealth, both connected to and distinct from the United States.

them from those nations, to give them a self-rule of tragedy? It would be like giving a razor to a babe and telling it to shave itself. It would be like giving a typewriter to an Eskimo and telling him to publish one of the great dailies of the world. . . .

Anti-Imperialism

Many Americans vigorously protested the creation of an empire as inconsistent with the nation's history and values. November 19, 1898, saw the founding of the Anti-Imperial League, which soon boasted 25,000 members. The league included some of the nation's most prominent citizens, including W. E. B. Du Bois, Jane Addams, Grover Cleveland, Samuel Gompers, Mark Twain, and Andrew Carnegie, who was one of the leading opponents of building an empire.

Because women were not allowed to hold office in the branch offices of the Anti-Imperial League, they formed their own organization, the Women's Auxiliary of the Anti-Imperialist League. In May 1899 they circulated the following petition.

We, women of the United States, earnestly protest against the war of conquest into which our country has been plunged in the Philippine islands. We appeal to the Declaration of Independence, which is the moral foundation of the constitution you have sworn to defend, and we reaffirm its weighty words:

We hold these truths to be self-evident that all men are created equal [before the law], that they are endowed by their Creator with certain inalienable rights, that among these are life, liberty and the pursuit of happiness; that, to secure these rights, governments are instituted among men, deriving their just powers from the consent of the governed; that, whenever any form of government becomes destructive of those ends, it is the right of the people to alter or abolish it, and to institute new government, laying its foundation on such principles and organizing its powers in such form as to them shall seem most likely to effect their safety and happiness.

And we unqualifiedly approve and support these resolutions of the anti-imperialist league:

First. That our government shall take immediate steps toward a suspension of hostilities in the Philippines and a conference with the Philippine leaders with a view to preventing further bloodshed,

The Philippine Colony

After considering various alternatives, President William McKinley finally concluded that the Philippines should be an American colony. He explained his decision as follows.

And one night late it came to me this way—I don't know how it was, but it came: (1) that we could not give them back to Spain—that would be cowardly and dishonorable; (2) that we could not turn them over to France or Germany—our commercial rivals in the Orient—that would be bad business and discreditable; (3) that we could not leave them to themselves—they were unfit for self-government—and they would soon have anarchy and misrule over there worse than Spain's was; and (4) that there was nothing left for us to do but civilize and Christianize them, and by God's grace do the very best we could by them, as our fellowmen for whom Christ also died. And then I went to bed and went to sleep and slept soundly. . . .

upon the basis of a recognition of their freedom and independence as soon as proper guarantees can be had for order and protection of property.

Second. That the government of the United States shall tender an official assurance to the inhabitants of the Philippine islands that they will encourage and assist in the organization of such a government in the islands as the people thereof shall prefer, and that upon its organization in stable manner, the United States, in accordance with its traditional and prescriptive policy in such cases, will recognize the independence of the Philippines and its equality among nations, and gradually withdraw all military and naval forces.

In those eternal truths of the Declaration of Independence lie the principles which we firmly believe ought to govern your action as a faithful servant of the American people. In those resolutions of the anti-imperialist league lies the clear application of those principles to the duty of the hour. In the name of justice, freedom, and humanity, and in the spirit of George Washington and Abraham Lincoln, we urge you to obey those principles, and cease at once this war of "criminal aggression" against a brave people fighting for their independence just as our forefathers fought for theirs and ours.

The Philippines

Sen. Henry Cabot Lodge of Massachusetts, one of the chief proponents of an American empire, attempted to ground his position in historical precedent—the nation's westward expansion. He made the following remarks on the floor of the Senate in March 1900. While Lodge stresses the "duty" of the United States to less "civilized" peoples, he also emphasizes the economic benefits of the Philippines to the United States.

I believe we are in the Philippines, as righteously as we are there rightly and legally. I believe that to abandon the islands, or to leave them now, would be a wrong to humanity, a dereliction of duty, a base betrayal of the Filipinos who have supported us . . . and in the highest degree contrary to sound morals. As to expediency, the arguments in favor of the retention of the Philippines seem to me so overwhelming that I should regard their loss as calamity to our trade and commerce and to all our business interests so great that no man can measure it. . . .

Some of us were beginning to hope that we were getting away from the ideals set by the civil war, that we had made all the presidents we could from men who had distinguished themselves in that war, and were coming to seek another type of man. That we were ready to accept the peace ideal, to be proud of our title as a peace nation; to recognize that the man who cleans a city is greater than he who bombards it, and the man who irrigates a plain greater than he who lays it waste. Then came the Spanish war, with its gilt and lace and tinsel, and again the moral issues are confused with exhibitions of brutality.

—Jane Addams
Address before the Chicago Liberty
Meeting, April 30, 1899

This cartoon from 1898, "The Cares of a Growing Family," portraying President McKinley with his childlike charges, reflects the racist attitudes used to justify the establishment of an American empire.

Our opponents put forward as their chief objection that we have robbed these people of their liberty and have taken them and hold them in defiance of the doctrine of the Declaration of Independence in regard to the consent of the governed. As to liberty, they have never had it, and have none now, except when we give it to them protected by the flag and the armies of the United States. . . .

The second objection, as to the consent of the governed, requires more careful examination, because of the persistency with which it has been made the subject of heated declamation. . . . Jefferson . . . took Louisiana without the consent of the governed, and he ruled it without the consent of the governed. . . . In 1819 we bought Florida from Spain without the consent of the governed. . . . We received a great cession of territory from Mexico, including all the California coast. . . . There were many Mexicans living within ceded territory. We never asked their consent. . . . In 1867 we purchased Alaska from Russia—territory, people, and all. . . . To the white inhabitants we allow the liberty of returning to Russia, but we except the uncivilized tribes specifically. They are to be governed without their consent, and they are not even allowed to become citizens. . . . If the arguments which have been offered against our taking the Philippine Islands because we have not the consent of the inhabitants be just, then our whole past record of expansion is a crime. . . . Does any one really believe it? Then let us be honest and look at this whole question as it really is. I am not ashamed of that long record of American expansion. I am proud of it. . . . The taking of the Philippines does not violate the principles of the Declaration of Independence, but will spread them among a people who have never known liberty, and who in a few years will be as unwilling to leave the shelter of the American flag as those of any other territory we ever brought beneath its folds.

The next argument of the opponents of the Republican policy is that we are denying self-government to the Filipinos. Our reply is that to give independent self-government at once, as we under-

stand it, to a people who have no just conception of it and no fitness for it, is to dower them with a curse instead of a blessing. . . . We have no right to give those islands up to anarchy, tyrannies, and piracy, and I hope we have too much self-respect to hand them over to European powers, with the confession that they can restore peace and order more kindly and justly than we, and lead the inhabitants onward to a larger liberty and a more complete self-government than we can bestow upon them. . . .

The Filipinos are not now fit for self-government. . . . The form of government natural to the Asiatic had always been a despotism. . . . You cannot change race tendencies in a moment. . . .

I conceive my first duty to be always to the people of the United States, and most particularly for the advantage of our farmers and our workingmen, upon whose well-being, and upon whose full employment at the highest wages, our entire fabric of society and government rests. In a policy which gives us a foot hold in the East, which will open a new market in the Philippines and enable us to increase our commerce with China, I see great advantages to all our people, and more especially to our farmers and our workingmen. . . .

William Jennings Bryan emerged as a leading spokesman for the anti-imperialists. Bryan ran as the Democratic candidate for President again in 1900, this time on an anti-imperialist platform. He once again lost overwhelmingly to McKinley. The following excerpts from his speeches rebut both the historical and economic arguments of Henry Cabot Lodge; as a longtime advocate of "the common man," Bryan denied that colonies would help either farmers or working people.

The forcible annexation of the Philippine Islands (and, in my judgment, even annexation by the consent of the people) would prove a source of pecuniary loss rather than gain.

Who can estimate in money and men the cost of subduing and keeping in subjection eight millions of people, six thousand miles away, scattered over twelve hundred islands, and living under a tropical sun? . . .

And even if the amount invested in ships, armament, and in the equipment of soldiers is returned dollar for dollar, who will place a price upon the blood that will be shed? If war is to be waged for trade, how much trade ought to be demanded in exchange for a human life? And will the man who expects to secure the trade risk his own life or the life of some one else? . . .

The Annexation of Hawaii

Hawaii had already been important for its sugar trade, but by 1898, as America turned its gaze outward, the island took on even more significance. Strategically located, Hawaii, if annexed to the United States, could serve as a crucial base of operations for economic and political expansion in the Pacific. With President McKinley's support, the United States annexed Hawaii on July 7, 1898, during the Spanish-American War.

The majority of Hawaiian natives did not support annexation. Their opinion is reflected in this cartoon, in which the bride, representing Hawaii, seems ready to bolt.

As illustrated in this 1898 cartoon, Uncle Sam's successful "fishing expedition" lands Cuba, Puerto Rico, the Philippine Islands, and Hawaii.

While the American people are endeavoring to extend an unsolicited sovereignty over remote peoples, foreign financiers will be able to complete the conquest of our own country.

Labor's protest against the black list and government by injunction and its plea for arbitration, shorter hours, and a fair share of the wealth which it creates will be drowned in noisy disputes over new boundary lines and in the clash of conflicting authority.

Monopoly can thrive in security so long as the inquiry "Who will haul down the flag" on distant islands turns public attention away from the question "Who will uproot the trusts at home?"

They tell us that trade follows the flag and that wider markets will be the result of annexation. . . . Our foreign trade is increasing, and that increase is not due to an expanding sovereignty.

The insignificance of the trade argument will be manifest to any one who will compare the consuming capacity of the Filipinos with that of a like number of Americans. The inhabitants of the torrid zones can never equal, or even approach, the inhabitants of the temperate zones as customers. . . .

It has been argued that annexation would furnish a new field for the investment of American capital. If there is surplus money seeking investment, why is it not employed in the purchase of farm lands, in developing domestic enterprises, or in replacing foreign capital? . . .

While the Philippines will not prove inviting to Americans, we shall probably draw a considerable number from the islands to the United States. The emigration will be eastward rather than westward. During the six years from 1889 to 1894 more than ninety thousand coolies left India, and we may expect an influx of Malays.

It is not strange that the laboring men should look with undisguised alarm upon the prospect of oriental competition upon the farms and in the factories of the United States. . . .

The farmers and laboring men constitute a large majority of the American people; what is there in annexation for them? Heavier taxes, Asiatic emigration, and an opportunity to furnish more sons for the army.

Will it pay?

While most African Americans supported the fight for Cuba's freedom, they rejected the colonial policy of the United States in the Philippines as another example of white Anglo-Saxons subjugating dark-skinned people. When black troops were sent to the Philippines in an attempt to quell Emilio Aguinaldo and the Filipino fight for independence, black Americans became even more upset. American black churches, as well as social and political organizations, passed numerous resolutions condemning imperialism. In a letter written to the *American Citizen* (Kansas City), Lewis H. Douglass, son of prominent African-American leader Frederick Douglass, expressed the feelings of many African Americans concerning the nation's imperialist policies as he linked the struggles of black Americans with the dark-skinned Filipinos.

President McKinley, in the course of his speech at Minneapolis, says of the Filipinos under American sovereignty: "They will not be governed as vassals, or serfs, or slaves. They will be given a government of liberty, regulated by law, honestly administered, without oppressing exaction, taxation without tyranny, justice without bribe, education without distinction of social conditions, freedom of religious worship, and protection of life, liberty, and pursuit of happiness."

I do not believe that President McKinley has any confidence in the statement above. It cannot be successfully asserted that the great tariff statesman is blind to the fact of the race and color prejudice that dominates the greater percentage of the soldiers who are killing Filipinos in the name of freedom and civilization.

President McKinley knows that brave, loyal, black American soldiers, who fight and die for their country, are hated, despised, and cruelly treated in that section of the country from which this administration accepts dictation and to the tastes of which the President, undoubtedly, caters. The President of the United States knows that he dare not station a regiment of black heroes in the State of Arkansas. He knows that at the race hating command of a people who sought destruction of the nation his administration rescinded an order to send black soldiers to Little Rock. The administration lacks the courage to deal with American citizens without regard to race or color, as is clearly demonstrated in the weak and contemptibly mean act of yielding to the demands of those who hold that this is a white man's government and that dark races have no rights which white men are bound to respect.

"My opinion is that the Philippine Islands should be given an opportunity to govern themselves. They will make mistakes but will learn from their errors. Until our nation has settled the Negro and Indian problems I do not believe that we have a right to assume more social problems."

—Booker T. Washington, *Indianapolis Freeman*, 1898

It is a sorry, though true, fact that whatever this government controls, injustice to dark races prevail. The people of Cuba, Porto Rico, Hawaii, and Manila know it well, as do the wronged Indian and outraged black man in the United States. . . .

The question will be asked: How is it that such promises are made to Filipinos thousands of miles way, while the action of the administration in protecting dark citizens at home does not even extend to a promise of any attempt to rebuke the outlawry which kills American citizens of African descent for the purpose of gratifying blood-thirstiness and race hatred? . . .

It is hypocrisy of the most sickening kind to try to make us believe that the killing of Filipinos is for the purpose of good government and to give protection to life and liberty and the pursuit of happiness. . . .

When the United States learns that justice should be blind as to race and color, then may it undertake to, with some show of propriety, expand. Now its expansion means extension of race hate and cruelty, barbarous lynchings and gross injustice to dark people.

The war to subdue Filipinos who demanded their freedom from the United States lasted four long years, from 1898 to 1902. The ferocity of the guerrilla warfare led many to question U.S. policy. More than 126,000 American soldiers fought against the Filipino nationalists. Around 4,200 Americans and 18,000 Filipinos died in battle, while as many as 100,000 Filipinos succumbed to disease and starvation as the U.S. government spent $400 million to quash the revolt. The United States finally granted the Philippines independence in 1946, after World War II. The following unsigned letter, from a black American soldier to the *New York Age*, a black newspaper, questions the treatment of Filipinos by the United States and reveals the racial dimension of the war to stifle Filipino independence.

Editor, New York Age:
I have mingled freely with the natives and have had talks with American colored men here in business and who have lived here for years, in order to learn of them the cause of their (Filipino) dissatisfaction and the reason for this insurrection, and I must confess they have a just grievance. All this never would have occurred if the army of occupation would have treated them as people. The Spaniards, even if their laws were hard, were polite and treated them with some consideration; but the Americans, as soon as they

saw that the native troops were desirous of sharing in the glories as well as the hardships of the hard-won battles with the Americans, began to apply home treatment for colored peoples: cursed them as damned niggers, steal [from] and ravish them, rob them on the street of their small change, take from the fruit vendors whatever suited their fancy, and kick the poor unfortunate if he complained, desecrate their church property, and after fighting began, looted everything in sight, burning, robbing the graves.

This may seem a little tall—but I have seen with my own eyes carcasses lying bare in the boiling sun, the results of raids on receptacles for the dead in search of diamonds. The [white] troops, thinking we would be proud to emulate their conduct, have made bold of telling their exploits to us. One fellow, a member of the 13th Minnesota, told me how some fellows he knew had cut off a native woman's arm in order to get a fine inlaid bracelet. On upbraiding some fellows one morning, whom I met while out for a walk (I think they belong to a Nebraska or Minnesota regiment, and they were stationed on the Malabon road), for conduct of the American troops toward the natives and especially as to raiding, etc., the reply was: "Do you think we could stay over here and fight these damn niggers without making it pay all it's worth? The government only pays us $13 per month: that's starvation wages. White men can't stand it." Meaning they could not live on such small pay. In saying this they never dreamed that Negro soldiers would never countenance such conduct. They talked with impunity of "niggers" to our soldiers, never once thinking that they were talking to home "niggers" and should they be brought to remember that at home this is the same vile epithet they hurl at us, they beg pardon and make some effeminate excuse about what the Filipino is called.

I want to say right here that if it were not for the sake of the 10,000,000 black people in the United States, God alone knows on which side of the subject I would be. And for the sake of the black men who carry arms and pioneer for them as their representatives, ask them to not forget the present administration at the next election. Party be damned! We don't want these islands, not in the way we are to get them, and for Heaven's sake, put the party [Democratic] in power that pledged itself against this highway robbery. Expansion is too clean a name for it.

Filipino rebels, under Emilio Aguinaldo, fought a bloody guerilla war against the United States for two years, demanding independence. After the capture of Aguinaldo ended the rebellion in 1901, Andrew Carnegie—who was adamantly opposed to colonizing the Philippines—sarcastically wrote to a friend in McKinley's cabinet: "You seem to have finished your work of civilizing Filipinos; it is thought that about 8,000 of them have been completely civilized and sent to Heaven; I hope you like it."

Chapter Ten

New Women, Strenuous Men, and Leisure

Beginning in the 1890s American society seemed to explode with physical activity. Both women and men participated in the bicycling craze that swept the country. Football and boxing, feeding a fascination for violent competition, nearly surpassed baseball as the most popular spectator sport. A new interest in nature and the wilderness spawned countless hiking, camping, and nature clubs as well as groups dedicated to preserving whatever wilderness remained in the United States. Even popular music reflected this new vigor, as white urban audiences listened to the syncopated rhythms of ragtime, a form of music invented by black Southern musicians, and danced the high-stepping cakewalk, also of African-American origin. John Philip Sousa's marches also captured the mood of the day. The exuberant "Ta-ra-ra-boom-der-e" was the most popular song of the decade.

This emphasis on sports and recreation marked a significant shift in U.S. culture, representing a deep-seated reaction to the regimentation of everyday life. Middle-class Americans, especially, had learned to conform to the discipline of factory work and the time clock, the restraints of urban-industrial life, and notions of respectability. But by the early 1890s, they reacted strongly, showing a deep desire to break out of the often dull routine of an urban culture.

This reaction took many forms. Middle-class and elite American men sharpened definitions of masculinity, stressing physical prowess. They even created new words to describe men who were considered insufficiently masculine: "sissy" and "pussyfoot." The enthusiastic response of American men to the Spanish-American War as an opportunity to test their virility, along with that of the nation, reflected the

The thrill of a ride on a popular roller coaster at Coney Island gave this proper Victorian young lady an excuse to publicly embrace a man.

"We Americans want either to be thrilled or amused, and we are ready to pay well for either sensation."
—George Tilyou, creator of Steeplechase Park, Coney Island

prevailing sentiment. But changes for upper- and middle-class American women were even more profound in the 1890s. Breaking from the restrictive middle-class ideal of the fragile homebody, the new woman discarded her confining corset, took up bicycling and tennis, and participated in vigorous activities alongside her male counterpart. As the physical awareness of middle-class American women deepened, so did their political consciousness. The suffrage movement gained momentum with the emergence of the new woman.

While physical activity became the rage in the 1890s, spectator sports also became enormously popular. Technological advances, in transportation and communications, helped make spectator sports a fundamental part of U.S. culture in the Gilded Age. Railroad networks made it possible for teams from around the nation to compete with one another. The telegraph instantaneously made available to newspapers scores and the latest sporting news. Newspapers devoted increasing space to sports coverage, ultimately creating the sports section. Sportswriters created national heroes through stories and pictures. Mass communications spawned a mass audience eager to keep abreast of the latest sporting news.

Working-class Americans also participated in new forms of leisure activity. Amusement parks, such as New York's Coney Island, attracted millions of people seeking fun. With increasing leisure time, higher incomes, and affordable transportation, via streetcar, working men and women flocked to amusement parks

On the beach at Coney Island in 1897, these young women pose playfully, rejecting the strict etiquette expected in other social settings.

all over the nation, all of which offered an inexpensive escape from the routine of modern life.

But not all Americans enthusiastically embraced the cultural developments of the 1890s. Some criticized assertive, physical women as "unnatural," fearing that they might injure themselves, making them unable to bear children. Others worried that the obsession of Americans with spectator sports and amusement parks kept the public in a mindless stupor. "'Looping the loop,'" noted Jane Addams, "amid shrieks of stimulated terror or dancing in disorderly saloon halls are perhaps the natural reactions to a day spent in noisy factories and in trolley cars whirling through the distracting streets, but the city which permits them to be the acme of pleasure and recreation to its young people commits a grievous mistake." Escapism, she and others argued, through this kind of activity, did little to educate or "improve" the public.

Despite criticism, the sports and leisure culture of the 1890s prevailed, deeply influencing American life to this day. That young people in the United States today routinely name a sports hero, rather than a political or religious figure, as their most admired American attests to the fundamental ways that the decade has shaped our society.

"The Strenuous Life"

In 1899 Theodore Roosevelt addressed Chicago's Hamilton Club on the topic of "The Strenuous Life." In this often-quoted speech, Roosevelt made "strenuosity," as well as an active foreign policy, the clarion call to the nation—particularly to his fellow members of the elite.

I wish to preach, not the doctrine of ignoble ease, but the doctrine of the strenuous life, the life of toil and effort, of labor and strife; to preach that highest form of success which comes, not to the man who desires mere easy peace, but to the man who does not shrink from danger, from hardship, or from bitter toil, and who out of these wins the splendid ultimate triumph.

A life of slothful ease, a life of that peace which springs merely from lack either of desire or of power to strive after great things, is as little worthy of a nation as of an individual. I ask only that what every self-respecting American demands from himself and from his sons shall be demanded of the American nation as a whole. Who among you would teach your boys that ease, that peace, is to be the first consideration in their eyes—to be the

Coney Island and the Creation of the Amusement Park

The amusement park was a Gilded Age creation first developed at Coney Island, New York. Made possible by an exploding urban population with increased leisure time and income, as well as the invention of the electric streetcar to transport visitors cheaply, parks like Coney Island were replicated in towns and cities across America. The amusement park represented a new kind of leisure activity. Not only did it provide fantasy, thrills, and fun, but it also challenged middle-class, Victorian conventions, offering an outlet to rigid codes of public conduct.

A series of three seaside parks—Steeplechase, Luna Park, and Dreamland—Coney Island provided cheap entertainment for the masses, even poor laborers. Fare to Coney Island on the trolley was a nickel and Steeplechase Park offered 25 rides for 25 cents. But even those who could not afford rides could enjoy Coney Island's festive atmosphere as well as luxuriate on the beach. Coney Island was especially attractive to young, single working people who relished the freedom and anonymity it offered, as well as release from the eyes of nosy parents or chaperones.

Coney Island's attractions were daring and racy in their day. Many rides challenged accepted etiquette between men and women. At Steeplechase Park, the Human Whirlpool and the Chair-O-Plane lifted women's skirts, exposing their legs. The Barrel of Fun, a revolving cylinder, rolled men and women, often total strangers, into each other. And the Blowhole Theater entertained viewers and participants as concealed air jets blew hats off and skirts up into the air. A popular amusement at Steeplechase Park was a booth with imitation china dishes, objects to throw at them, and a sign: "If you can't break up your own home, break up ours!" Other attractions appealed to fantasy: Illuminated by 250,000 lights at night, Luna Park featured "oriental" palaces, complete with elephant rides, an Eskimo village, and a Japanese garden.

Coney Island and other amusement parks came under fire from critics who deemed them a sign of American civilization's decline. Some claimed that the "thrills" promoted by the parks led to mental illness. Others worried that the loosening of social standards might lead to social chaos. Yet, the amusement park survives to this day. Coney Island fell into decline with the arrival of the motion picture in the 1920s, but Walt Disney and other entrepreneurs built upon the concept, providing fantasy and fun for present-day Americans who seek diversion and escape just like their Gilded Age ancestors.

Now that Thanksgiving day is close at hand, the great game of football, perhaps the greatest game in America to-day, is in every boy's mind throughout the United States. There is no other sport which gives you a better respect for yourself and for the boys against whom you are playing than this hardy game. Your anxious mother is terribly worried, and tears come into her eyes day after day when she sees one of your shins barked for two or three inches or a big scratch down your cheek. . . .

It will always be a rough game, but you can tell your family at home, with a clear conscience, that the bumping and bruising you get each afternoon, while it looks pretty bad, is healthy and not nearly as bad as the bumping and bruising you are sure to get when you leave school or college and begin to fight out your own battles with the busy world.

—from "The Great Autumn Sport,"
in *Harper's Young People*, November 1893

ultimate goal after which they strive? . . . You work yourselves, and you bring up your sons to work. If you are rich and are worth your salt, you will teach your sons that though they may have leisure, it is not to be spent in mere idleness; for wisely used leisure merely means that those who possess it, being free from the necessity of working for their livelihood, are all the more bound to carry on some kind of non-remunerative work in science, in letters, in art, in exploration, in historical research—work of the type that we most need in this country, the successful carrying out of which reflects most honor upon the nation. . . .

In the last analysis a healthy state can exist only when the men and women who make it up lead clean, vigorous, healthy lives; when the children are so trained that they shall endeavor, not to shirk difficulties, but overcome them; not to seek ease, but to know how to wrest triumph from toil and risk. The man must be glad to do a man's work, to dare and endure and to labor; to keep himself, and to keep those dependent upon him. The woman must be the

Football embodied the martial spirit of "the strenuous life." Developed by American college students—members of the upper and middle classes—in the 1880s, football became one of the most popular sports in America by the 1890s, although it was often criticized for its violence. In 1887, Alexander Johnston wrote an article for Century Magazine, introducing the sport to the public and explaining the rules and subtleties of the game. Johnston argued that "this outdoor game is doing for our college-bred men, in a more peaceful way, what the experiences of war did for so many of their predecessors in 1861–65."

housewife, the helpmeet of the homemaker, the wise and fearless mother of many healthy children. . . . When men fear work or fear righteous war, when women fear motherhood, they tremble on the brink of doom; and well it is that they should vanish from the earth, where they are fit subjects for the scorn of all men and women who are themselves strong and brave and high-minded.

As it is with the individual, so it is with the nation. . . . Far better it is to dare mighty things, to win glorious triumphs, even though checkered by failure, than to take rank with those poor spirits who neither enjoy much nor suffer much, because they live in the gray twilight that knows not victory nor defeat. . . .

I preach to you, then, my countrymen, that our country calls not for the life of ease but for the life of strenuous endeavor. The

20th century looms before us big with the fate of many nations. If we stand idly by, if we seek merely swollen, slothful ease and ignoble peace, if we shrink from the hard contests where men must win at hazard of their lives and at the risk of all they hold dear, then the bolder and stronger peoples will pass us by, and will win for themselves the domination of the world. Let us therefore boldly face the life of strife, resolute to do our duty well and manfully; resolute to uphold righteousness by deed and by word; resolute to be both honest and brave, to serve high ideals, yet to use practical methods. Above all, let us shrink from no strife, moral or physical, within or without the nation, provided we are certain that the strife is justified, for it is only through strife, through hard and dangerous endeavor, that we shall ultimately win the goal of true national greatness.

Sports

Dr. James A. Naismith invented the game of basketball at the YMCA Training School in Springfield, Massachusetts, in 1891. Asked to create a game that could be played indoors during the winter months, Naismith formulated a noncontact sport that combined some characteristics of soccer, football, and field hockey. An instant hit, basketball appealed to men and women alike. This article, from _Harper's Weekly_, features basketball teams at women's colleges.

In the gymnasiums of the majority of girls' colleges and schools, basket-ball is one of the principal methods of pastime and exercise. In the cities like New York and Brooklyn, the winter is, in fact, the regular playing season, and more than the usual number of matches have already taken place. But in the larger colleges throughout the country, such as Vassar, Wellesley, Bryn Mawr, Newcomb, Smith, and others, the winter gymnasium practice is only preliminary to the class games and matches that are played out-doors in spring and early summer. These games are largely attended by the relatives and girl friends of the teams, but are in no sense public gatherings like the football contests of the girls' brothers.

The college girl who goes in for athletics is just as much in earnest as her big brother, but she goes about the matter in a different way. The boy is proud of his athletic inclinations and ability, and fond of displaying his prowess to an admiring public. His sister may be no less conscious of her skill and strength, but it is not good form to court notoriety, and thus it is that we hear much

This illustration from Harper's Weekly _depicts John G. Clarkson, a member of the National League and one of baseball's stars in 1890._

Baseball Unionizes

Despite the surge of interest in football, baseball maintained its standing as the national pastime in the Gilded Age. Magazines and daily newspapers regularly featured articles about baseball stars and other athletes, creating the modern cult of the sports celebrity. Baseball players in 1890 were in the midst of a labor dispute. As early as 1885 the players—like many of their working-class counterparts—organized a union, the National Brotherhood of Base-ball Players, in an attempt to offset the near-absolute power of team owners. Among players' grievances were a salary cap of $2,000, set by National League owners, and the standard "reserve clause" that bound a player to his original team, prohibiting him from negotiating a better deal with another. In 1890 most union players withdrew from the National League to create the Players' League. Reflecting the fate of many Gilded Age unions, the Brotherhood and League soon collapsed in the wake of the owners' seemingly limitless wealth and power.

less of the girl athlete. Nevertheless, in college circles and among the girl's intimates, her reputation as a star player is as well known and discussed as are the feats of her sturdier relative.

If the girl is in a position to acquire less of fame than her brother, she is, on the other hand, recompensed by the fact that she probably gets more fun and real pleasure out of her athletic exercise with less of work and hardship. The long, trying days of training and abstinence are not considered as necessary in the case of the girl as with the boy. The athletic reputation and supremacy of the college are not at stake, as is the case among Yale, Harvard,

The *1897* Sears, Roebuck and Company Catalogue *featured bicycle suits for women.*

281

1897 TAILOR MADE WALKING and BICYCLE SUITS

24993 $6.75

24990 $3.75

24980 $3.15

24982 $4.25

SUITS FOR HIGH SUMMER WEAR.

24980 Made of Washable Linen Crash, Blazer style with newest sleeves and cuffs, very finest skirt. Price....................$3.15

24981 Very Stylish, made of high grade plaid washable linen crash, big sailor collar fancy front. Our price, only............$4.00

24982 This Beautiful Summer Suit, is made of fancy checked washable linen crash, sailor collar and fronts of white linen, newest sleeves and cuffs. Very rich. Price.........................$4.25

24983 $6.00 Would not be too much for this Elegant Suit, made of fancy washable linen crash, big sailor collar, front and cuffs of blue linen, making a very pretty combination.
Price only..$5.00

BICYCLE SUITS.

24989 Consists of five pieces, Jacket, Skirt, Bloomers, Leggins and Cap, made of Austrian covert cloth in brown or gray mixtures. Blazer Jacket very nobby. Price........................$3.75

24990 This Nobby Suit (illustrated) is made of five pieces in double breasted Reefer style, full skirt in either tan or gray mixed Austrian covert cloth. Would be cheap at $7.50.
Only...$4.00

24991 Very Similar to 24993, made of very stylish novelty cloth, in five pieces consisting of cap, jacket, skirt, leggins and bloomers. Only..$4.25

24992 Blazer Style made of Imported Tiger Cloth, consisting of five pieces. Material durable and will outwear any material. Others sell it for $8.00, we sell it for.........................$4.75

24993 This Handsome Suit (illustrated) is made of brown or blue Repellant cloth, bound in leather all around and consists of five pieces, Jacket, half lined with silk. Can't be beat..............$6.75

24983 $5.00

24981 $4.00

Professional baseball, reflecting American society at large, became segregated in the Gilded Age when some white players refused to compete against blacks. Beginning in the 1880s, blacks established their own professional teams, such as the Cuban Giants (New York) and the St. Louis Black Stockings. Amateur baseball was also especially popular among African Americans, including these members of Atlanta's Morris Brown College team, around 1900.

Cornell, Columbia, and other universities. The girl's athletic contests are more for fun and real sport, and while there is a healthful rivalry between classes and schools, a defeat is not of serious importance.

The college girl has her own way of training. She believes, and rightly, too, that there should be no violent exercise without a period of preliminary practice and preparation. The physical instructor sees to it that the girl has no constitutional defect or impediment before she is allowed to join the regular gymnasium class and participate in the more strenuous work that comes later. Her heart must be sound and her general health good. With this foundation, she is welcomed and encouraged to take her place among the others, no matter how frail and weak she may be. It is argued that a certain amount of exercise, always in moderation, will be beneficial to her, and when this exercise is combined with pleasurable recreation, the effect cannot be otherwise than good. . . .

Bicycling was the most popular participant sport of the 1890s—one that middle-class women especially embraced with enthusiasm. Approximately 1 million Americans owned bicycles in 1893; by 1900 10 million bicycles proliferated along streets and roads.

Bicycling was also a popular spectator sport in the 1890s. Massive crowds of Americans from all classes and backgrounds assembled to watch highly competitive cyclists compete for lucrative prize money. Marshall W. "Major"

"A few years ago the spectacle of a woman on a bicycle brought a flush of indignation to the face of the average matron; to-day thousands of ladies in our great cities are enjoying this health-giving exercise."
—B. O. Fowler, *Arena*, 1892

Corsets

In 1875 Don Salvador Vallejo criticized the Americanization of Californio women, members of the landed elite who had resided in California when it was part of Mexico and continued living there after it became part of the United States. He cited their adoption of cosmetics, high-heeled shoes, and especially whalebone corsets, which he called "veritable instruments of torture."

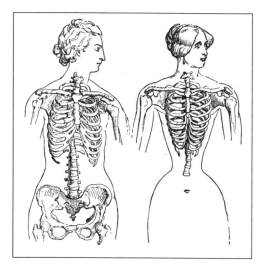

As a result of their heightened physical activity in the 1880s, a group of elite and middle-class American women pressed for dress reform. These drawings, which appeared in the Arena *in 1892, display the disfigurement caused by the corset. Despite these criticisms, American women would not abandon this type of corset until after 1910.*

Taylor was one of the most famous cyclists of the time. He turned professional at the age of 18, in 1896. Only three years later, Taylor became a world champion as well as American sprint champion in 1899 and 1900. Although barred from some tracks in the United States because of his color, Taylor nevertheless won honors and acclaim all over the world. In an era of segregation, extreme discrimination, and racial violence, Taylor provided an invaluable example of achievement to black Americans. The following is an excerpt from Taylor's autobiography, *The Fastest Bicycle Rider in the World,* **1928.**

Despite the fact that I was at the top of my form that summer [1897], I was not able to make a fight for the championship that season because the circuit extended into the South, and my entry had been refused by all southern promoters. They claimed it would be folly for me to compete with white riders in that section of the country.

I found that the color prejudice was not confined to the South entirely, in fact it had asserted itself against me even in and around Boston. It would be difficult for me to narrate all the unpleasant experiences which I underwent in my long racing career and also to call to mind all the vicious attempts that were made in vain to eliminate me from bicycle racing. I was the only colored rider ever permitted to compete in the professional class, and one may well surmise the obstacles I had to overcome against prejudice and narrow-minded opponents.

Rebellious Women

This excerpt from an 1881 editorial in *Scribner's* **reminded "rebelling" middle-class women of their "proper" place, as wives and mothers.**

A woman has a right to do everything she can do, provided she does nothing which will unfit her for bearing and raising healthy children. The future of the nation and the race depends upon the mothers, and any woman who consents to become a mother has no moral right to engage in any employment which will unfit her for that function. We speak, of course, of women whose circumstances give them the control of themselves. It is pitiful to think that there are multitudes who have no choice between employments that unfit them for motherhood and want. It is pitiful to

think that there are mothers who live their whole married lives in conditions which utterly unfit them for the functions and responsibilities of maternity.

We have a theory, which we regret to say, is not only unpopular among a certain class of women, but exceedingly offensive to them, viz., that every one of them ought to be mistress of a home. Women have a fashion in these days of rebelling against the idea that marriage is the great end of a woman's life. They claim the right to mark out for themselves and achieve an independent career. We appreciate the delicacies of their position, and we bow to their choice and their rights; nevertheless, we believe that in the millennium women will all live in their homes, and that men will not only do that which is regarded as their own peculiar work, but much of that which is now done by women. There has been in these late years a great widening out of the field of women's employments. We have been inclined to rejoice in this "for the present necessity," but we are sure the better time is to come when man, the real worker of the world, will do the work of the home, and that woman will, as wife and daughter and domestic, hold to the house and to that variety of employments which will best conserve her health and fit her for the duties and delights of wifehood, and the functions of motherhood. Quarrel with the fact, as she may, woman's rights must all and always be conditioned on her relations to the future of humanity. . . .

Annie Peck and the New Woman

Annie Peck epitomized the new woman of the 1890s. Well-to-do and college educated, Peck taught Latin at Purdue and Smith College and was an accomplished mountain climber and a suffragist. Her accomplishments undermined commonly held views that women were the weaker sex, incapable of physical and intellectual challenges.

Soon after, we reach what would be the most dangerous part of the journey, if the whole distance were not hung with ropes. I had received various reports of its difficulty, some declaring that there were chains to be mounted hand over hand; others, that it was all as easy as possible. My own experience was that this was the nicest part of the climb. The ropes, with two exceptions, seemed new and strong, and in two places there were iron chains in addition. Then I had always the additional support of the rope around my waist, if one of the others had broken or the fastening staple gave way. So one at a time we scrambled up the rocks with ease and rapidity, though the incline was from forty to eight degrees, mostly eighty. . . . Now we advance over an easier grade of rocks, more or less sprinkled with snow, until we arrive about half-past nine at the summit. It was indeed a moment of satisfaction to stand at last upon this famous peak, fourteen thousand seven hundred and five feet above the sea. . . .

[S]uch a climb is enjoyable, not simply for the exercise, varied and exciting though it may be, and for the elation that victory inspires; but also for the intimate acquaintance thus gained with the mountain.

—Annie S. Peck, "A Woman's Ascent of the Matterhorn," *McClure's*, July 1896

The members of this basketball team at Newcomb College, New Orleans, put into practice the new emphasis on vigorous exercise for women, a groundbreaking concept in the 1890s.

Timeline

1869
Knights of Labor established

1870
Standard Oil Company founded by John D. Rockefeller

1873
Financial panic leads to economic depression that lasts approximately five years

Andrew Carnegie and partners establish Carnegie Steel

1875
First Farmers' Alliances organized in Texas

1876
Battle of Little Big Horn

1877
Rutherford Hayes elected President after an election dispute

Reconstruction ends as last of federal troops are withdrawn from the South, and white Democrats regain control of Southern state governments

Railroad strike disrupts rail service from Baltimore to St. Louis, resulting in violence

1879
Carlisle Indian School founded, the model for subsequent government-sponsored schools for Indian children

1881
American Federation of Labor founded

1882
Chinese Exclusion Act passed by Congress

1886

Bombing at Haymarket Square in Chicago damages labor movement

1889

Hull House opened in Chicago by Jane Addams

1890

Ghost Dance revival ends with massacre of Native Americans at Wounded Knee South Dakota

Jacob Riis publishes *How the Other Half Lives*

Sherman Antitrust Act passed by Congress

Mississippi passes first disfranchisement law excluding black voters; other Southern states follow

1892

Lockout of steelworkers at Homestead results in violence

People's Party (Populist Party) formed in Omaha

1893

Financial panic leads to severe depression that continues through most of decade

1896

In *Plessy* v. *Ferguson*, the Supreme Court upholds "separate but equal" facilities for blacks as constitutional

Republican William McKinley defeats Democrat/Populist William Jennings Bryan for the Presidency

1898

Spanish-American War

Treaty of Paris cedes Puerto Rico, Philippines, and several other Spanish possessions to the United States

United States annexes Hawaii

1898–1902

Filipinos, led by Emilio Aguinaldo, revolt against U.S. rule

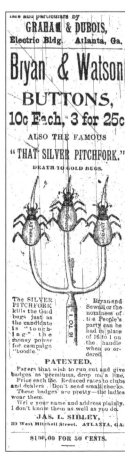

Further Reading

Overviews

Calhoun, Charles W., ed. *The Gilded Age: Essays on the Origins of Modern America*. Wilmington, Del.: Scholarly Resources, 1996.

Cashman, Sean D. *America in the Gilded Age: From the Death of Lincoln to the Rise of Theodore Roosevelt*. 3rd. ed. New York: New York University Press, 1992.

Takaki, Ronald. *A Different Mirror: A History of Multicultural America*. Boston: Little, Brown, 1993.

Wiebe, Robert. *The Search for Order, 1877–1920*. Hill & Wang, 1980.

Farmers

Goodwyn, Lawrence. *The Populist Moment*. New York: Oxford University Press, 1978.

Immigration

Antin, Mary. *The Promised Land*. 2nd ed. Boston: Houghton Mifflin, 1969.

Archdeacon, Thomas J. *Becoming American: An Ethnic History*. New York: Free Press, 1983.

Howe, Irving, and Kenneth Libo, eds. *How We Lived: A Documentary History of Immigrant Jews in America, 1880–1930*. New York: Richard Marek, 1979.

Metzker, Isaac, ed. *A Bintel Brief: Sixty Years of Letters from the Lower East Side to the Jewish Daily Forward*. New York: Ballantine, 1971.

Nee, Victor G., and Brett DeBary Nee. *Longtime Californ': A Documentary Study of an American Chinatown*. New York: Pantheon, 1973.

Weber, David, ed. *Foreigners in Their Native Land: Historical Roots of the Mexican Americans*. Albuquerque: University of New Mexico Press, 1971.

Imperialism

Gatewood, Willard, ed. *"Smoked Yankees" and the Struggle for Empire: Letters from Negro Soldiers, 1898–1902*. Urbana: University of Illinois Press, 1971.

LaFeber, Walter. *The New Empire: An Interpretation of American Expansion, 1862–1898*. Ithaca, N.Y.: Cornell University Press, 1963.

Roosevelt, Theodore. *An Autobiography*. New York: Macmillan, 1913.

Industry

Carnegie, Andrew. *Autobiography of Andrew Carnegie*. Boston: Houghton Mifflin, 1948.

Rockefeller, John D. *Random Reminiscences of Men and Events*. New York: Doubleday, Doran & Company, 1937.

Wall, Joseph. *Andrew Carnegie*. New York: Oxford University Press, 1970.

Labor

Demarest, David P., Jr. *"The River Ran Red": Homestead, 1892*. Pittsburgh: University of Pittsburgh Press, 1992.

Gompers, Samuel. *Seventy Years of Life and Labor*. Ithaca, N.Y.: Industrial and Labor Relations Press, 1984.

Jones, Mary Harris. *The Autobiography of Mother Jones*, 3rd ed. Edited by Mary Field Parton. Chicago: Charles H. Kerr, 1978.

Leisure

Kasson, John. *Amusing the Million: Coney Island at the Turn of the Century*. New York: Hill & Wang, 1978.

Peiss, Kathy. *Cheap Amusements: Working Women and Leisure in Turn-of-the-Century New York*. Philadelphia: Temple University Press, 1986.

The South

Aptheker, Herbert, ed. *A Documentary History of the Negro People in the United States*, Vol. 2. New York: Citadel Press, 1964.

Ayers, Edward. *The Promise of the New South*. New York: Oxford University Press, 1993.

Gatewood, Willard. *Black Americans and the White Man's Burden*. Urbana: University of Illinois Press, 1975.

Greenwood, Janette Thomas. *Bittersweet Legacy: The Black and White "Better Classes" in Charlotte, 1850–1910*. Chapel Hill: University of North Carolina Press, 1994.

Harlan, Louis. *Booker T. Washington: The Making of a Black Leader, 1856–1901*. New York: Oxford University Press, 1972.

Lewis, David Levering. *W. E. B. DuBois: Biography of a Race, 1868–1919*. New York: Henry Holt, 1993.

Washington, Booker T. *Up from Slavery.* New York: Doubleday, 1901.

Wells, Ida B. *Crusade for Justice: The Autobiography of Ida B. Wells.* Edited by Alfreda M. Duster. Chicago: University of Chicago Press, 1970.

Urban Life

Addams, Jane. *Twenty Years at Hull House.* New York: Penguin, 1981.

Eastman, Charles. *From the Deep Woods to Civilization.* Lincoln: University of Nebraska, 1977.

Hales, Peter B. *Silver Cities· The Photography of American Urbanization, 1839–1915.* Philadelphia: Temple University Press, 1984.

Kessler-Harris, Alice. *Out to Work: A History of Wage-Earning Women in the United States.* New York: Oxford University Press, 1982.

Langley, Winston E., and Vivian C. Fox, eds. *Women's Rights in the U.S.: A Documentary History.* Westport, Conn.: Greenwood Press, 1974.

Riis, Jacob. *The Making of an American.* New York: Macmillan, 1931.

Thomas, John L. *Alternative America: Henry George, Edward Bellamy, Henry Demarest Lloyd and the Adversary Tradition.* Cambridge, Mass.: Belknap, 1983.

Warner, Sam Bass, Jr. *Streetcar Suburbs: The Process of Growth in Boston.* New York: Atheneum, 1972.

———. *The Urban Wilderness.* New York: Harper & Row, 1972.

The West

Allen, Charles Wesley. *Autobiography of Red Cloud: War Leader of the Oglalas.* Helena: Montana Historical Society, 1997.

Armitage, Susan, and Elizabeth Jameson, eds. *The Women's West.* Norman: University of Oklahoma Press, 1987.

Judson, Phoebe Goodell. *A Pioneer's Search for an Ideal Home.* Lincoln: University of Nebraska Press, 1984.

Milner, Clyde, ed. *The Oxford History of the American West.* New York: Oxford University Press, 1994.

Moquin, Wayne, ed. *Great Documents in American Indian History.* New York: Praeger, 1973.

Painter, Nell Irvin. *Exodusters: Black Migration to Kansas After Reconstruction.* New York: Knopf, 1977.

Reps, John W. *Cities of the American West: A History of Frontier Urban Planning.* Princeton, N.J.: Princeton University Press, 1979.

Siringo, Charles. *A Cowboy Detective: A True Story of Twenty-two Years with a World Famous Detective Agency.* Albuquerque: University of New Mexico Press, 1988.

Utley, Robert M. *The Lance and the Shield: The Life and Times of Sitting Bull.* New York: Henry Holt, 1993.

Text Credits

Main Text

pp. 16–17: Andrew Carnegie, *Autobiography of Andrew Carnegie* (Boston: Houghton Mifflin, 1920), 130, 172.

pp. 17–18: John D. Rockefeller, *Random Reminiscences of Men and Events* (New York: Doubleday, Doran & Co., 1937), 87.

pp. 18–20: Henry Demarest Lloyd, "The Story of a Great Monopoly," *Atlantic Monthly* (March 1881): 317–34.

pp. 21–23: Andrew Carnegie, "Wealth," *North American Review* (June 1889): 653–64.

pp. 23–24: Henry Demarest Lloyd, *Wealth Against Commonwealth* (New York: Harper & Brothers, 1899), 494, 496, 498, 500, 503.

pp. 24–25: Andrew Carnegie, "Wealth," *North American Review* (June 1889): 653–64.

pp. 25–26: Washington Gladden, "Mr. Rockefeller and the American Board," *Outlook* (22 April 1905): 984–86.

pp. 26–27: Horatio Alger, *Ragged Dick and Mark, the Match Boy: Two Novels by Horatio Alger* (London: Collier Macmillan, 1962), 108–9.

pp. 33–34: Abraham Cahan, *The Rise of David Levinsky* (New York: Harper & Row, 1960), 86–87.

pp. 34–35: Juanita Hermandes Garcia, from American Life Histories: Manuscripts from the Federal Writers' Project, 1936–1940, Library of Congress.

pp. 36–38: Mary Antin, *The Promised Land*, 2d ed. (Boston: Houghton Mifflin, 1969), 180–81; 184–85; 186; 187–88; 198; 202–5.

pp. 38–39: Robert Ferrari, from American Immigrant Autobiographies, Part I: Manuscript Autobiographies from the Immigration History Research Center, University of Minnesota, General Editor Rudolph Vecoli, Microfilm, University Publications of America.

pp. 40–42: Thomas Vivien, "John Chinaman in San Francisco," *Scribner's* (October 1876): 866.

p. 42: Saum Song Bo, *American Missionary* (October 1885): 10.

pp. 43–44: James Sargent, *Why I Am an A.P.A., or the American Protective Association Explained and Justified* (Rochester, N.Y.: n.p., 1895), 4.

pp. 44–45: "The Mischief of the A.P.A.," *Century Magazine* (May 1896): 156.

pp. 45–47: Isaac Metzker, ed. *A Bintel Brief: Sixty Years of Letters from the Lower East Side to the Jewish Daily Forward* (New York: Ballantine, 1971), 76–78; 36–37; 66–68.

pp. 51–53: T.V. Powderly, *Thirty Years of Labor, 1859 to 1889* (Philadelphia: n.p., 1890), 128–130.

p. 54: George Frederic Parsons, "The Labor Question," *Atlantic Monthly* (July 1886): 97–113.

pp. 56–57: Samuel Gompers, *Seventy Years of Life and Labor* (New York: E. P. Dutton, 1925), 68–70; 79–80; 97–98. Copyright 1925 by Samuel Gompers, renewed © 1953 by Gertrude Gleaves Gompers. Used by permission of Dutton, a division of Penguin Putnam Inc.

pp. 57–59: Mary Harris Jones, ed. Mary Field Parton, *The Autobiography of Mother Jones*, rev. 3d ed. (Chicago: Charles H. Kerr, 1996) originally published in 1925, 30–39. Used by permission of the publisher.

pp. 60–62: Marie Ganz with Nat. J. Ferber, *Rebels: Into Anarchy—And Out Again* (New York: Dodd, Mead and Company, 1920), 38–42; 93–95.

pp. 63–64: Emma E. Brown, "Children's Labor: A Problem," *Atlantic Monthly* (December 1880): 787–92.

pp. 71–72: Jane Addams, *Twenty Years at Hull House.* (New York: Macmillan, 1910. Reprint, New York: Penguin, 1981), 72, 74, 88–89.

pp. 73–74: "Minutes of the Second Convention of the National Association of Colored Women: Held at Quinn Chapel, 24th Street and Wabash Avenue, Chicago, Ill., August 14th, 15th, and 16th, 1899," Daniel A.P. Murray Collection, Library of Congress.

pp. 75–76: Jacob Riis, *How the Other Half Lives: Studies Among the Tenements of New York* (New York: Charles Scribner's Sons, 1890).

pp. 76–78: William Graham Sumner, *What Social Classes Owe to Each Other* (New York: Harper's, 1883), 15–17; 20–24.

pp. 78–79: William L. Riordon, *Plunkitt of Tammany Hall* (New York: E. P. Dutton, 1963), 91–93.

pp. 80–81: "Men of Mecklenburg," *Charlotte Observer*, 2 August 1881.

pp. 94–96: Grimes Family Papers (#3357), 1882, Southern Historical Collection, University of North Carolina, Chapel Hill.

pp. 97–99: Henry Grady, "The New South," speech at New York, December 1886. Reproduced in *The New South Writings and Speeches of Henry Grady* (Savannah, Ga.: Beehive Press, 1971), 3–13. Permission granted by Mills Lane.

pp. 99–100: From *These Are Our Lives*, as told by the people and written by members of the Federal Writers' Project of the Works Progress Administration in North Carolina, Tennessee, and Georgia (New York: Norton, 1967), 131–37; 181–83. Copyright © 1939, 1967 by the University of North Carolina Press. Used by permission of the publisher.

pp. 101–103: *Plessy v. Ferguson*, 163 U.S. 537 (1896).

pp. 105–6: *Public Laws of North Carolina*, 1899, ch. 218.

pp. 106–7: Ida B. Wells, *Crusade for Justice: The Autobiography of Ida B. Wells*. Ed. Alfreda M. Duster (Chicago: University of Chicago Press, 1970), 64–66; 69–71. © 1970 by The University of Chicago. All rights reserved.

pp. 107–10: Booker T. Washington, *Up from Slavery* (New York: Doubleday, 1901), 217–37.

pp. 110–13: W. E. B. Du Bois, *The Souls of Black Folk*, 2d ed. (Chicago: A. C. McClurg, 1903), 41–59.

p. 121: "An Indian Victory," *New York Times*, 7 July 1876.

pp. 122–23: Hamlin Garland, "General Custer's Last Fight as Seen by Two Moons," *McClure's Magazine* (September 1898): 443–48.

pp. 124–25: Zitkala-Sä, "Impressions of an Indian Childhood," *Atlantic Monthly* (January 1900): 37–41.

pp. 125–27: Zitkala-Sä, "School Days of an Indian Girl," *Atlantic Monthly* (February 1900): 185–94.

pp. 127–29: Phoebe Goodell Judson, *A Pioneer's Search for an Ideal Home* (Lincoln: University of Nebraska Press, 1984), 222–23; 225–29; 227; 278.

pp. 129–30: *Negro Exodus: Report of Colonel Frank H. Fletcher* (Topeka: Kansas Freedman's Relief Association, 1880).

p. 131: Reproduced in David J. Weber, ed. *Foreigners in Their Native Land: Historical Roots of the Mexican Americans* (Albuquerque: University of New Mexico Press, 1973), 234–36.

pp. 138–40: Ocala Demands of the Farmers' Alliance (1890). National Farmers' Alliance and Industrial Union. *Proceedings*. Washington, 1890, 25.

pp. 140–42: Annie L. Diggs, "The Women in the Alliance Movement," *Arena* (July 1892): 161–79.

pp. 142–43: *Progressive Farmer*, 10 July 1888.

p. 143: *Progressive Farmer*, 31 July 1888.

pp. 144–46: *People's Party Paper*, 19 August 1892.

pp. 146–48: Tom Watson, "The Negro Question in the South," *Arena* (October 1892): 540–50.

pp. 148–49: William Jennings Bryan, "The Cross of Gold," *The First Battle: A Story of the Campaign of 1896* (Chicago: W. B. Conkey Co., 1896), 199–206.

pp. 157–58: Theodore Roosevelt, *An Autobiography* (New York: Macmillan, 1913), 227–28.

pp. 158–59: H. H. Proctor, *A Sermon on the War: 'The Duty of Colored Citizens to Their Country': delivered before the Colored Military Companies of Atlanta, Sunday evening, May 1st, 1898, at the First Congregational Church, Atlanta, Ga.* (Atlanta: Mutual Printing Co., 1898), Daniel A. P. Murray Collection, Library of Congress.

pp. 160–62: Albert Beveridge, "The March of the Flag," speech by the Honorable Albert Beveridge Opening the Indiana Republican Campaign, at Tomlinson Hall, Indianapolis, Friday, September 16, 1898 (Indianapolis, 1898).

pp. 162–63: Women's Auxiliary of the Anti-Imperialist League, "Women Make an Appeal in Behalf of the Foundation Principles of the Republic," *Springfield Republican*, 30 May 1899.

pp. 163–65: *Congressional Record*, 56th Cong., 1st sess., 1900, 2618–21; 2627–29.

pp. 165–66: William Jennings Bryan, *Republic or Empire: The Philippine Question* (Chicago: Independence, 1899), 59–68.

pp. 167–68: Lewis Douglass, letter to the *American Citizen* (Kansas City), 17 November 1899.

pp. 168–69: Willard B. Gatewood, ed. *"Smoked Yankees" and the Struggle for Empire: Letters from Negro Soldiers, 1898–1902* (Urbana: University of Illinois Press, 1971), 279–81.

pp. 173–75: Theodore Roosevelt, "The Strenuous Life": Speech Before the Hamilton Club, Chicago, April 10, 1899, reproduced in *The Strenuous Life: Essays and Addresses* (New York: Century Co., 1903), 1–21.

pp. 175–76: "College Girls and Basket-Ball," *Harper's Weekly*, 22 February 1902.

p. 178: Marshall W. "Major" Taylor, *The Fastest Bicycle Rider in the World* (Worcester, Mass.: Wormley, 1928).

pp. 178–79: *Scribner's* (February 1881).

Sidebar Credits

p. 16: Quoted in David Traxel, *1898: The Birth of the American Century* (New York: Knopf, 1998), 43.

p. 20: Andrew Carnegie, *Autobiography of Andrew Carnegie* (Boston: Houghton Mifflin, 1920), 130, 172.

p. 24: Quoted in David Brody, *Steelworkers in America* (Cambridge, Mass.: Harvard University Press, 1960), 94.

p. 26: *New York Sun*, 1905.

p. 38: "The Greenhorn Cousin," from *How We Lived: A Documentary History of Immigrant Jews in America, 1880–1930* by Irving Howe and Kenneth Libo, copyright © 1979 by Irving Howe and Kenneth Libo. Used by permission of G. P. Putnam's Sons, a division of Penguin Putnam Inc., 134–35.

p. 39: Abraham Cahan, *The Education of Abraham Cahan*. Trans. Leon Stein et al. (Philadelphia: Jewish Publication Society of America, 1969), 401.

p. 40: Diane Mel Lin Mark and Ginger Chih, *A Place Called Chinese America* (Dubuque, Iowa: Kendall/Hunt, 1982), 6.

p. 60: J. M. Lizarras to Samuel Gompers, June 8, 1903. Quoted in John Murray, "A Foretaste of the Orient," *International Socialist Review* 4 (August 1903): 78.

p. 61: Carroll D. Wright, Chief of Bureau of Labor Statistics, Massachusetts, 1882.

p. 93: William C. Smith, *Charlotte Messenger*, 2 March 1883.

p. 96: Frederick Douglass, "Decoration Day," May 1894, reel 17, Frederick Douglass Papers.

p. 98: The Reverend H. L. Atkins, "Overworked Factory Workers," *Daily Charlotte Observer*, 8 January 1895.

p. 100: W. S. Mallory, "Reply to Mr. Atkins," *Daily Charlotte Observer*, 9 January 1895.

p. 116: From W. Fletcher Johnson, *Life of Sitting Bull and History of the Indian Word 1890–91* (Philadelphia: Edgewood Publishing Co., 1891), 201.

p. 117: From *American Indian Poetry: An Anthology of Songs and Chants*, ed. George W. Cronyn (New York: Liveright, 1962), 64; 66–67. Copyright 1918 and renewed 1962 by George W. Cronyn. Reprinted by permission of Ballantine Books, a division of Random House Inc.

p. 134: "Notes from Alliances," *Progressive Farmer*, 5 June 1888.

p. 135: C. H. Otken, *The Ills of the South, or Related Causes Hostile to the General Prosperity of Southern People* (New York: G. P. Putnam's Sons, 1894), 21–22.

p. 138: L. Frank Baum. *The Wonderful Wizard of Oz* (New York: Bobbs-Merrill, 1900), 1–2.

p. 141: Mary Elizabeth Lease, *Macon Telegraph*, 11 August 1891.

p. 143: "Secretary Rusk and the Farmers," *North American Review* CLII (June 1891): 751–53.

p. 144: *New York Times*, July 5, 1892.

p. 145: "Leaving the Party," in *American Labor Songs of the Nineteenth Century*, ed. Philip S. Foner (Urbana: University of Illinois Press, 1977), 277.

p. 146: Tom Watson, "The Negro Question in the South," *Arena*, October 1892: 542.

p. 162: Quoted in Charles S. Olcott, *The Life of William McKinley*, vol. 2 (Boston: Houghton Mifflin, 1916), 111.

p. 163: Jane Addams, "Democracy or Militarism," *Chicago Liberty Meeting*, Liberty Tract No. 1 (Chicago: Central Anti-Imperialist League, 1899).

p. 168: Booker T. Washington, *Freeman* (Indianapolis), 24 September 1898.

p. 172: George Tilyou, quoted in Reginald Wright Kaufman, "Why Is Coney," *Hampton's Magazine* 23 (August 1909): 224.

p. 174: "The Great Autumn Sport," *Harper's Young People*, November 1893.

p. 177: B. O. Fowler, "The Next Forward Step for Women; or Thoughts on the Movement for Rational Dress," *Arena*, November 1892: 635–42.

p. 179: From Annie S. Peck, "A Woman's Ascent of the Matterhorn," *McClure's Magazine*, July 1896.

Picture Credits

Courtesy, American Antiquarian Society: 54, 152; Courtesy: Arizona Historical Society/Tucson (AHS# 51185): 131; Bishop Museum Archives: 165; Brown Brothers: 23 bottom, 32; California Section, California State Library: 41; Carnegie Company of New York: 15; Carnegie Library of Pittsburgh: 65; CORBIS-BETTMAN: 44; Dorothy Hill Ethnographic Photo Collection, CSU Chico, Merriam Library, Chico, Calif.: 119 bottom; Emory University: cover (text), 144, 148, 181; Ericson Photograph Collection, Humboldt State University Library: 125; Forward: 46; Frank Leslie's, July 24, 1886: 171; The Granger Collection, New York: 49; Janette Greenwood: 92; Harper's Young People, June 19, 1894: 27; Institute of Texan Cultures: 36; Jacob Rader Marcus Center of the American Jewish Archives: 28; Kansas State Historical Society, Topeka, Kansas: 126, 127, 141; Kheel Center for Labor-Management Documentation and Archives,

Cornell University, Ithaca, NY 14853-3901: 61; Library of Congress: cover, 2, 12, 42, 52, 70, 81, 90, 97, 104, 108, 111, 116, 132, 139, 155, 157, 160, 166, 169, 174, 177, 180; Minnesota Historical Society: 80; Montana Historical Society, Helena: 121; Museum of the City of New York: 3, 69 (The Byron Collection), 84 (Gift of Joseph Verner Reed), 85 (Gift of Joseph Verner Reed), 115 (The Harry T. Peters Collection), 172, 181; Museum of the City of New York / Jacob A. Riis Collection: 66 (#108), 77 (#244), 82–83 (#1491/2), 86 top (#154), 86 bottom (#187), 180 right (#187), 87 top (#129), 88 (#157), 89 top (#148), 89 bottom (#230); Courtesy Museum of New Mexico, Photo by John K. Hillers, Neg. No 16096: 119 top; National Archives: 33 (Northeast Branch), 63, 124; National Parks Service, Ellis Island: 31; Nebraska State Historical Society: 9 bottom, 114, 129; New York Journal, 1896: 151 bottom; New York Public Library: 43,

64, 95, 98, 107 (Photographs & Prints Division, Schomburg Center for Research in Black Culture, Astor, Lenox and Tilde Foundations), 151 top, 164 (Photographs & Prints Division, Schomburg Center for Research in Black Culture, Astor, Lenox and Tilden Foundations), 170 (General Research, Astor, Lenox and Tilden Foundations), 175 (Harper's Weekly, May 3, 1890), 178 (Arena, Nov. 1892), 179; Newport Historical Society: 23 top; Sears Roebuck & Company: 21, 176; Smithsonian Institution: 56 (National Portrait Gallery), 72, 124; State Historical Society of Wisconsin: 93; Swarthmore College Peace Collection: 71; U.S. Department of the Interior, National Parks Service, Edison National Historic Site: 14; Valentine Museum, Richmond, Virginia: 134; Verdict, January 22, 1900: 9 top, 17, 18; Yale Collection of Western Americana, Beinecke Rare Book and Manuscript Library: 118.

Index

Acknowledgments

I would especially like to thank my editors at Oxford University Press, Nancy Toff and Karen Fein, for their care in shepherding this book through the process of publication. I am indebted to Sally Deutsch for suggesting me for this project, and for her thoughtful criticism of the manuscript as well as her encouragement and helpful advice. I would also like to thank Jenean Rombola, who provided valuable research assistance, and Nicole Dupont for her help in transcribing documents.

About the Author

Janette Thomas Greenwood is Associate Professor of History and Director of the Higgins School of Humanities at Clark University, where she teaches a course on the Gilded Age and other classes in U.S. social history. She is the author of *Bittersweet Legacy: The Black and White "Better Classes" in Charlotte, 1850–1910*, selected as an Outstanding Academic Book by *Choice* in 1995.